Helping entrepreneurs and their leadership
teams clarify, simplify and achieve their vision.

A gift for you from Bobi Siembieda.
I hope this book gives you clarity in your business.

Here to help,

Bobi Siembieda
EOS Implementer
bobi@conradbusinessresults.com
630.728.4177

www.conradbusinessresults.com

PRAISE FOR *GET A GRIP*

"Gino Wickman's first book, *Traction*, describing his Entrepreneurial Operating System (EOS), is already one of the great improvement game plans for business owners in America. Here, in his new brainstorm with coauthor Mike Paton, he takes entrepreneurial readers through a single story to show how every advantage of implementing EOS can actually become a practical reality in their own businesses. I would absolutely read both books together."

—DAN SULLIVAN, Founder of Strategic Coach®

———

"Over the years I've heard countless testimonials from entrepreneurs who swear by Gino Wickman's first book, *Traction*, but only after reading *Get A Grip* did I see clearly how implementing his Entrepreneurial Operating System could truly transform a business and put it on the road to greatness. This book will change your company—and your life."

—BO BURLINGHAM, Editor-at-Large of *Inc.* magazine,
Author of *Small Giants: Companies That Choose to Be Great Instead of Big*

GET A GRIP

HOW TO GET EVERYTHING
YOU WANT FROM YOUR
ENTREPRENEURIAL BUSINESS

GINO WICKMAN • MIKE PATON

BENBELLA

BENBELLA BOOKS, INC.
DALLAS, TEXAS

BenBella

BenBella Books, Inc.
10300 N. Central Expressway
Suite 530
Dallas, TX 75231
www.benbellabooks.com
Send feedback to feedback@benbellabooks.com

Printed in the United States of America
10 9 8 7 6 5 4 3

ISBN 978-1-937856-08-3

Copyediting by Rebecca Logan
Proofreading by Michael Fedison and Jenny Bridges
Cover design by Facout Studio
Text design and composition by John Reinhardt Book Design
Printed by Lake Book Manufacturing

Distributed by Perseus Distribution
(www.perseusdistribution.com)

To place orders through Perseus Distribution:
Tel: 800-343-4499
Fax: 800-351-5073
E-mail: orderentry@perseusbooks.com

Significant discounts for bulk sales are available.
Please contact Glenn Yeffeth at glenn@benbellabooks.com or 214-750-3628.

To my mom, Linda Wickman, the strongest person I know.
—*Gino Wickman*

To "Pop," Art Pfeil, the storyteller and teacher in me.
—*Mike Paton*

CONTENTS

Introduction

THIS IS A BUSINESS FABLE, but it's not like any business fable you've read before. Though fictional, *Get A Grip* is a gritty, real-world story about an entrepreneurial company that has hit the ceiling. Tired and frustrated, its leaders respond by implementing a practical, proven system that dramatically improves the performance of their business and the quality of their lives.

That system is called EOS, the Entrepreneurial Operating System. It's not theory. It's not full of abstract concepts. It's not about one big idea. Rather, it's a complete system full of simple, practical tools that has helped thousands of entrepreneurs worldwide get what they want from their businesses.

We've personally taken hundreds of companies through this process. If the details ring true it's because we really didn't make up anything. Any similarities to issues you face with your organization, leadership team, or people are pure coincidence. This book isn't based on a true story; it's actually based on hundreds of true stories. There isn't one situation you will read about that we haven't experienced at least twenty times with various clients.

We hope these realistic characters and familiar situations help you see how to solve the most important and common issues you face as a leader. These practical tools will help you simplify, clarify, and achieve your vision. We're confident they will because—over and over again—we've seen that the results of implementing EOS are truly remarkable. But don't take our word for it. We'll let the business owners who've implemented it speak for themselves:

"In the ten years prior to implementing EOS, our company experienced substantial and consistent revenue growth year after year. But we hit a ceiling. Our leaders weren't on the same page, there was confusion about direction and roles, finger pointing, and turf protecting—profit dropped considerably. It wasn't fun. EOS has helped us develop a trusting, engaged, focused, and empowered leadership team. We're growing again, expanding our facilities, acquiring companies, and delivering more consistently to our customers. Best of all, we've been profitable, even through the tough years, and I am able to truly strategize our long-term path instead of concentrating on present-day issues. On a one-to-ten scale, I give the whole experience a ten (and I don't give many tens)."

JOE CEKOLA
President, Imperial Beverage

"Prior to beginning our EOS journey, issues small and large often got in the way of our growth. Implementing EOS has helped us see these issues and resolve them. We now have a phenomenal (and very clear) vision for our firm, the right structure to take us to the next level, and are hiring strategically based on our Core Values so that we have the right people in the right seats. We've grown 25 percent or more in each of the last three years and, perhaps more importantly, are enjoying the ride. We look forward to working hard with a great team, but are increasingly able to disengage at the end of the day and spend quality time with our families. It doesn't get much better."

DAVE KOLB
CEO, Global Tax Network

"After twenty-seven years of business, a downturn in the economy, and a new management team, adopting EOS was exactly what we needed at Brogan & Partners. Through the process, we have expedited our decision making, enabling us to get far more done in a shorter period of time. Simply, the process has helped us make the

hard decisions that are right for our business. Not only has EOS helped us uncover our true culture, it has helped our company live by those values. Brogan & Partners is stronger, the management team is more accountable, and we are seeing the results with an influx of new clients, more income, and a better bottom line."

ELLYN DAVIDSON
Managing Partner, Brogan & Partners

"Five years ago we ended the year at $5 million in revenue and a 3 percent net loss. Things weren't awful, but we definitely wanted to do better, so we implemented EOS. It felt a little awkward at first, but as we began to master the system, things became simpler and everything began to work better. As a result, we ended the next year at $7,500,000 with a 6 percent net profit! The whole leadership team is so much more confident about the future now, and we've never been so unified as a team. I guess the big 'WOW!' in all of this is knowing that our dreams are attainable. We're on pace to close out this year at $18 million with a nice profit. EOS works."

STEVE SPIECH
Spiech Farms

"Though growing quickly, profitable, and entirely self-funded after three years in business, my partner and I realized things weren't perfect. We had a murky vision, plenty of stress, and a strained partnership. Implementing EOS changed all that. For the first time we had clarity and accountability. We began managing our growth in a way that wouldn't cost us our friendship or financial stability. Two short years after seriously doubting the future of our business, it is stronger and growing faster than ever. The results speak for themselves. Sales have grown from $2.2 million to more than $7 million in two short years, and we are #258 on the Inc. 500. Best of all, we run a stable, profitable business and we're still having fun."

ANDREW DUNEMAN
Owner, Bulk Reef Supply

"Dietz Property Group (DPG) has been implementing EOS for just over two years coming out of the Great Recession. During this period, we grew 44 percent by picking up six new third-party engagements and acquiring three new properties—after being stagnant for a couple of years. EOS has also helped position us for future growth. We are a much stronger, clearer, simpler, more cohesive organization than before we started with EOS."

BRIAN DIETZ
President, Dietz Property Group

"Lowry Computer Products is celebrating our one-year anniversary of being engaged in the EOS process and have committed to the process for our future. The process has helped us solidify our vision and streamlined the execution of our vision. As a result, our company has accomplished major milestones in propelling growth and employee satisfaction, and reaching all of our goals successfully. We grew three times the rate of our industry average this year."

MIKE LOWRY
President/CEO, Lowry Computer Products

"Our business had enjoyed sixty-plus years of success prior to implementing EOS with a 'shoot from the hip' way of doing business. As we grew, however, that approach created inconsistency and inefficiencies as each of our locations developed their own way of doing things and each became like separate businesses. We realized that would make it very difficult for us to continue growing profitably. EOS has given us the structure, discipline, and accountability to get everyone in the organization on the same page and working hard to achieve a common vision. We waste less time, identify and resolve issues as a healthy, cohesive team, and we get more done."

TOM BOHLS
Vice President, Buckeye Power Sales

"EOS was the catalyst for one of the most remarkable changes in my company. My leadership team has integrated the EOS tools into our everyday work habits. Our vision is clear, and strategies are well-executed and communicated to all. EOS taught my leadership team how to plan, act, and communicate in a system that is easy for all to adopt and follow. Within the first year of

integrating EOS, my company was able to achieve a record revenue growth of 87 percent over the prior year."
RANDY PRUITT
President, Randall Industries, Inc.

Get A Grip is not designed to just give you something to think about. It's thorough enough to help you and your leadership team fully implement the tools described in this fable and achieve results like those of the companies above. We could have written this book as a straightforward description of EOS (in fact, its companion book, *Traction,* does exactly that). But we believe that for many readers, observing a company actually implementing EOS will make the process easier to follow and apply. It also provides greater insights into the realities of implementation.

When we decided to write this book, it was a true passion project. As we started to write, the words and situations flowed out of us like water. The reason is that this is what we do. Every day we are in the real world, helping entrepreneurial leadership teams of small to mid-sized companies achieve the results you will read about. Nothing is made up. There is not one ounce of theory. Together we have delivered almost two thousand full-day sessions with almost two hundred companies.

Our passion and obsession is you, the entrepreneurial leader. You take risks, you build remarkable things, and you suffer. Helping you get everything you want from your business is why we exist. We are here to help you permanently resolve the root cause of your issues, to build something greater, and live the life you want and deserve. EOS was created for you by someone just like you. You are real, raw, and lay it on the line every day with no safety nets and no BS. We feel you deserve a solution worthy of who you are and how you operate.

We believe *Get A Grip* will give you everything you need to transform the performance of your business. But if you need more resources, like free downloadable tools and an entrepreneurial community to access, or you want to find a Certified EOS Implementer in your area, you can access them at www.eosworldwide.com. But let's not get ahead of ourselves. Turn the page, start reading, and begin the process of truly getting a grip on your business.

CHAPTER 1

THE INCIDENT

S ITTING IN HER CAR, Eileen Sharp stared intently at Vic's SUV parked across the lot. For a brief moment, she envisioned gunning the engine and ramming it. The hint of a smile appeared at the corners of her mouth.

Eileen was angry and frustrated with Vic. For the first time, she thought of ending the partnership with her childhood friend. After a few moments, she gathered herself and regained some resolve.

"I'm not walking away from what we've built these last ten years," Eileen said under her breath. "You don't just turn your back on a $7 million company and thirty-five employees."

Still, what her business partner had done in the meeting was a new low. The fact that he had said it in front of the other leaders was unforgivable. She couldn't just let it go.

Suddenly Eileen realized she was late for the Business Roundtable reception. She took a deep breath and checked herself in the rearview mirror. As she pulled out of the parking lot, she muttered, "That son of a bitch."

Four hours earlier, at 1:00 P.M., Eileen had rushed into the conference room carrying her laptop and a mound of paperwork. Determined to begin Swan Services' quarterly executive committee meeting on time for once, she had scurried around all morning and skipped lunch to prepare the presentation and numerous reports that would tell the story of the last eighteen months.

This had been the first tough stretch in Swan Services' history. Until the last year and a half, the company had been profitable and had grown quickly. Swan was still doing well, but the steady growth had stopped. Everything seemed to be getting more difficult: winning new customers, keeping them happy, operating profitably—you name it. She had always taken pride in her work ethic, but recently the demands of her business required so much attention that she regularly missed important events with her husband and two children. For the first time, Eileen was frustrated, and she could tell that other members of the team were frustrated, too.

Eileen burst through the conference room door ready to apologize, once again, for being late. Instead, she found only two of her five colleagues. Sue Meecham, Swan's vice president of sales, was reviewing the latest pipeline numbers. Eileen's longtime friend and business associate and the acting director of marketing, Art Pearson, was stowing his overcoat and briefcase in the corner of the conference room.

"Hello, Sue. Hi, Art. Any sign of the others?" she asked.

"No," replied Sue. "Unless you count Evan racing by a minute ago and looking relieved to see he wasn't the only one late."

Eileen rolled her eyes, dropped her materials at the front of the table, and asked Art to help connect her laptop to the LCD projector. In walked Carol Henning, Swan's controller. Eileen distributed presentation folders to the three executives and began bringing up the PowerPoint presentation she had prepared. Vice President of Operations Evan McCullough entered looking rushed and disheveled. And then the team waited.

Vic finally strolled through the door at 1:14, still in the middle of an animated phone conversation with what sounded like a prospective client. He made a few exaggerated gestures to the rest of the team, making it clear he was attempting to end the call. Eventually he hung up, sat down, and apologized as only Vic could.

"Sorry, guys. That was the procurement guy at Shoreline Industries," he said. "I've been trying to pry that deal out of his hands and back under the control of our buyer for so long, I think we used a slide rule to put the bid together."

The entire team laughed—even Eileen. She tossed her founding partner and CEO a folder, strode to the front of the room, grabbed the remote control, and launched into her presentation. Over the next sixty minutes, she detailed the troubling signs that had developed in the five quarters since the company's breakout year:

- In Swan's eighth full year, revenues grew at a record pace and exceeded $7 million for the first time. However, the company hadn't managed to hit its quarterly revenue goals since. Against projected growth of 14 percent, revenue had grown only 1.5 percent in the previous year and was flat in Q1 this year.
- Profitability had taken a beating. On the heels of a great year, the team had invested heavily in a foundation for further growth. Those investments had not yet paid off.
- Pinpointing the cause of these problems had been difficult. Eileen had been studying the issue for three quarters and now felt comfortable sharing her findings with the team:
  - Swan's sales team had missed its new revenue goal in three of the last five quarters.
  - Existing customers had begun leaving—a new phenomenon. At first the occasional defections seemed trivial, but the trend was disconcerting.
  - Labor costs had increased significantly. Swan had begun adding people and upgrading talent last year in an effort to ramp up to its five-year goal of $20 million in revenue.
  - Despite the company's paying more for talent, a couple key employees had resigned abruptly in recent months. Neither cited internal issues in exit interviews, but Eileen had come to believe that Swan's once great culture—one devoted to being a genuinely fun place to work hard and get great results—had begun eroding.

None of these issues was new. The team had discussed each one at some length in prior quarterly meetings, often staying late into the night and ordering pizza, but rarely reaching agreement on anything, much less a plan of action. The prevailing sense was that the primary cause of all of these issues was somehow outside of their control.

One quarter, the economy was to blame. The next, it was the software conversion. Last quarter, Vic had actually used the terms "bad mojo" and "funk" in an attempt to quantify the problem, suggesting that the company had lost its "Midas touch."

"Dwelling on all this bad news drags us down," he had said, staring directly at Eileen. "We've lost our swagger, and—while I know some of you will dismiss this as metaphysical mumbo jumbo—I'm convinced that we have to get that swagger back at all costs."

At the time Eileen had taken Vic's observation in stride. She had learned long before to ignore his constant baiting and avoid getting sucked into titanic battles over trivial matters. Instead, Eileen had analyzed the situation thoroughly and carefully prepared her plan of attack for today's meeting. She had entered the conference room intent on staying positive and focusing on solutions to the thirteen things she believed the executive committee actually *could* control. But first, she needed to present her mountain of evidence to convince them that Swan had a right to expect more.

Eileen methodically made her case; the data was irrefutable. Despite a larger budget, Swan's marketing efforts had produced fewer qualified leads. The sales team's close ratio had declined, and it had more frequently offered discounted pricing on the deals it *had* won. In operations, revenues per employee had fallen, while errors and missed deadlines were up.

As she walked through the troubling details, Eileen saw the mood in the conference room change. Arms were uncrossed. Heads began to nod. Notes were taken. Near the end of her presentation, Vic pushed himself away from the conference table and held his hands up dramatically, as though he had eaten too much at Thanksgiving dinner.

"No mas, boss," he said with a smile. "We get it."

When the laughter subsided, Eileen suggested the team take a quick break and return ready to start solving problems. In high spirits, she headed for the ladies' room. That's where a nightmare scenario began to unravel.

Eileen heard someone slide quickly into the restroom before the swinging door closed behind her.

"Um, Eileen?"

"Yes, Sue—what is it?" said the startled leader.

"I don't know exactly how to say this," she began. "So I'll just spit it out. I think it would be best for all concerned if I left Swan, effective immediately."

Eileen was floored. She considered Sue a shining star—and an integral part of Swan's future. Since joining the company two years before, after a successful stint selling for a competitor, the young VP of sales had been a tireless and skilled asset. She consistently worked harder and got better results than anyone else in the organization and had recently been rewarded with a promotion.

"Wha—I mean, *why?*" Eileen stammered.

"It's clear to me that I'm the problem," Sue said, straining. "You and Vic promoted me nine months ago. Since then our team hasn't hit a single sales goal. I haven't even hit my *own* sales goals! On the rare occasion that we *do* win a deal, we seem to be screwing that up, too." She turned and splashed cold water on her face.

"What in the world do you *mean*, Sue?" she cried. "Of all the people in that room, you're the *least* of my worries!"

"I don't know how you can say that, Eileen. Every slide in your presentation hit me like a ton of bricks! We're not selling enough, margins are down, and the customers we do sell seem to be putting undue stress on the ops team. What's more, all of this seemed to start about the same time I was promoted! If the sales team and I aren't to blame, who is?" she asked.

Eileen started to sweat. Was she about to drive away her most promising ally—the young leader she believed Swan could least afford to lose?

"Sue," she said gently. "I appreciate the way you take responsibility for everything you do. Candidly, I wish the other members of the executive committee felt the same way. But..." she trailed off, unsure of what to say next.

After an awkward pause, Eileen continued. "Please, Sue, give me a week or so to sort things out," she said. "I just *can't* let you resign."

"Well, um..." Sue seemed surprised that Swan's capable leader was at a loss for answers. "Okay, thank you. I'm grateful for your confidence in me."

"You have nothing to say 'thank you' for," Eileen replied. "I feel terrible about making you doubt your value to this team."

Before exiting the restroom, Eileen thought about how best to proceed. She had originally planned to focus first on marketing and sales performance but decided to switch gears.

"Let's discuss client retention first," Eileen said as the meeting resumed, distributing a large Excel spreadsheet. Vic stared at the endless rows of numbers and sighed audibly. Undaunted, Eileen walked the team through a detailed accounting of the spending habits and life cycles of every client in Swan's history. Eileen explained the conclusions she had drawn: Two years ago, Swan's average client had engaged the firm for 2.5 projects and spent an average of $174,000 over its life cycle. Today, both of those numbers had dropped. Two of the largest clients on the spreadsheet had decreased their spending by more than 10 percent, and one of those clients hadn't spent a dime with Swan for over a year.

Evan began to sweat as all eyes turned his way. He glanced nervously at his colleagues—the passionate founder with a short attention span; a young, hard-charging sales leader; an annoying marketing guy; a curmudgeon from accounting; and the other founder waving an incriminating spreadsheet. By all accounts, the day had taken a nasty turn.

"Hold on here, guys," he stammered. "This is the first I've seen of this information. I'll admit it sounds pretty bad, but until I look into the numbers and talk to my people, I have no idea where to even begin."

"*Relax*, Evan," said Vic. "Weren't you paying attention to Eileen's feel-good movie of the year? Every one of us is sucking wind right now!"

Evan chuckled halfheartedly. The rest of the group stared at their spreadsheets, waiting to see how Eileen would respond to Vic's attempt to lighten the mood.

"He's right, Evan," she said coolly. "This isn't a witch hunt. I just hoped we could work together this afternoon to figure out how to get these numbers headed back in the other direction. Perhaps I should have shared this data with you before our meeting today. You're so busy already that I didn't want to bother you."

"But I'm not even sure the numbers are accurate," he protested.

"The numbers *are* accurate," said Carol abruptly. "I put the spreadsheet together myself. And isn't it your *job* to know what the numbers mean?"

As usual, a cutting remark from Carol brought the discussion to a standstill. A capable and dedicated resource, Swan's controller had never been admired for her interpersonal communication skills. Even when accurate, her blunt feedback often drove others away and shut down meetings—which was just fine by Carol.

The room was uncomfortably silent. Eileen's blood pressure began to rise. The executive committee's discussions had been derailed too many times by petty bickering, and she wasn't about to let that happen today.

"Just a minute, Carol," she said sternly. "Remember, today is about staying positive and working through our problems together, not arguing or casting blame."

Eileen turned back to her VP of operations. "Evan," she said, "I'm guessing the whole team supports your desire for more information, but we need to spend a few minutes brainstorming today to see if we can identify any obvious opportunities to improve. We should also talk about the best way to quickly get more reliable information on why our clients seem to be leaving faster and spending less than they did before."

"Right," said Art. "Great idea, Chief. Maybe my firm can conduct a focus group with some clients whose spending has declined or stopped?"

Eileen shot glances at both Art and Sue. The two had been arguing a lot recently about marketing priorities and Art's enthusiasm for costly new marketing projects. Before Eileen could say something, Evan interjected.

"Sorry, Eileen, I didn't mean to be so defensive," he said. "I've just been swamped lately with my own projects and babysitting my staff. There's hardly any time to come up for air as it is, and then to be confronted with this..." his voice trailed off.

"I get it, Evan," said Eileen gently, suddenly feeling very tired. Despite the lack of progress, she decided to take another short break. This dead end with Evan had sucked the energy out of the room. She needed to get him (and the rest of the team) reengaged. "Let's take ten. We'll reconvene at four."

Eileen made eye contact with Vic as she broke the meeting. She cocked her head in the direction of their offices, and he nodded his understanding. Vic ducked into the restroom and then quickly headed back to Eileen's office, where he found his talented, driven partner leaning back in her chair with eyes closed and arms crossed behind her head. Through the years he had rarely seen Eileen stand still, much less meditate.

"Hey, Vic," she said dejectedly.

"What's up, Eileen?" he replied.

"Well," she began, "I know you're going to say, 'I told you so,' but I'm really worried this team wasn't prepared for what I shared with them today."

"You mean Evan?" asked Vic. "He's just being a defensive control freak, like always. Don't let it—"

"Not just Evan," Eileen interjected. "Sue tried to resign in the restroom during the last break."

"*What?*" cried Vic. "Why didn't you tell me? Why didn't *she* tell me? What the hell is going on here?"

Eileen responded wearily, "Slow down, Vic. It just happened an hour ago—there was no time to tell you. Besides, I talked her out of it, at least for a week."

"Well that's just *great*," said Vic sarcastically. "At least one of our best young minds is happy here for another *week*! Great job, Eileen."

The more Vic thought about it, the angrier he got.

"I still can't believe you didn't involve me in this conversation!" he shouted. "We're *partners*, for one thing. And Sue works for *me* in sales. She's my only direct report, for God's sake. Why on earth would she resign to *you*?"

Listening to Vic's histrionics, Eileen regretted her decision to put glass walls and doors on all the executive offices. Anyone from the rows of cubicles outside her office would know the two partners were arguing yet again.

"Vic, please sit down. I called you back here to bring you into the loop and get your help. I couldn't have called you into our impromptu conference in the *ladies' room*! Please?" she pleaded, her tone softening.

Vic quickly checked the office behind him and sat down.

"Okay," Vic replied more calmly. "But shouldn't we go get her and work this out?"

"I don't think so," said Eileen. "I've been watching Sue since the last break, and it looks like she's calmed down a bit. If we stop the meeting to rehash our conversation, we'll just reopen the wound. Let's give her some time to rethink things and speak with her again later in the week."

"I guess that makes sense," said Vic.

"I'd really like to finish this meeting, Vic," said Eileen. "We've *got* to respond to these challenges we face, and we have to do it *together.* That said, I underestimated how personally the team would take my matter-of-fact approach."

"Is that what you call it?" asked Vic. "How about hair-on-fire approach?"

"Stop it," she said with a smile.

"I'm with you, partner," said Vic, getting serious. "But I'm begging you to ease up a little. Sue and Evan responded the way they did because it sometimes seems nothing is ever good enough for you."

"I know," Eileen acknowledged. "But we can't just sweep these problems under the rug."

"Agreed," replied Vic as they left the office. "But let's focus on forming a plan rather than dwelling on problems."

Later, when she looked back, Eileen would remember that conversation with Vic as the only bright spot in easily the worst day of her professional career. From there, it took less than twenty minutes to drive the bus off a cliff.

Back in the conference room, she asked the executives to jot down five to ten potential solutions to the client retention problem. Then she stepped to the whiteboard and asked the executives to share their lists, beginning with Carol.

"Better quality control," she began. Eileen recorded the idea.

"Make fewer mistakes. Manage projects better. Quit making up stuff during the sales process. Sell at higher margins so we can hire better people."

Eileen winced at Carol's blunt criticisms of nearly everyone else in the room.

"Thank you for your usual candor, Carol," she said, forging ahead. "Sue?"

"Clearer statements of work," Sue began. "I also had selling at higher margins. And, Evan, please don't take this personally, but I do think we need a better project management system. It's too hard to get information out of your department when clients ask for status updates."

"That's okay, Sue. I had the same thing on my list," said Evan.

"I also had better invoicing," said Sue, bracing for Carol's response.

"How so?" Carol responded, folding her arms across her chest.

"Well, we get a lot of complai—um, inquiries, about our invoices. If they were delivered more promptly and included clearer detail about the work being performed, I think our clients would appreciate it," she said gently.

"Well, just how do you think I can do that when we aren't defining the project properly during the sales process," Carol barked, "and when I'm sorting through emails and Post-it notes from operations to figure out what the heck to bill each month?"

Vic stopped doodling on his legal pad and cut in suddenly. "Whoa there, Carol," he said. "Let's just get the ideas on the list."

"But I—" protested Carol.

"Damn it, Carol," interjected Eileen, surprised by her own temper. "We're just brainstorming possible solutions. Sue's got a valid point. Can we move on?"

"Whatever," the testy controller said dismissively. She settled back in her chair and glared at Sue.

"Art, anything to add?" Eileen continued.

"Just focus groups or some kind of market research, Chief," said Art, again getting looks from Sue and Carol.

"Very well," Eileen said. "Vic?"

"Just three things, Eileen," he said. "First, I think we need new offices."

"What?" Carol said reflexively.

"New offices. I know we have a couple of years left on our lease. But this place is dark, too corporate, and not conducive to fostering the kind of teamwork we need to knock our clients' socks off. I said that when we moved out here to the 'burbs three years ago, and I think it's more true now. Plus, we have to do something radical to shake this run of bad luck."

Wanting to be fair, Eileen dutifully recorded "new offices" on the whiteboard. She heard Carol murmur "Oh boy" under her breath. Undaunted, Vic continued.

"Second, I think we might be in the wrong business."

Everyone in the room suddenly fixed his or her complete attention on Swan's unpredictable CEO.

"You heard me correctly," Vic continued. "We need to reinvent this company from the ground up with a renewed focus on what clients are going to need over the next ten years. We're still selling plain old business and technology projects, and our clients are just not buying those anymore."

"Okay," Eileen said slowly. She looked skeptically at Vic, poised to write something. "How, exactly, would you say that for the list?"

"How would I say that for the list? C'mon, Eileen, I just suggested we scrap our business model and start over, and you want to know how to write that on your *list*?"

"Well, yes. I do," replied the surprised president. "What's wrong with that?"

"Because your list," he said, "is a waste of time—trivial details. We might as well whitewash the fence while the house is burning!"

A switch had been flipped in Vic's brain. When he looked back on this moment later, it would never be clear exactly what had set him off. He did recall feeling absolutely certain that Swan Services had been going about things in precisely the wrong way for all these years. He was suddenly seized by an overwhelming desire to convince his longtime partner that incremental progress was not enough.

"Call it 'reinvent Swan,'" he said sharply.

"And the third thing," he said, "is that you and I need to admit that the way we're running this company isn't working."

Immediately the mood in the room shifted from painfully awkward to panic-stricken. The executives worked hard to avoid eye contact. The fan on the LCD projector hummed loudly. A throat was cleared nervously. Eileen opened her mouth to speak but said nothing.

"Face it, partner," Vic continued. "Running this company has gotten *hard*. We're not having fun anymore, and we're not hitting our numbers like we used to. I think we've been asleep at the switch for the last year, and we need to make some radical changes or we're screwed."

Eileen's head was swimming. "How do you mean?"

"We've been running this company together for a long time—me at thirty thousand feet, you in the trenches. Clearly, that hasn't worked as of late," he said loudly. "So I'd propose we switch it up."

Eileen glanced at the other executives. Four sets of wide eyes darted back and forth between her and her partner, trying to figure out what was going to happen next. Eileen agreed that something was broken, but Vic running day-to-day operations? That was truly crazy!

"You're suggesting that *you* run the company day to day?" she asked, trying in vain not to sound defensive.

"Sure, why not?" he asked.

That did it. Eileen felt the heat rising into her face.

"Why not?" she hissed. "I'll tell you why not! You have absolutely *no idea* what 'day to day' *is*. It means being in this office nearly every day for the last six months. It means seventy-hour workweeks. It means spending more time with your kids on a cell phone than in person—missing baseball games, parent-teacher conferences, and *birthdays*, for God's sake! It means paying attention to detail. It means discipline and sacrifice."

"Maybe the way *you* do it," Vic said firmly.

"C'mon, Vic, you're a *sales guy*!" She regretted the words as soon as she said them.

"First of all, Eileen, I'm a hell of a lot more than a 'sales guy.' For starters, I'm your cofounder and partner—we've built this business *together*, and you know it."

"You're right, Vic," said Eileen, backpedalling futilely. "I didn't mean—"

"And being a 'sales guy' means I understand people," Vic continued. "I know how to build and leverage relationships, how to get things done through others. Those things *matter*! You've spent the last three months locked in your office with your spreadsheets, intent on convincing us all that the sky is falling. And what has it gotten us? Your most promising executive resigned in the restroom. Evan's so overworked he keeps a *cot* in his office, and today he spent three hours with us focused on everything he's doing wrong. Your old friend Art the vulture is circling our carcass hoping for more work, and Carol's here to point out what everyone else is doing wrong."

Vic jumped up and drew a tangled series of lines and swirls on the whiteboard. "What it's gotten us," he shouted, "is a big, hairy, dysfunctional *mess*!" Vic handed his marker to Eileen on his way out the door, leaving the stunned president alone with her wide-eyed executive committee.

"I think we're done here," she said in a barely audible whisper.

The team filed silently out of the conference room. Eileen sat for a moment, stunned. She and Vic had argued many times before, but something about this blowup felt different. The severity of Vic's attack had surprised and hurt her.

Having just seen her partner beeline toward his office, Eileen elected to gather her things and head straight to the parking lot. She wasn't sure exactly where to go; she just knew better than to risk further escalating the confrontation. Arriving at her car, she chucked her things on the passenger seat and noticed the hastily scribbled Post-it note affixed to the steering wheel:

Biz Roundtable
Cocktail Event

Walker Museum 6-8

Eileen had been a member of the Twin Cities Business Roundtable—a peer group for small business owners—for three years. These days she rarely had time to attend the group's regular social and education events. She had written the note earlier that morning after promising several people she would make it tonight. Still seething, Eileen stole one last glance at Vic's vehicle before pulling slowly out of the lot.

"I'd rather chew glass than make small talk right now," she thought grimly. "On the other hand, maybe a stiff drink will do me some good."

HOPE

Vic slammed open his office door, replaying the last few minutes in his head. Gradually coming to grips with what he had just done to his partner, he slumped into his chair, dropped his head, and rubbed his temples. Slowly Vic allowed himself to acknowledge how scared and unhappy he had become these last few months.

He'd been having trouble sleeping for the first time in his life. His trademark confidence had begun to erode, causing him to play it safe and avoid conflict, another first. Vic began to realize his own frustrations and self-doubt had caused the sudden attack. He had lashed out at Eileen because her relentless focus on the negative made it impossible to ignore the fact that he and the rest of the team at Swan just weren't getting it done.

"Damn," thought Vic. He hit Eileen's speed dial, hoping for the chance to make things right.

Eileen checked her vibrating smartphone at a stoplight.

She pressed the "ignore" button when the name "Vic Hightower" popped up on the display. After thirty years she knew well how he operated. He was calling to apologize.

Their "professional" relationship had begun on a whim, when Vic suggested they start a lemonade stand in their neighborhood, the City Lakes district near downtown Minneapolis. With Vic on a street corner reining in passersby and Eileen managing the stand, the "business" was a success from the start.

Throughout their many entrepreneurial adventures, Vic had been the front man and Eileen the backbone of their operations. The two ran numerous ventures as teens—a lawn-care business, a bike repair shop, and even a stint reselling bulk candy to other middle-school students. Although they pursued different tracks through college, the pair made an effort to stay connected. Eileen studied business and graduated with honors from the University of Minnesota's Carlson School of Management. Vic changed schools and majors three times, all the while less interested in studying than in running a series of remarkably profitable ventures from his dorm rooms and apartments.

Eileen secured a high-profile job with a prestigious investment banking and management consulting firm right out of school. For nine years she moved up quickly in several of the firm's practice areas and ultimately worked closely with more than sixty companies. From the beginning, she had planned to eventually leave the firm to buy a business—or start her own.

Vic's postcollegiate career was as fluid as Eileen's was stable. He took his first sales job as a fourth-year junior and was immediately successful. Over the next few years he replayed the same story several times—excelling in his first several months as a business developer only to later become bored, frustrated, or both. Despite the frequent job changes, though, Vic's talent and drive to win always helped him perform at a high level.

Although on divergent paths, the two friends spoke often. During one such call eleven years earlier, Eileen had first sought feedback regarding her plan to start a technology consulting business. Within days, the two had cobbled together a compelling business plan and had committed to making it happen—together.

Eileen snapped out of her walk down memory lane when she arrived at the Walker Art Center. She parked and went inside.

"Well, I'll be," said a familiar voice from the registration table. "I was beginning to think you were a figment of my imagination!"

Eileen smiled at Bill Pullian, executive director of the Business Roundtable, and extended her hand sheepishly. "I figure I'd better show up every once in a while," she replied. "Otherwise you're going to think my membership fee is a charitable contribution."

Walking away, Eileen wondered if Bill could tell she was still reeling after her train wreck of an afternoon. She glanced to her right to see Miguel Gutierrez zeroing in on the open bar.

"Hello, stranger, can I buy you a drink?" he asked.

"Very generous of you, Miguel," she answered. "I'll be sure to return the favor when we're at some high-priced fund-raiser."

Eileen was genuinely glad to see Miguel. He had been a member of her roundtable since she joined the group more than three years ago. Although he ran one of the largest and fastest growing companies in the Twin Cities chapter, he had always been generous with his time and counsel.

"How ya been?" he said, extending his arms for a hug.

"I've had better days," she said.

"Well, let's grab a drink and talk about it," said Miguel.

The pair collected their cocktails and retreated to a less crowded spot.

"So what's happening?" Miguel asked.

"It's really just the same old story..." Her voice trailed off, and Miguel raised an eyebrow to invite more.

Eileen hesitated. On the one hand, Miguel was the *perfect* confidant—very successful but humble enough to share his trials and tribulations with other members of his roundtable. On the other hand, by sharing what had happened this afternoon, Eileen worried she would be admitting that the company she had painstakingly built was falling apart.

Miguel motioned to some nearby chairs. "Why don't you start at the beginning?"

"Well," Eileen said with a heavy sigh, "you know how much harder things seemed to have gotten since our $7 million year."

Miguel nodded; Eileen had shared a few details in prior discussions.

"I've spent most of the last year trying to figure out why and to get my team to respond. Until today they'd been mostly ignoring me, blaming the problem on stuff outside our control. Today I finally convinced them otherwise," she said ruefully.

Miguel looked confused. "That sounds like *good* news."

"You'd think so, wouldn't you?" replied Eileen with a sarcastic laugh. "In less than three hours, my best executive tried to quit—in the ladies' room, no less. My ops guy pretty much ran screaming from the room when we started talking about ways to improve customer satisfaction. Our marketing guy cares more about generating revenue for his own agency than our survival, and my controller spent the whole meeting pissing everyone else off."

"Sounds awful," Miguel said soothingly.

"Those were the *bright spots*!" said Eileen. Both she and Miguel had a good laugh at her expense. More comfortable telling the story now, she went on to describe the private discussion and public conflict with Vic. Miguel listened intently, asked a few clarifying questions, and then grabbed a business card from his coat pocket.

"You're right, Eileen, that is one lousy day," he acknowledged. "But it might be the best thing that ever happened to you."

Eileen was puzzled. "How is *that* possible?"

"Because it happened to me," said Miguel, smiling.

"One of your people resigned in the *ladies' room*?" she joked.

Miguel laughed and continued, "About five years ago, I had—by far—my worst day in business. The company was really struggling, and it had been unbelievably hard on my family and me. I was working all the time, waking up at all hours of the night—it was awful."

Eileen was shocked. Of all the entrepreneurs she knew, Miguel seemed like the calmest and most balanced.

"Finally, on that terrible day, I decided I'd had enough. I realized that everything about the way my company operated needed to change. Luckily, a friend and mentor helped me understand I probably couldn't make that kind of change on my own. So I took his advice and, as he had done a few years earlier, asked for help."

Miguel took his business card and wrote down a phone number on the front, then flipped it over and wrote something else on the back. He slid the card to Eileen.

"When you're ready to make things better—permanently—call my friend Alan Roth," Miguel said, standing.

"Wait, Miguel—who is this Alan?" Eileen said, standing as well. "Why do you think he can help me?"

"Because that's what he does, Eileen. He helps people like us get what we want from our businesses," he said.

"He's a consultant?" she said with a sour look. "Listen, Miguel, I really respect you, but if I walk back into my business tomorrow suggesting we hire another consultant, I'll have a full-scale mutiny on my hands!"

Miguel nodded reassuringly. "I get it, Eileen. I felt the same way about consultants, which is why it took me six months to call Alan myself. But he's not a consultant—he calls himself an 'implementer.' All I can tell you is that his system and approach are completely different from anything you and your team have experienced. And it'll flat-out work."

"I don't know, Miguel," protested Eileen.

A mutual friend walked by, and Miguel held up a finger to get her attention.

"I have to run, Eileen—Melanie and I have been trying to connect for weeks," he said. "I really do think Alan can help. Call him."

"Thanks, Miguel," she said, fingering the business card. "You've definitely given me something to think about."

Before placing Miguel's card in her bag, she noticed her friend had written something intriguing on the back:

CHAPTER 2
FIT

B Y THE TIME Eileen pulled her car into the garage that evening, Vic's email had appeared in her inbox. Flagged as "urgent" and copied to the entire executive committee, the message was a long, heartfelt apology.

Despite Vic's attempt to patch things up with Eileen and reestablish himself as a team player, the next two weeks were unsettling. The others saw no evidence that anything significant had happened since what was now being referred to as "the incident." As a result, conflict and confusion hung in the air like a stubborn fog.

Eileen grew more frustrated with each passing day. Remembering her ten years' experience helping other companies resolve much bigger problems, she now completely understood how difficult changing an organization from the inside could be.

"Besides," she wondered aloud, "what if *I am* the problem?"

With that in mind, Eileen pulled the dog-eared business card that Miguel had given her from her purse and placed it on her desk. She'd repeated this step several times but hadn't yet mustered the courage to go public with the company's issues. Finally, Eileen picked up her receiver and dialed.

"Alan?" she inquired. "This is Eileen Sharp of Swan Services. I got your—"

"Eileen," interjected Alan. "I've been looking forward to talking with you ever since Miguel told me to expect your call. How are you?"

"Oh," said Eileen, surprised that Alan knew who she was. "What, um, what did Miguel share with you?"

"Not much really," replied Alan. "He just said you were a success-ful entrepreneur who wanted to get more from your business."

"Well," said Eileen, relieved. "I guess that's right. In fact, you could call it an understatement."

Alan chuckled knowingly. He asked a few questions, and Eileen shared a brief history of Swan. She also talked more frankly than she had planned about the past fifteen months, especially the difficult events of the last few weeks.

"Sounds frustrating, Eileen," Alan said. "If you have just a few more minutes, I'd like to tell you why Miguel thought I could help."

"Sure," said Eileen, relieved to stop talking about Swan's problems.

"My passion is helping entrepreneurs get what they want from their businesses," he began, "by working with their leadership teams to help them master a simple, complete system for running an entre-preneurial company."

"Is that what you did for Miguel's company?" Eileen asked.

"Yes, it is."

"Okay," said Eileen carefully. "So how does it work?"

Alan took a few minutes to explain his system. He described it as a straightforward, holistic "way of operating" an entrepreneurial company—a blend of timeless concepts and simple real-world tools.

"Okay, Alan," interjected Eileen. "This all sounds great, but our experience with consultants has not been stellar. If I recommend bringing in another outside resource, my team may walk out on the spot. How can I be sure this will work for us?"

"Well, you can't, Eileen—not after one phone call," replied Alan. "And frankly, this works best when your whole team is sure, not just you. So if you're curious about whether I can help, let's just take the next step."

"Which is?" queried Eileen.

"I'd like to give you and your leadership team ninety minutes of my time," continued Alan. "Afterward you'll all be fully equipped to make a decision about whether there's a fit."

After exchanging some basic information, the two agreed to talk again later in the week. Eileen hung up, sat back in her chair, and thought carefully about her next move. Later that evening, Eileen called Vic at home.

"Hey, partner," Vic said quietly.

"Hi, Vic," Eileen replied. "I figure it's time we bury the hatchet and get back to business. Agreed?"

"You bet. When?"

"Any chance you could meet me this evening? I'm still at the office, so we could meet at Ruby's."

"I can make that work," Vic replied. "Can you give me about forty-five minutes to help Lisa put the kids down?"

"Of course. See you there."

Ruby's was a dark, quiet bar five minutes from the office. Eileen arrived first and took a table near the back. She ordered vodka on the rocks for herself and a pale ale for her partner. Vic sailed through the door a few minutes later wearing shorts and a rumpled T-shirt.

Eileen pointed at the large spot on Vic's shorts with a quizzical look on her face.

"Oh, that," said her partner instantly. "Bath time got a little ugly."

Eileen chuckled openly, though she struggled to avoid becoming resentful whenever Vic demonstrated his deep commitment to family time so matter-of-factly.

"Glad you could make it, Vic. Be sure to thank Lisa for me," said Eileen.

"Will do. Same to Dan," replied Vic.

"So," began Eileen. "How are we going to fix all this?"

Vic smiled deeply. He loved her ability to get right to the point. He also knew she rarely asked a direct question without having prepared an answer herself.

"I've certainly got some ideas, Eileen. But seeing as how that's what got us in this mess in the first place—" Both partners chuckled. "Why don't you tell me what you're thinking?" finished Vic.

"Glad to," replied Eileen. She talked about what he had said about their losing their mojo and the fact that even after a year, neither of them could come up with a plan the whole team could get behind.

"So," said Eileen quietly. "What would you think of bringing someone in?"

"Someone who?" asked Vic warily.

"Well," Eileen began, choosing her words carefully. "I spoke to Miguel Gutierrez the other day."

Vic nodded, acknowledging that he knew Miguel.

"I didn't share any of the specifics," said Eileen, "but I made it clear that we had hit a rough patch."

"I'd call that a minor understatement," said Vic, smiling.

"Right," she agreed. "Anyway, Miguel's response really surprised me. He admitted that he had been at a similar spot in his business five years ago. And—"

"Really?" said Vic, surprised. "Optimal Distribution? I thought they'd *breezed* to $50 million! And word on the street is that their margins are the best in the industry."

"That was *exactly* my reaction!" responded Eileen. "Miguel's in my roundtable, and in three years of talking about our businesses every month, I've never gotten the feeling he was the least bit frustrated. But he assured me that the problems Optimal faced five years ago were just as severe as ours."

"So what'd he do to fix things?" asked Vic.

"Well, that's the thing. When I asked him that question, he just handed me this business card and told me to call Alan Roth," replied Eileen cautiously. She pushed the card across the table.

"What the heck is 'traction'?" asked Vic.

Eileen recounted her conversation with Alan.

"I don't know, Eileen," protested Vic. "We've had some *lousy* experiences with consultants."

"I hear you," agreed Eileen. "I shared that with Miguel. He assured me Alan is not a consultant and nearly guaranteed that meeting with him would be worth our while. When I pressed him for more details yesterday, Miguel mentioned several other successful companies from different industries Alan has helped. I knew a couple of the owners and made a few calls. Vic, every single one of them had nothing but good things to say."

The partners sat quietly, letting the information settle. Eileen swirled the ice in her vodka.

"So how do you see this working?" Vic asked.

"Alan said he'd start by meeting with the executive committee for ninety minutes," she replied.

"I don't know," said Vic skeptically.

"Remember, Miguel did say he was different," replied Eileen. "I think it's worth ninety minutes of our time. If you and I feel strongly enough about this, the rest of the team will support it."

Vic thought long and hard as he finished his pint. He had always had a dim view of consultants. Still, he was intrigued by Alan's track record with Miguel and the other companies Eileen had mentioned.

"You really want to do this?" Vic asked.

"Yes, I do," replied Eileen.

"Then I'm in."

CONTEXT

The meeting was scheduled for ten o'clock on a Tuesday morning at Alan's office in suburban Minneapolis, a comfortable conference room with wall-mounted whiteboards surrounding a large conference table. Alan asked Eileen to make sure the entire team arrived on time. He greeted each executive at the door and invited the team to sit. Alan waited until everyone got comfortable and then began, about seven minutes after ten.

"Welcome and good morning. Thank you for giving me ninety minutes of your precious time. This meeting is known as the Ninety-Minute Meeting," he said, "which means we will be together for about...ninety minutes."

Most of the group chuckled. Carol rolled her eyes.

"The reason I know that," he continued, "is that we find that covering four simple points is the best way to answer all the questions a team like yours might have about whether my system and I can help you. The first point is 'About Us.' I'll give you a quick history, just so you know I'm not here practicing on you. The second is 'About You.' I'll ask you a few questions to get a sense of where you've been, where you are, and where you're going as an organization. The third point is called 'The Tools.' Here, I'll open my toolbox and share with you some of the real-world tools we use to help you resolve all your issues. My goal is to give you all a clear sense of what a company running on this system really looks like. Finally, we'll review 'The Process' we'll follow to help your leadership team get the most out of your business."

Alan paused for a moment and surveyed the team. "At the end of this meeting," he continued, "we'll both be able to determine if there is a fit and what steps, if any, to take after today. Any questions before we begin?"

"Are we going right to eleven thirty?" asked Art. "I have a call scheduled at that time, and if you need me to move it—"

"I'll make sure we conclude right at eleven thirty, Art," Alan replied immediately.

With that, he began the meeting by sharing a quick professional history with Swan's executive committee. Alan himself had been a lifelong entrepreneur. As he had worked to build his own company, he had discovered a series of simple, practical tools that really seemed to help. He began sharing those tools with other business owners in his network and ultimately found that he had a real passion for helping other entrepreneurs succeed. He sold his business, and a little more than ten years later, Alan decided to pursue that passion full-time.

"Okay, let's talk about Swan Services," he said. "Can someone give me a two-minute history of the organization?" Alan scanned the room, looking for a response. He noticed that Evan's, Sue's, and Art's eyes were darting between Eileen and Vic, wondering which owner was going to answer the question. Vic jumped in to provide a quick overview, and Alan followed up with a series of specific, high-level questions regarding revenues, number of employees, greatest strengths, and biggest challenges. He was careful to draw responses out of each executive in the room. Alan's last questions really hit home.

"I'd like an answer from all of you to these next three questions," he said. "In each case, answer with a number between one and ten. One is worst; ten is best. Ready?"

The team nodded. For some reason she couldn't pinpoint, Eileen got a little nervous about this impromptu assessment of the company she had built.

"On a scale of one to ten, how effective are your *internal* meetings?" Again, nobody wanted to answer first. Alan simply gazed at each leader until someone decided to speak up.

"Seven?" said Evan delicately.

"Seven!" exclaimed Sue. "What meetings are *you* attending?" The whole team laughed loudly, including Evan. "I say two."

Alan chuckled and went around the room quickly. In the end, the average score was a four.

"Okay," he continued. "On a scale of one to ten, how aligned is the entire organization around your plan?"

Again Vic broke the tension. "You're assuming we *have* a plan," he said, smiling. "Two."

"That's a little harsh, Vic," replied Eileen. "We publish a strategic plan annually, and everyone in the organization hears us present the plan and gets an executive summary. I say eight."

"Carol?" said Alan quickly.

"Five," she replied indifferently. Sue said four, acknowledging the existence of the plan but questioning whether the entire organization was aligned around it. Evan said three; Art said six.

Alan recorded the scores in his notebook and moved on to the third question: "How would you rate the level of accountability that exists in your organization?"

Clearly this question struck a nerve, as each leader squirmed a bit while sharing a score of two, three, or four. Alan recorded the average of three and continued.

"Thank you for your candor," he said. He approached the whiteboard at the front of the room, where he had drawn the following diagram:

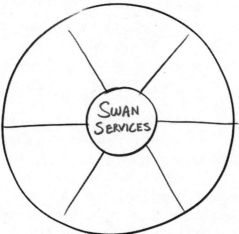

"I'd like to begin by showing you what things will look like at the end of our journey together," he said. "At that point you'll be running

Swan Services using this simple operating system, and your business will have become strong in what I call the 'Six Key Components.' We call the first Key Component 'Vision.'" Alan wrote "VISION" into the top wedge in the diagram. "Strengthening the Vision Component is simply getting everyone 100 percent on the same page with exactly where our organization is going and how we're going to get there."

As Alan turned back to face the group, he noticed several leaders looking furtively at one another. Vic chuckled.

"If you can do that," he said loudly, "name your price!"

Alan laughed along with the group and then introduced the other five Key Components, each with a one-sentence explanation, writing "PEOPLE," "DATA," "ISSUES," "PROCESS," and "TRACTION" into the diagram as he went along.

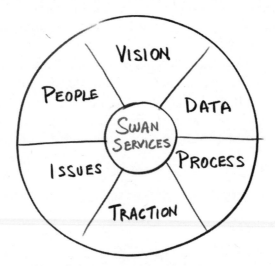

That introduction set the stage for a thorough second pass around the model. In the forty minutes that followed, Alan helped the Swan Services team understand just what "strong" meant for each Key Component, and he introduced a set of practical tools to help the leaders strengthen each Component.

Eileen was intrigued by the simplicity of the system but worried that her team might consider the tools Alan described too basic. While with Anodyne Consulting, she had put together dozens of comprehensive and articulate business plans, dashboards, and organizational development tools that were now being used by dozens of Fortune 1,000 companies. She had attempted to replicate those tools within Swan, to no avail. Was it truly possible that these simple tools could somehow transform her company?

For example, Alan presented the team with a streamlined strategic planning tool called the "Vision/Traction Organizer (V/TO)." He claimed that agreeing on the answers to the eight questions on the V/TO would help the team create a single compelling vision for the organization and get everyone "rowing in the same direction." After ten years of trying, Eileen knew that was a lot more difficult than Alan made it sound. Still, she was drawn to the idea that simplifying things might help.

"I've yet to encounter a company with *no* vision," Alan had explained. "Most of the time there's *too much* vision. In other words, if I were to ask each of you where Swan Services is going and how it's going to get there, I'd likely get six different answers."

Eileen noticed Sue nodding and realized how often she and Vic gave what must seem like conflicting directions to the young executive. Alan's comments really hit home a few minutes later, when he introduced the first question on the V/TO: "What are your Core Values?"

Vic and Eileen had both been through countless hours of leadership training with dozens of organizations. By the time Swan Services was founded, the importance of building a culture around Core Values had become commonplace—even a little clichéd. Dutifully, though, the leaders had agreed on a set of key principles early on. Over time, those Core Values gradually faded into the background, and today, neither partner could recite them without checking the company website. So when Alan talked about the need to live and breathe these few guiding principles every day in order to make sure they define the company's culture, Eileen felt guilty.

"What culture?" she thought to herself.

Worse yet, she noticed that Evan and Sue were nodding vigorously as Alan described the need to "walk the talk" when building an enduring culture. After discussing the V/TO, Alan moved on, and things *really* got interesting.

"When we work on the People Component," Alan began, "we try to cut through all the jargon—'A' Players,' 'Superstars,' 'Platinum

Team,' and so on. Put simply, you need two things to be 100 percent strong in this Component."

He turned to the whiteboard and put two bullets below "PEOPLE" on his diagram. He then wrote the following words as he spoke them:

"Jim Collins popularized these terms by helping us understand that to succeed in business, you need the right people in the right seats," Alan explained. "You've got to have both. But what do those terms really mean? Well, 'right people' share your Core Values—they fit your culture. 'Right seats' means everyone has the skills and experience to excel in a job that's truly important to your organization. Once those definitions are clear and tangible, we use two tools to strengthen your People Component. A simple tool called the People Analyzer will help you clearly identify everyone in the organization who fits your culture like a glove and will also expose those who *don't* share your Core Values."

Evan and Sue stole a glance at Carol, who had pushed herself away from the conference table and sat staring straight ahead, her arms crossed tightly.

"To help you build the ideal structure for your organization and clearly determine the right seats," Alan continued, "we use a very powerful tool called the Accountability Chart."

"We already have an org chart," volunteered Carol icily.

"Of course, Carol, lots of my clients do," Alan said kindly. "And that may save us some time if we decide to work together. But the Accountability Chart is like a supercharged org chart because it absolutely crystallizes everyone's roles and responsibilities. It establishes clear ownership of and accountability for everything that's important to your business and plainly illustrates who reports to whom."

Carol seemed satisfied with that response, and Eileen was relieved. Alan then walked the team through a basic Accountability Chart to demonstrate the process.

"When we build an Accountability Chart, we start with a clean slate by figuratively 'firing' everybody," he said.

"Carol's been waiting more than five years for that day!" shouted Vic.

"Just you, Vic," replied Carol, smiling.

Eileen shook her head. "Children," she thought to herself. Still, it was nice to see the team having fun again—especially Carol.

"We take a big step back and start from scratch," explained Alan, "because we have to focus all of our attention on getting the *simplest* and *best* structure for the organization. When you're stuck thinking about the way things have always worked or the people you have in certain seats today, you simply *can't* focus on structure first. So with a clean slate, we start with the fundamental belief that there are only three major functions in every business." Alan walked to a blank section of the whiteboard and drew three rectangles side by side.

"There's a sales and marketing function," he said, writing "S/M" into one of the rectangles. "You have to generate a lead and close a sale before anything happens."

"There's an operations function," he said, placing an "O" in the center rectangle, "in which you make the product or provide the service."

"And there's finance. You have to keep track of the money flowing in and out of the organization," Alan continued, filling the third rectangle with the letter "F."

"Now, when we build *your* Accountability Chart, we'll customize it. Sometimes the sales and marketing function splits into two seats. There may be two or more distinct operations seats; occasionally finance splits into HR, IT, and admin. This is just a basic structure to illustrate the concept. What's really important is getting the simplest and best structure for you."

He drew a fourth rectangle above the others and placed a large "I" at the top of it. "The next critical function is someone we call the 'integrator.' Simply put, the integrator is the glue—the person who harmoniously integrates the major functions of the business, who runs the day-to-day. In many organizations, these four seats make up the company's leadership team."

Alan then drew a fifth rectangle above the integrator seat and placed a "V" in it. "About half the time," he explained, "there's another critical seat called the 'visionary.' This is the person with lots of ideas. I always say they have twenty ideas a week—nineteen aren't so great, but one is *awesome*. It's that one idea that will take the company to the moon. Often this is the founding entrepreneur. Visionaries are great at relationships and at creating and preserving a good culture. They're creative, strategic thinkers and builders."

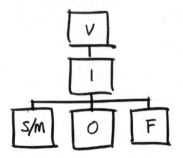

Alan now had the group's complete attention—he had just described Vic perfectly.

"I see two common problems in entrepreneurial companies when the roles of the visionary and integrator haven't been clearly defined," Alan explained. "The first occurs when a visionary is trying to run the company. You can't have a visionary in the integrator seat because what you'll get are these wonderful ninety-day spikes where everybody's excited about a new idea or direction, but then the visionary gets bored running the day-to-day and starts to create chaos. The second problem happens when two or more partners trip all over one another trying to co-run the company. In the world of the Accountability Chart, only one person can ultimately be accountable for a major function. Because when you have two people accountable, nobody is accountable."

Vic and Eileen looked at one another, both feeling a strange mix of emotions. In a few concise sentences, Alan had nailed the essence of their complex thirty-year relationship.

"Once we've identified all the critical functions in the organization," Alan went on, "we then define the five roles for each seat. In other words, what do we need the person who owns each seat to excel at in order to achieve our vision? From there, we'll build out the Accountability Chart for the entire organization. Only *after* we've detailed the critical functions we need and the five roles for each function do we identify the right people for each seat. We do that by comparing the demands of the seat to what people love to do and are best at. Following this process will potentially expose two people issues that need to be resolved. The first is *right person, wrong seat*. You'll have someone who shares your values—they've been around forever, you love 'em—but they're in the wrong seat. Hopefully there's a different seat for that person, but if there's not, assuming you're a for-profit business, you must make a tough people decision."

The team laughed uneasily, and Alan continued. "The second issue is *wrong person, right seat*—you have a talented, productive person who just doesn't share your Core Values. As tough as it is, you *must* let these people go. They're *killing* your culture—chipping away at what you're trying to build in little ways you can't even see. They're consuming your time and energy; they're making other people in the company miserable. Long term they do far more damage than good."

Again Carol drew a few careful glances and scowled.

"Using these tools and making those tough decisions," Alan continued, "you'll ultimately get to a point where all thirty-five people on your team are the right people in the right seats. Only then will you be getting the most from everyone in the organization—working together well and achieving your full potential. The third Key Component is Data. To be 100 percent strong in the Data Component you need two things: Scorecards and measurables for everyone in the organization."

Alan went on to explain that great Scorecards contain five to fifteen weekly numbers—leading indicators that give leadership teams an "absolute pulse" on the business. By looking at thirteen weeks of history each week, he promised, Swan's leaders would see patterns and trends develop, gain insight from those numbers, and make better decisions.

Eileen grinned; nobody liked data more than she did. But the mountains of reports she pored over each day, week, and month didn't give her a "pulse" on the business. Worse yet, she couldn't get anyone else on Swan's leadership team to use that data.

"Ultimately, this discipline will spread throughout the organization," continued Alan. "Every department will have its own Scorecard, and every single person will have at least one measurable. You're 100 percent strong in the Data Component when you have a great leadership team Scorecard and when everyone in the organization is connected to achieving Swan's vision by at least one number he or she has to keep on track each week. With Scorecards and measurables, you'll cut through feelings, subjectivity, personalities, opinions, and egos and instead manage objectively. That creates a peace of mind. You'll sleep better at night. You'll no longer have to talk to six people to get the real story. When a number is off track, you simply make the appropriate adjustment to get that number back on track."

Alan paused to invite questions before continuing. "When you're strong in the Vision, People, and Data Components," he said, "you have a transparent organization. All of your challenges become crystal clear. There's no place to hide, and you start to smoke out the *real* issues. That brings us to the fourth Key Component."

Alan explained how his clients strengthened the Issues Component by first creating a culture in which everyone feels comfortable being open and honest about what he or she believes is holding them back. They get those problems, challenges, ideas, and opportunities out of their heads and onto an "Issues List" for each team. Next, Alan introduced a simple tool called "IDS" that would help those teams make their issues go away forever.

"The 'I' stands for 'identify,'" Alan explained, "the 'D' stands for 'discuss,' and the 'S' stands for 'solve.' This stems from our discovery that when tackling issues, even talented leadership teams spend most of their time discussing. They rarely identify anything and almost never solve anything."

"Oh, that's not us," said Sue sarcastically.

The team laughed, but the thought stuck with Sue for a while. Her single biggest frustration at Swan had been the pervading sense that the organization was stuck. Quarter after quarter the executive committee met for hours to discuss the same challenges over and over again. They'd complain, argue, and even cobble together "solutions" during lengthy meetings, but three months later, they'd be back in the same conference room discussing the same issues.

"Before we start discussing anything," Alan said, "we first have to dig down to identify the root cause of the issue. Then we discuss it openly and honestly—with everyone saying what needs to be said only once, because more than once is politicking. Finally, we solve the issue by agreeing on a plan that will make it go away forever. We take the time to get every member of the team's support for and commitment to that plan before moving on. Ultimately, this simple discipline will create a habit in your organization—top to bottom—that will help *everyone* become an expert at solving his or her own problems so these issues no longer linger for days, weeks, months, and years. You'll stop the endless rehashing."

Alan went on to describe the fifth Key Component—Process. Evan listened carefully as he walked them through an approach for documenting the company's handful of "Core Processes" at a high level and then getting those steps "followed by all." For most of his eight years at Swan, Evan had been trying to finish a thorough standard operating procedures (SOP) manual, to no avail.

"As Jim Collins said, 'Magic occurs when you combine a spirit of entrepreneurialism with a culture of discipline,'" Alan explained. "Most of my clients believe that's far easier said than done, so we take a very simple approach to systemizing your business. Even without a massive procedural manual, everything will quickly become easier to manage, more consistent, more scalable, more profitable, and more fun."

Encouraged but skeptical, the VP of ops concluded things were never as simple as they seemed.

"The last Key Component is Traction," said Alan, "the weakest link in most businesses. Being 100 percent strong in this Component means that everyone in your organization is disciplined and accountable, staying focused on the right stuff and getting done what needs to be done to bring your vision down to the ground and move your organization forward."

Alan then introduced two tools—"Rocks" and an efficient, productive "Meeting Pulse"—that his clients used to strengthen the Traction Component. He added those terms to the board under "TRACTION."

"The term 'Rocks' was first used to describe an organization's top priorities in Stephen Covey's book *First Things First* and popularized further in *Mastering the Rockefeller Habits* by Verne Harnish," Alan explained. "My clients define Rocks as the three to seven most important things they have to get done in the next ninety days. When your business is running on this system, every person in the organization will have at least one Rock each quarter. In years of working with all kinds of entrepreneurial leadership teams from every conceivable industry, I've found that it's human nature to get distracted about every ninety days. We all get sucked into the day-to-day, lose focus, or just get bored. Setting and achieving Rocks each quarter creates a ninety-day world for everyone in your organization. You come together, see how you did last quarter, recheck the vision, and then set new priorities for the next ninety days. This keeps everyone laser focused. Everyone owns a piece of the vision and is working together to achieve it. We come up for air every ninety days and repeat that same pulse forever.

"Inside that ninety-day world, we'll also help you create a healthy, productive Meeting Pulse with weekly 'Level 10 Meetings.' This means you will elevate the meetings you rated earlier at a four to a ten. Level 10 Meetings follow a set agenda with a specific psychology behind it that will help you communicate regularly and productively, stay focused on what's important, and solve issues effectively throughout the quarter."

Alan put down his marker and faced the team.

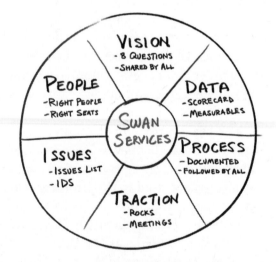

"That's Traction," he continued, "and those are the Six Key Components. Our journey together is designed to help you get to 100 percent strong in each of them—which will never happen. We'll keep striving for it, but 100 percent is utopia. Fortunately, 80 percent or better in each Key Component *is* possible, and most teams reach it. When you're 80 percent strong, everything seems to fall into place. You can grow the business to whatever size you choose. Running the company becomes more peaceful, more profitable, and more fun. That's the goal, and when you get there, you're truly a great organization."

Alan invited questions before continuing on to describe his process.

"The first step in the process is this Ninety-Minute Meeting," he said while drawing on the whiteboard. "If you believe I can help Swan Services, we simply schedule the next step—a full-day off-site session with the leadership team called the 'Focus Day®.' In that session we'll cover five tools that will help you get a grip on your business."

Alan walked through the five Focus Day tools in detail before introducing the next steps in his process—Vision-Building Days One and Two.

"If you like what happens in the Focus Day and want to continue," Alan explained, "we'll schedule two Vision-Building Sessions about thirty and sixty days after the Focus Day. In each of those sessions, we'll first carefully review the tools you've already learned to make sure they're working well. Then we'll begin working through the eight questions on the V/TO."

"These are *all* full-day sessions?" asked Eileen.

"Yes," replied Alan, "seven hours each day, give or take an hour." Eileen looked concerned but nodded to Alan to continue.

"So, after three sessions and about sixty days," he said, "you'll all be 100 percent on the same page with where you're going and exactly how you plan to get there. Things will really start to feel different as you gain traction and make real progress toward achieving your vision. From there, we'll meet every ninety days. I'll conduct your Quarterlies and Annuals for as long as you need me. This is where we create that ninety-day world. We come together, see how you did last quarter, get clear and aligned around the vision, solve all your problems, and set priorities for the coming quarter. Then you go back into the business for ninety days—all rowing in the same direction—and execute." Alan stepped back to show them what he had drawn on the whiteboard.

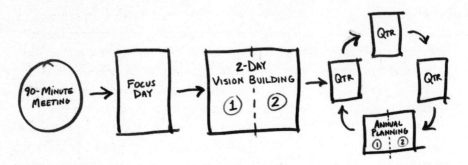

"Ultimately, you and your team will understand and have implemented every tool in my toolbox. Your business will be running on this system. At that point, you'll be ready to graduate and begin conducting your own Quarterlies and Annuals. My job is to get you there quickly—and then get out of your way and let you run your business using this system and these tools. That defines success for me."

"How long does that take?" asked Vic.

"Clients are with me on average for two years," answered Alan. "But if you decide to move forward, you won't sign any engagement letters or pay any retainer fees. You simply commit to moving forward one session at a time."

"So we can fire you if we're not happy?" asked Evan.

"Yes," replied Alan. "In fact, every session is fully guaranteed—if you ever feel that the time we spend together doesn't create value, you won't pay. And of course, you can leave the process at any time. But if you do elect to move forward, it's important that you make a commitment to sticking with the process for the duration. This is a way of life I'm teaching you, not a seminar. You can't come to the Focus Day thinking you're going to solve all your problems and see things magically change overnight."

"So that's my show," Alan concluded. "Any questions?"

There were none. Carol looked at her watch; it read 11:25. She hurriedly collected her things.

Eileen offered to call Alan back later in the week with the team's decision about moving forward, and the group shuffled out of the conference room. Wanting to discuss what the team had learned with the information still fresh, Eileen had arranged lunch near Alan's office. Once everyone was seated, she posed a simple question.

"Well, what did you think?"

"This may surprise you, Eileen," started Vic. "But I'm in. I like it. Simple stuff; there's a beginning, middle, and end. And I love the fact that this system is something we can master and use to run *our* company rather than turning over control to some consultant."

"Thank you, Vic," replied Eileen. "Anyone else?"

"A total waste of time," said Carol without looking up.

"How so?" replied Eileen, trying to mask her frustration.

"We're gonna pay this guy to teach us how to play with blocks and take naps?" she blurted. "That's highway robbery!"

Again Eileen worked hard to stay open to Carol's point of view.

"You're saying it's so basic that we should be able to do it ourselves?" she asked.

"*Yes*," replied Carol, finally looking up. "And anyone on our so-called leadership team who can't do this stuff themselves ought to be replaced with someone who can!"

Eileen felt herself getting flushed with Carol's lack of tact.

"Well," she stammered, "those are certainly two dramatically different perspectives. Art, what did you think?"

"It's up to you," Art said quickly. "I'm just a hired gun."

"Sue?" asked Eileen.

"I like it, and I like him," she replied. "Clearly we need to get better as a team; I think Alan's approach may actually work for us."

"Evan?" she asked.

"I don't know what to think," admitted Evan after a long pause. "I *am* drawn to the simplicity of it. We all have a tendency to overcomplicate things—especially me. But I'm concerned about the time this will take. We're already slammed, and this sounds like a ton of work. More important, I wonder if we're *really* committed to changing the way things are done here. Alan said that was the key. Are we really willing to do that?"

Eileen was pleased. Evan spoke less than the other executives, but he was always thoughtful and on point. She put down her pen and waved away the approaching waitress.

"I'm frightened about that, too," Eileen replied. "I love the simple, practical system that Alan describes. And I've already spoken with a half-dozen entrepreneurs who confirmed what Alan said—this system works. But Evan is right. I don't know if we're—I don't know if

I'm—ready for change of this magnitude. However, I realized today that I'm also terrified of the status quo. As much as it ticked me off, what Vic said a few weeks back is entirely accurate. The way he and I are running this company is not working."

Eileen looked around the table slowly.

"So I think we absolutely *must* change," she said. "The worst thing we can do is to decide not to do anything. And frankly, much of what Alan said strikes me as a very good antidote to the things that are driving us all crazy."

Eileen watched the team react to her comments. Sue was nodding her approval. Vic was smiling knowingly, having watched his partner succinctly summarize many situations over the years. Carol was still crossing her arms, but she *was* paying attention. Evan and Art both seemed ready to move forward.

"I say let's do it," she concluded. "We'll take Alan up on his offer to commit one day at a time. I have a good feeling about how well his operating system fits what we need. And if we decide he's a raving lunatic or the system isn't working for us, we can walk away."

And so Swan Services began its journey to simplify, clarify, and achieve its vision.

CHAPTER 3
FOCUS

T HREE WEEKS LATER at 9:00 A.M., the Swan team found itself back in Alan's meeting room. Art was the first to arrive, followed by Carol, Sue, Eileen, and Evan, all on time. Vic walked in at 9:08. Alan checked his watch, stepped to the front of the room, and pointed at two diagrams on the whiteboard.

"Welcome back," he began with a smile. "I'd like to start your Focus Day with a quick reminder of where we're going and how we're going to get there."

"In hundreds of sessions with entrepreneurial leadership teams," he explained, pointing at the diagram on the whiteboard, "I've seen thousands of frustrations and obstacles get traced back to weakness in one or more of these Six Key Components." Alan reviewed his proven process for mastering these tools and then directed them to the objectives and agenda for the Focus Day.

OBJECTIVES

- HAVE FUN
- UNDERSTAND HEALTHY AND SMART
- THINK AND WORK ON THE BUSINESS
- IMPLEMENT PRACTICAL TOOLS—GET MORE DONE

AGENDA

- CHECK IN
- HITTING THE CEILING
- ACCOUNTABILITY CHART
- ROCKS
- MEETING PULSE
- SCORECARD
- NEXT STEPS
- CONCLUDE

Alan invited questions after walking the team through each item. Hearing none, he continued to the check-in by asking everyone to take a few minutes to jot down the answers to three questions he had written on the board:

- NAME AND ROLE?
- GOOD NEWS?
- EXPECTATIONS?

"Okay," Alan said when the team members had finished writing. "We're going to start with the brave one and go to the left from there. Who'd like to begin?"

Silence.

Finally Evan cleared his throat and said, "I'll go."

"Thank you, Evan," replied Alan.

"Evan McCullough, VP of operations," began Evan. "Good—"

"Hold on, Evan," interrupted Alan. "I apologize for not making myself clear. When I asked for your role, I was looking for a little more than your title. Can you help me understand what a VP of ops does at Swan Services?"

"Oh," said Evan, a little startled. "Well, I manage all of our developers and other technical resources. I keep all of our projects—the work we do for our clients—on track, and I try to keep those clients happy."

"Perfect. Thanks, Evan," replied Alan. "How about good news?"

Evan shared his personal and professional good news with the team and then looked back up at the board.

"Expectations," he continued. "Well, I hope we get through the agenda way before five. I have a ton of stuff waiting for me at the office."

"Fair enough," replied Alan. "Going to Evan's left—Sue?"

"Sue Meecham. I sell and I lead the sales team," she began. After recounting her good news, she said, "For expectations I wrote down two words: 'clarity' and 'harmony.' Let's just say I think we can use lots more of both."

Vic, Art, and Eileen followed. Carol went last.

"Carol, controller," she began abruptly. "Accounting, financials, billing, collections. I can't really think of any good news. Expectations? Same as Evan—that we get through what you wrote on the board as quickly as possible. I have work to do."

"We'll not waste any time today, Carol," replied Alan, "but the quality of our work is always more important than speed. Okay?"

"I suppose," she replied warily.

Alan then checked in himself, concluding with one clear expectation.

"My expectation of you at this and every session is that you be open and honest," he said. "Open means both open with one another and open-minded. When somebody else on the team has something to say, you don't have to agree, but you do need to hear it, so we can consider everyone's perspective. Honest means *just say it*. We can't deal with an issue unless we get it out of your heads and on the table. Everything will move a lot faster and we'll do better work if we all agree to just say it. As far as I know, nobody's ever been fired or killed because they were honest in one of these sessions."

The team chuckled lightly; Carol shifted uncomfortably in her chair. Alan reminded the team that it had started a journey to become its best as a leadership team and clearly explained what the trip would entail.

"At the end of this journey," he concluded, "you'll be operating with one vision, with one voice, and as one team. Each of you will be proud to look across the table into the eyes of your fellow leaders, knowing you can implicitly trust one another and be completely confident that together, you can achieve your vision."

Carol rolled her eyes, but Sue and Evan seemed intrigued. Vic sat back in his chair, realizing clearly that Swan still had a long way to go to achieve that dream.

After each member of the team committed verbally to the journey ahead, Alan started in on the day's agenda with a concept called "hitting the ceiling."

"Whether your definition of growth is rocketing to $200 million or just growing *internally* by becoming more profitable and operating more smoothly," Alan explained, "it's inevitable that you will occasionally get stuck. Growing, making money, and running your business will get harder. You'll get frustrated. You won't know exactly why you're stuck or what you need to do about it; you'll just know you've hit the ceiling."

"We have absolutely no idea what you're talking about, Alan," Vic said with a wry smile. The group erupted with laughter.

Alan went on to explain that hitting the ceiling is inevitable and often necessary before an organization can advance to the next level. He challenged the team to rise to those occasions and help the company break through those ceilings by mastering five leadership abilities.

"If you can't," Alan continued, "the company will flatline or fail—like so many small businesses." As he walked through each of the five leadership abilities, Alan was recording them on the whiteboard:

- SIMPLIFY
- DELEGATE
- PREDICT
- SYSTEMIZE
- STRUCTURE

He explained the importance of the first leadership ability by helping the group understand how quickly growing organizations become complex and just how hard it can be for leaders to keep things simple.

"*Everything* about this system you're about to learn is designed to help you simplify," he explained. "And throughout our journey together, you'll hear me say '*less* is *more*' quite often."

Alan moved on to the second leadership ability. He made it clear that all leaders must learn to build extensions of themselves—to truly "let go" and stop trying to do everything themselves—for growing organizations to break through the ceiling.

"We're going to introduce several tools over the course of our journey that will help you 'delegate and elevate,'" Alan explained. "So you can spend far more time doing those things you love to do and are best at. It's where you'll all be happiest and where you'll each be able to add the most value to the organization. The Accountability Chart that we create this morning will be the first and most important step in that journey."

Alan continued with his third point: "The third leadership ability is the ability to predict. Leadership teams predict on two levels—long-term and short-term—and you have to be good at both."

Alan introduced the V/TO and Rocks as tools to help the team master long-term predicting, meaning everything ninety days out and beyond. He stressed the value of creating a clear long-term vision for the company and a plan to achieve it. He then defined short-term predicting as the ability to effectively solve daily and weekly issues. He promised to later equip the team with IDS, a simple tool to help them master the discipline of short-term predicting.

"If you're normal, you're getting hit with five or six issues every single day," said Alan. "You have to get better at predicting which of those issues needs to be tackled right away and then predicting the right solution that solves them forever. Leaders entangled in the day-to-day often ignore issues, or push them aside, or cobble together half-baked, makeshift solutions. They're just hoping to make it to next week. As a result, the company ends up being held together by duct tape and twine; it will eventually implode."

Eileen chuckled quietly. She knew Swan Services was chock-full of duct tape and twine. While people like Vic and Art seemed perfectly comfortable as all that pressure and worry built up, she had become anxious and frustrated.

Moving to the fourth leadership ability, Alan explained that systemizing an organization results in consistency and scalability. He helped the team understand how to get there by documenting its Core Processes at a high level using a tool called the "Three-Step Process Documenter."

"Every company has a handful of Core Processes—the essential things that make the organization run," he explained, drawing as he spoke. "Every company has an HR process, a marketing process, a sales process, two or three operations processes, an accounting process, and a customer service or customer retention process. Once defined, these processes become your unique business model, the Swan Services way of operating. Soon we're going to help you document these processes at a high level, simplify them, and get them followed consistently by everyone in the organization. That will make things easier to manage, more predictable, and more fun. You'll be better able to scale this business to any size you choose."

"Do you really think it's that easy?" asked Evan.

"I didn't say easy," replied Alan. "I said simple. Systemizing works best when you keep it simple. That's why we use the 20/80 Rule—documenting 20 percent of the high-level steps in a Core Process to get 80 percent of the results. If you're trying to document 100 percent of the steps to get 100 percent compliance, that project is probably never going to be truly done. And even when it does get done, it usually provides you with a low return on your investment of time."

Evan considered Alan's point and then signaled his willingness to move on with a nod.

"The ability to structure your organization properly is the fifth leadership ability," Alan continued. "The Accountability Chart will help you create the right structure to get you to the next level. It creates simplicity and absolute clarity, crystallizing the roles and responsibilities in your organization. Which leads us to our next Focus Day tool."

Alan put down his marker and invited the team to take a five-minute break. Sue, Evan, and Eileen jumped onto their mobile devices to check emails and voice mail. Vic and Art excused themselves and headed for the restroom. Carol grabbed some coffee and scribbled some notes in her manual.

"Two-minute warning," Alan said three minutes later, looking at his watch. Eileen watched with amazement as, one by one, the executives sat down and reengaged.

ACCOUNTABILITY

RIGHT STRUCTURE

Alan began the exercise by leading the team through the basic Accountability Chart, reminding them that there are three major functions—sales/marketing, operations, and finance—that make every organization work. He stressed the importance of having a single leader responsible for ensuring each major function stays "strong."

"You can't have two people accountable for a single major function," he explained, "because when two people are accountable, nobody is accountable. We need one person with the authority to make that function strong, to get us consistently great results. They'll need people to help and support them, but we need one champion driving it. When things are going well, we'll know this person helped pull everyone together to make great stuff happen. And when things are off track, we'll be able to look into one set of eyes and ask that leader to get us back on track."

Vic and Eileen both nodded, warming to the idea.

Illustrating on the whiteboard as he spoke, Alan reminded the team that all organizations have a fourth critical function at the leadership team level.

"The integrator is the glue," he explained. "The one person who beats the drum, runs the day-to-day, and is ultimately accountable for harmoniously integrating the other major functions so that the company achieves its goals. Because when you have strong, talented people in each of the major functions, there's often healthy friction between two or more of those leaders. When the team can't agree on something, the integrator breaks the ties."

The looks around the table made it clear that this team had known its share of friction.

"What makes this an *Accountability* Chart," Alan said as he drew five bullets in each rectangle, or "seat," "is that we clearly define the five major roles the owner of each major function must obsess about and excel at in order to take us to the next level. Remember, we're going to customize *your* Accountability Chart in two ways. First, we have to determine whether you have three or more major functions on your leadership team. And second, we have to decide whether or not there's a visionary at Swan Services."

Alan drew a fifth seat at the top of the Accountability Chart, placed a "V" in that seat, and reminded the team about the differences between a visionary and an integrator.

"Whereas integrators love rolling up their sleeves and digging into the day-to-day," he explained, "visionaries are attracted to big ideas—they may have twenty or more before breakfast every day. They're great with big relationships. They're driven by creativity, and they consider culture, principles, and values very important. Much of what exists today—enduring companies, world-changing innovations, cultural advancements—exists because of visionaries."

Everyone turned to look at Vic.

"Clearly we don't have one of those, Alan," Vic said dryly. He paused a moment before smiling broadly. The whole team burst into laughter.

"We're about to start with a blank slate and create the right structure for *your* company," Alan continued, grinning. "When we do, these three major functions may split into more than three. For example, you might have a marketing seat and a separate sales seat on your leadership team. Operations may split into two or more distinct functions, and sometimes the finance seat splits into maybe HR, finance, and IT. All that matters is that you arrive at the simplest and best structure to get you to the next level."

Alan erased the sample Accountability Chart and faced the group. "So, please detach yourselves from your current roles, your ego, and your past beliefs," he said. "Act as a board of directors—fight for the greater good of the company. A rule of thumb with the Accountability Chart is to think about the next six to twelve months. What major functions do you need to take your company where you want it to go? You have to get the structure right *before* we work on getting the right people in the right seats. Always think structure first and people second; that's the only way to get it right."

Alan paused before asking, "So what does it look like? What are the major functions that make Swan work?"

The team was silent. Eileen made a conscious decision to let someone else speak first and hoped that Vic would have the sense to do the same. Carol and Evan glanced nervously at the two owners, not daring to speak first.

"Well, we definitely need to sell something," said Sue finally.

Her comment elicited a few nervous giggles that seemed to release the pressure building around the conference table. Alan drew a square near the left edge of the whiteboard and waited for Sue to continue.

"But I don't know whether sales and marketing are two major functions or one," she admitted.

"Well, today it's two seats," volunteered Art, a little too quickly. "But I know we're not supposed to think about history or people."

Art and Sue both looked at Alan for guidance.

"Carol, Evan—what do you think?" Alan asked.

"Seems like having one person would be less expensive than two," Carol said, staring directly at Art. Evan just shrugged.

"I think it's one seat," Vic said.

"What makes you feel that way?" asked Alan.

"You said 'simplest and best structure,'" replied Vic. "Having one person responsible for everything that goes into generating revenue seems simpler and better than having two. We'll never have to worry about those two functions not working well together."

"I see your point, Vic," injected Eileen. "But those seem to me to be two totally unique jobs requiring vastly different skill sets. Do you really think it's possible for one person to lead both the marketing and sales functions well?"

Vic paused to contemplate the question, and Art chimed in.

"I don't," he said flatly. "I don't know the first thing about managing salespeople. And in all my work with senior sales executives from lots of large, successful businesses, I've never met a single one of them who would make a good leader of a *real* brand development team."

Alan glanced at the leaders gathered around the conference table, pleased at the way each member of the team had joined the discussion.

"But we're *not* a big company," countered Sue. "There is no marketing team to lead here, Art. You *are* the marketing team. Couldn't one leader actively manage the sales team and, at the same time, rely on *you* to do the marketing we need?"

"I thought we weren't supposed to think about people," Carol said bluntly.

"That's correct, Carol," agreed Alan. "So, Sue, without assuming Art is the owner of the marketing function, do you still believe the right structure is to have a single leader of sales and marketing?"

"Yes, I think that makes sense at our current size," she replied. "It's a simpler structure, and I think it'll help us market and sell better."

"How so?" asked Vic, intrigued.

"Well," began Sue warily, "don't take this the wrong way, Art. But sometimes it seems as though what we're really selling and your marketing pieces are two different things. We salespeople feel as though the important tools we need to sell more are put on the back burner in favor of pet projects that you believe are important."

Eileen's eyes got wide. She couldn't believe how direct Sue was being, and she wondered how Art would react. She didn't have to wait long to find out.

"Whoa there," protested Art. "What is *that* supposed to mean? My agency submits a marketing plan each year, and you guys pick what you want from that plan. We don't decide anything on our own!"

"Why does Sue feel the sales team's needs aren't being met?" asked Alan.

"I don't know," Art said slowly. "This is the first time anyone's told me our stuff is missing the mark. Eileen and I meet regularly, and—"

"That's the problem," interjected Eileen. "Maybe you and Sue should be meeting regularly."

"Or you and I," said Vic, suddenly feeling left out.

Art sat back in his chair, confused. He wasn't even a formal part of the Swan team, yet he suddenly felt like the problem.

"We're getting a little caught up in people," said Alan. "Let's refocus on the ideal structure for the organization."

He walked to the left front corner of the room, where "Issues List" was written in green at the top of the whiteboard. He wrote "Art and Sue Same Page" and turned to face the group.

"Congratulations," he said. "You've broken the seal on your Issues List. There will be more today. I only ask you to resist the temptation to try to solve them all right away. Today is about solving the root causes of your biggest issues. So, can we move on with the Accountability Chart and come back to this issue later?"

Sue and Art looked at one another and nodded their agreement. Eileen smiled, thinking of countless hours the team had wasted on similar issues in their own meetings.

"What we're trying to decide," Alan said, "is whether sales and marketing is a *single* major function or *two* major functions."

After a few moments of uneasy silence, Vic spoke up. "Now I'm thinking two seats, Alan," he said. "I think we need a marketing leader and a sales leader on our executive committee. If something's not working, we ought to deal with that as a team, not in the sales department."

"Does that feel right to everyone?" Alan asked. Hearing no objections, he recorded "MARKETING" in the seat and drew another square to the right and wrote "SALES" in that seat. He turned to face the team again. "What's the next major function?"

Similar discussions ensued as Alan led the team through the major functions. After some occasionally testy debate, the team decided there was a single operations seat rather than four distinct seats—account management, project management, business analysis, and development. A similar debate about the finance function surprised Eileen and led to an epiphany of sorts.

As the discussion began, Eileen advocated splitting the finance function into two or three distinct roles—with one leader (probably Carol) owning the accounting function and two other leaders heading the IT and HR functions—all at the leadership-team level on the Accountability Chart. Art and Carol seemed to agree, but she was challenged by Vic, Sue, and Evan to explain why such a large leadership team made sense for their $7 million company.

Eileen realized she was structuring the company around Carol's limitations. As the discussion wore on, she came to understand that a fully capable finance seat owner would easily be able to lead those other major functions as part of a single department at Swan's current size. Carol's narrow focus and limited people skills had obscured that fact. Once Eileen relented, the team quickly concluded that a single finance seat should have HR and IT reporting to it.

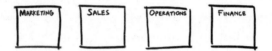

"Well done," Alan said, drawing the integrator seat above the four others. "Every great organization has an integrator," he went on. "Someone to run the day-to-day, to lead and manage the leadership team. I take it from your earlier comments that there may also be a visionary in this organization?"

The team chuckled. Alan drew the visionary seat at the top of the chart.

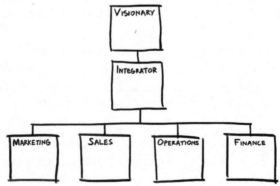

"Now that we've settled on the six major functions of your company," Alan continued, "the next step is to define the five roles for each seat. Let's take them one at a time, again focusing on structure rather than people or history. Where shall we start?"

The team began with the marketing seat, agreeing through discussion and debate to add the following five roles:

MARKETING
- BUILDING THE SWAN BRAND
- MARKETING PLAN
- GENERATE LEADS
- MARKET RESEARCH
- MARKETING TOOLS/ WEBSITE

"Sue," Alan asked about the next seat, "does the owner of the sales function manage people in your organization?"

"Yes," she replied, "we have four sales executives today. I'm not sure that's the right number in our ideal structure, but it's safe to say that the sales leader will have to manage somebody."

Alan recorded "LMA" next to the first bullet in the sales seat. "LMA stands for 'leadership, management, and accountability,'" he explained. "We use this acronym to describe everything you do to get the most from your people. It becomes the first role in your seat. You have to lead well and manage well to create an environment where organizational accountability just happens. That takes time and effort, and it's often done poorly because leaders don't devote enough of either. With all of the tools you'll be learning on our journey together, you'll be better at this than ever."

After further discussion, the team agreed to these roles for the sales leader:

SALES
- LMA
- SET & ACHIEVE REVENUE GOALS
- SALES PROCESS
- SELLING ("A" PROSPECTS)
- SET REASONABLE CLIENT EXPECTATIONS

The last role in this seat—"set reasonable client expectations"—resulted from a spirited discussion. With the first four bullets done, Alan triggered the debate by asking the team who should be accountable for client satisfaction.

"Operations," replied Vic immediately.

"Not if you sell stuff that we can't deliver on," shot back Evan.

"Good point," replied Sue. "So do we share responsibility for client satisfaction?"

"That's against the rules," said Carol. "You can't have two people accountable for a single role."

"Exactly right, Carol," said Alan, smiling. "We need one person to accept accountability for everything important in the organization. But if I understand this situation correctly, it sounds like sales owns one very specific piece of client satisfaction, and operations owns another. Can we agree on a simple way to describe what the sales leader is responsible for?"

"Well, we already have 'sales process' up there," said Sue. "If we make sure everyone follows the sales process, aren't we holding up our end of the bargain?"

"I don't know," replied Evan. "I'd feel better if we made it clearer that the salespeople—and maybe other departments, too—accept some responsibility for satisfying clients. My team feels like it's always blamed when a client is unhappy, and most of the time there is plenty of blame to go around."

Evan glanced nervously around the room. He was surprised when nobody took issue with his opinion.

"So how would you express the sales leader's responsibility clearly?" Alan asked. After a quick discussion, the team settled on "set reasonable client expectations."

Before moving on, Alan walked to the Issues List and wrote "Define 'Reasonable' Client Expectations."

"Do you agree this is an issue?" he asked the group.

Everyone nodded. Eileen chuckled once again, appreciating Alan's knack for capturing meaningful issues like that one without letting it bog down the team.

Alan continued on to the operations seat. Everyone agreed that the first role was "LMA" and the second was client satisfaction, but the discussion ground to a halt from there. Despite repeated reminders from Alan, Evan held tightly to the past and seemed to resist the idea that a high-level summary of the operations leader's roles was even possible. Instead, he kept itemizing every aspect of his job.

"It's just not that simple," he said passionately when Vic suggested that the third role be described as "deliver projects on time and on budget." "To do that, I need greater control over the quote process," he explained. "I can't be accountable for something that I don't control!"

"Why not?" asked Vic. "We're accountable for hitting sales numbers, and we sure as heck don't control the clients!"

"It's more complicated in my department," replied Evan defensively. "You don't have any idea how—"

"I'm sorry to interrupt, Evan," said Alan. "Remember, nobody here has a job yet, so this isn't your department we're talking about. We're focusing first on structure, *then* on people. Let's take a quick break and clear our heads. When we resume, let's stay focused on the way we want the operations function to be structured going forward. No people, no history, and no egos."

Although the break was necessary and well-timed, it didn't help Evan. Instead of clearing his head, he spent the break responding to urgent emails and voice mails. Still distracted by events at the office and threatened by this exercise, Evan stopped expressing his views after the break. Alan recognized this shift and tried to get Evan to challenge another team member's assumptions or suggest an alternative, to no avail.

"Okay, Eileen," Alan finally said, "besides LMA and client satisfaction, what are the roles you need your operations leader to own?"

After some prodding and suggestions from Sue, Vic, and Carol and very passive approval from Evan, the team settled on five roles for the seat:

Next, the team focused its attention on the finance seat and added the following roles:

```
┌─────────────────────────────┐
│  FINANCE                     │
│  - LMA                       │
│  - BUDGETING & REPORTING     │
│  - ACCOUNTS PAYABLE/         │
│      ACCOUNTS RECEIVABLE     │
│  - HR                        │
│  - IT                        │
│  - OFFICE MANAGEMENT         │
└─────────────────────────────┘
```

Before settling on these six roles, the team spent several minutes discussing IT, trying to decide whether that role belonged in the ops or finance seat. Ultimately, the leaders decided that *internal* IT—the technology needs of Swan and its employees—belonged in the finance department. The ops seat owner would be accountable for the technology needs and issues of Swan's clients.

Carol was thrilled when what she viewed as her seat was defined. She had never been given complete authority of functions outside of accounting, a source of regular conflict between her and Eileen.

Next, Alan drew attention to the integrator and visionary seats, respectively. He reiterated the difference between the two and helped the team define the integrator seat as follows:

```
┌─────────────────────────────┐
│  INTEGRATOR                  │
│  - LMA                       │
│  - ACHIEVE P&L,              │
│      BUSINESS PLAN           │
│  - REMOVE OBSTACLES &        │
│      BARRIERS                │
│  - SPECIAL PROJECTS          │
│  - LEGAL & COMPLIANCE        │
└─────────────────────────────┘
```

"I'm going to ask you to talk about people for a moment," Alan explained as he pointed at the visionary seat, "because this seat is always customized for the individual who owns it. So, team, what do you want Swan's visionary to do? How can Vic add the most value every day?"

He was greeted by silence. Alan had seen this happen many times before—team members unsure of what a visionary might do for a growing business and reluctant to suggest *anything* to a company owner.

"Vic, what do you love to do most?" he asked. "What are you best at?"

"I think I'm best at the high-level stuff—big ideas, big relationships, solving big problems. The smaller and more detailed things become, the less I care."

Alan smiled and began writing. "What else?"

"Vic's also passionate about our 'vibe,' as he calls it," answered Sue.

"When you say 'vibe,'" Alan asked, "are you describing morale, the way people in the company fit with one another and engage in the mission of the organization?"

"Absolutely," Vic replied.

"I commonly see that expressed as 'culture,'" Alan remarked. "Does that work for you, or do you prefer 'vibe'?"

"Culture's great," replied Vic, laughing a little as Alan recorded the role.

"Anything else?" Alan asked the team.

"Vic's also great at turning his best ideas about the future into a plan," suggested Art.

Eileen grinned. "As long as he doesn't have to *implement* any of those ideas and plans," she added, getting a hearty laugh from everyone in the room.

"Would you call that 'R&D'?" asked Alan.

"More 'R' than 'D,'" replied Eileen with a straight face. "Art's right. Vic keeps his finger on the pulse of our industry and on the future technology needs of our clients. He has always been the guy who helps the rest of us understand what's possible and what's going to be necessary to stay current. But turning those possibilities into a plan of action is another matter."

Vic smiled knowingly. Eileen was right, of course.

"Why don't we call the role 'industry trends'?" asked Vic.

"Works for me," replied Alan. "Does everyone here have a clear sense of what that means?"

The team nodded its approval, and Alan completed filling in the roles of the visionary seat:

```
VISIONARY
- BIG IDEAS
- BIG RELATIONSHIPS
- SOLVING BIG PROBLEMS
- CULTURE
- INDUSTRY TRENDS
```

"Is that what we want Swan's visionary to be accountable for?" Alan asked.

The team agreed and took a ten-minute break before settling in for a working lunch. Once Alan had regained everyone's attention, he continued facilitating the Accountability Chart exercise.

RIGHT PEOPLE IN THE RIGHT SEATS

"Now that we've defined your ideal structure—at least at the leadership-team level—let's put the right people in these seats," Alan began. "To do that, we must elevate everyone into seats where they'll spend most of their time doing what they love to do and are best at. We're going to take these seats one at a time, starting with the four major functions—marketing, sales, operations, and finance. Are there any clear-cut owners of those seats?"

The group was eerily silent. Art and Carol each waited for someone else on the team to suggest their names for the marketing and finance seats, respectively. Sue wanted to nominate herself for the sales seat but didn't want to offend Vic. Eileen almost suggested Evan for the ops seat, but his awkward behavior earlier in the session left her wondering whether he was really capable of leading such a critical function. She finally broke the silence.

"Art clearly owns the marketing seat," Eileen said.

"That's right," agreed Vic, and the rest nodded. Alan wrote Art's name into the marketing seat and then surprised the leaders with what he said next.

"Art, it's time for a real-time performance review. Are you ready?"

"Uh, sure," Art replied unsteadily.

"You're going to get some candid feedback from your peers. Starting from your left, I'll ask each leader to tell us whether they think you 'GWC' the five roles in the marketing seat. 'GWC' stands for 'gets it, wants it, and capacity to do it.'

"When someone 'gets it,' their brain is innately hardwired in a way that matches the demands of the five roles in their seat," Alan explained. "When someone 'wants it,' they genuinely spring out of bed every day—wanting to excel in their roles. And when someone has the 'capacity to do it,' they have acquired the intellectual and emotional maturity, education, training, and on-the-job experience to consistently perform well in the seat.

"So with that context set," he continued, "we are looking for everyone to say 'yes' three times. If someone feels they don't GWC the seat, you'll hear at least one no, and I'll ask that person to explain."

Alan looked around the suddenly tense conference room to invite questions, but nobody spoke up. Alan looked to Art's left and began.

"So, Evan," he said calmly, "being completely open and honest, do you think Art gets, wants, and has the capacity to own the five roles in the marketing seat?"

Petrified, Evan stared intently at the whiteboard.

"Hold on," Eileen interjected, sensing Evan's discomfort. "Are you really suggesting that we just come right out and tell someone if we feel they can't do their jobs well? In front of their peers?"

"Yes," Alan replied, "although I should make it clear that we're not inviting personal attacks, just asking for candid feedback. We have to stay focused on the greater good of the organization. Nonetheless, I absolutely understand your concern, Eileen. In many companies this kind of feedback is provided confidentially, if at all. Is that the way things work at Swan?"

"Well," Eileen began to respond and then stopped. She suddenly realized it didn't happen at all. She had doubts about Carol and Evan that she hadn't properly conveyed to them, and she had no idea what the other leaders thought about their peers.

"It's natural to feel uncomfortable during this exercise," Alan assured Eileen and the rest of the team. "But getting your open and honest feelings about one another out on the table is what allows us to identify any people issues that exist and resolve them *together*, as a team. If we don't do that here and now, these issues left unsaid tend to fester and grow. Ultimately, they really hold you back as a team and as a company."

"Come *on*," Carol said harshly. "Personnel matters should be handled in private, period. This is ridiculous! Certainly you have other clients who feel the same way?"

"Well," Alan said carefully, "I *can* tell you that even those who were uneasy about real-time performance appraisals quickly realized the value of this candid approach to providing feedback. I can't think of a single client who regretted doing it in the Focus Day or repeating it whenever a people issue arose in a session."

"What's the big deal?" Vic chimed in. "This is part of the system we signed up to learn. I'm no more comfortable hearing what you all think of me than you are hearing what others think of you, but if we can't be honest with one another, we shouldn't be here!"

"You're right," Eileen agreed. "It's time we all do a better job of saying what's on our minds. Go ahead, Alan."

"Thank you—all of you," Alan replied. "Evan?"

"Well," Evan said, "I don't see Art often enough to know any better. But I'd say he gets it, he wants it, and he has the capacity to do it."

"Okay, that's three yeses. What about you, Carol?" asked Alan, continuing to Evan's left.

Carol agreed, also claiming that she didn't see enough of Art's work to really know the answer. Eileen quickly said, "Yes, yes, yes," without any qualifications.

"Vic?" asked Alan.

"Well," Vic said very slowly. Art's heart skipped a beat. Despite having taken plenty of constructive feedback in his life, he found this exercise nerve-racking. "I wonder whether you want it and have the capacity, Art," Vic explained. "After all, you have your own agency to run. The seat we defined carries with it some significant responsibilities. Can you really get it done well working for us one day a week?"

Alan let the question linger, waiting for Art to respond. Sue chimed in first.

"Alan," Sue asked, "do you have any other clients with people on the leadership team who aren't full-time employees?"

"Yes," Alan replied. "It's rare, but it does happen. Whether a seat is owned by a full-time employee or by a part-time contractor, we *must* hold the person who owns it to the same standards as everyone else in the organization. So, Art, can you step up and GWC the marketing seat?"

"That's a fair question," he said finally. "My answer is yes, but I'd like to learn more about exactly what 'owning' that seat really means before I commit to doing it well in just one day a week."

Vic asked, "Sue, what do you think?"

Sue took a deep breath. "Being open and honest," she said slowly, "I'd like to hear Art say that he's committed to Swan and to owning the seat. We're paying his firm more than $50,000 per year. That may not make us one of their biggest or most important clients, but it's a lot of money for us."

"Art," Alan asked calmly, "are you able to fully commit to this team and accept accountability for the marketing seat? Looking at the five roles and based on your current agreement with Swan, do you GWC the seat?"

Art's face was red, and he had to gather himself before answering. "If you need an answer today, then yes, I GWC the seat," he said, staring directly at Sue. "All I'm saying is that Eileen and I will have to review our contract and make sure we agree on exactly what each of those bullet points in the seat means. We'll have to agree on priorities. No matter how many hours my colleagues and I put in, we can't meet un-limited expectations."

"Vic, Sue, is that a fair request?" Alan asked.

"Yes," replied Vic, "but this isn't something Eileen and Art should work out behind closed doors. I know the two of them go way back, but this is business. If there's a concern about whether or not Art is meeting the company's needs, I think Sue and I ought to be involved in that discussion."

"I agree," said Eileen quickly. This wasn't the first time she was forced to consider that her friendship with Art might complicate matters.

"Great," Alan said as he walked to the Issues List. "It seems like you agree that Art's the best person for the marketing seat, but there's an issue." The leaders quickly agreed, so he added "Art—Define Role/Enough Time?" to the Issues List. Despite the tension-filled discussion, the team was able to continue without disruption.

"All right," Alan said cheerfully, "who is the right person for the sales seat?"

Each leader's eyes darted from Sue to Vic and back again.

"I'd have to say Sue," Eileen jumped in. "As I look at those bullets in the seat, she's the one who GWCs those things. I think Vic could do it, but he's a much better fit for the visionary seat, and I don't think he wants most of those roles. Is that fair, Vic?"

"I guess that's right," said Vic reluctantly. "But I wouldn't say I don't want the seat. If the company needs me to own it or to help Sue own it, I'll do it. Alan, are you sure we can't share the seat?"

"No," said several people simultaneously. Everyone laughed, including Alan.

"Why do you think we need to share the seat, Vic?" asked Sue abruptly.

"Well, um, I'm not sure I said that, exactly," stammered Vic. "I just think maybe my experience and your energy and organizational skills makes us a great team."

Sue frowned. She thought carefully about how to respond, took a deep breath, and spoke directly to Vic. "Being honest *again*, that really ticks me off," she said. "Do you think that all I bring to the table is youth and detail-orientation? Haven't you any respect for my knowledge, my leadership and sales skills, and my track record? I may be young, but I've succeeded in every position I've had in this industry before Swan. Do you really feel I can't lead the sales function without your sage advice and constant guidance?"

"Of course not, Sue!" said Vic immediately. "I have tremendous confidence in you, and I never meant to say otherwise. But when we work together, great stuff happens. I'd hate to lose that."

Sue seemed reassured, but that wasn't really her point. "Thank you for the vote of confidence. But I've been thinking a lot about why we're not hitting our numbers, and I really think this is part of the reason. We've been trying to share responsibility for sales leadership. Every time we get a major lead or have to deal with a problem, just figuring out who should respond requires a half-dozen emails and a couple of meetings. It's confusing to everyone, including me."

Vic realized that his constant "helping" could be misconstrued—by Sue and other members of the sales team—as a lack of confidence in his young leader. "Damn," he thought. "This is *hard*."

"It's definitely Sue," Vic finally said with conviction. "She GWCs the role, and I have to work hard to stay the heck out of the seat so she can really own it."

"That sounds like an issue to me, Vic," replied Alan, writing "Vic Letting Go of Sales Seat" on the Issues List. "Thank you for being so candid about how difficult it will be to let go of that seat. You're already getting better at delegating."

Alan added Sue's name to the seat and conducted another impromptu performance appraisal, moving left around the table. After getting unanimous agreement that Sue GWC'd the sales seat, he called for a five-minute break.

Eileen caught Vic's attention with her eyes and motioned for him to join her in the hallway. "Are you *really* okay with this?" she whispered.

Vic smiled. Despite Eileen's hard-charging demeanor, his longtime partner had a knack for knowing exactly what everyone was thinking.

"Yes," he said slowly, "and no."

Eileen gave Vic a reassuring look and invited him to continue.

"On the one hand," he said, "I *do* think this is right for the company. Sue's definitely more organized and disciplined than me."

"But?" Eileen queried.

"But," replied Vic, "part of me feels like I'm being put out to pasture."

Eileen couldn't help but laugh. "Oh, Vic," she said. "Don't be ridiculous—you know that's never going to happen!"

"I know," he replied. "I'm just letting you know how hard it's going to be for me to let go."

"Fair enough," responded Eileen. "We'll get through it together."

After the break, Alan resumed the session by asking, "Who's the right owner of the operations seat?" Several seconds passed. Everyone seemed to be sneaking glances at Evan, but nobody said a word for what seemed like a very long time.

"Well," Art finally said, "Evan owns that seat today."

"Does that mean he should own it tomorrow?" asked Alan. "Remember, we have to build this chart looking forward—no history and no people. If you think Evan is right for the operations seat, let's give him a real-time performance review."

After Art wrote Evan's name into the seat, Carol began by offering three unenthusiastic yeses for GWC.

"Eileen?" continued Alan. "Do you feel Evan GWCs the five roles in that seat?"

A long, agonizing pause followed. Evan started sweating.

"Here's the thing, Evan," Eileen finally said. "I think you definitely GWC the last three roles—delivering on projects, managing resources, and developing processes. But I don't think you *want* to lead and manage people or be held accountable for client satisfaction. I'm not sure you have the capacity for those two things, either."

As tough as the previous two discussions had been, Eileen's comments about Evan seemed to elevate the tension to a new level. He was bright red and almost vibrating.

"Evan," Alan said calmly, "what is your reaction to that assessment?"

"Well, it hurts," he said shakily, "because frankly, this is the job I'm here to do. And on the whole I think I'm doing it damn well. It's just that—" Evan went silent. He folded his arms and stared at his notes.

"It's just that what?" Alan asked kindly.

"*Nobody* around this table understands just how hard this job is!" he exclaimed. "Am I great at managing people? No, I'm not. Am I great with clients? No. Frankly, sometimes they annoy the heck out of me! But there are lots of things at this company that make managing people and making clients happy *way* harder than it needs to be! If we fix those things, I'll be a heck of a lot better at LMA and client satisfaction than you guys think I am."

Alan was impressed—both with Eileen's willingness to confront Evan with her concerns and Evan's ability to come out of his funk and clearly express his frustrations. Moving to Eileen's left, Alan drew each executive into the dialogue. The debate continued at a fevered pitch for several minutes before Alan helped the team conclude.

He made it clear that before leaving the room today, the team needed to identify someone who would own the operations seat, even if temporarily. He explained that a seat on the leadership team was too important to leave open. Once again, Alan asked the team to suggest the best right person for the ops seat.

"Clearly it's Evan," said Eileen emphatically. "I just wanted to be open and honest about my concerns, Evan. And just like we did with Art and Vic, I think there's an issue here that we need to add to the list. I hope you can understand that."

Evan nodded, still shell-shocked by this very public review of his strengths and weaknesses.

Alan added "Evan—LMA/Customer Satisfaction?" to the Issues List and continued. "Evan," he said, "you'll be given ample opportunity to prove that you're the right person for this seat. But the team's concern about LMA and customer satisfaction is an issue. As with all issues, it's better on your list and in the open than in someone's head. Okay?"

Evan narrowed his eyes. "Okay," he said.

"Who owns the finance seat?" Alan continued, seemingly unfazed by all the conflict.

"That would be me," said Carol immediately.

"Carol feels she GWCs the six roles in the finance seat," Alan said. "LMA, budgeting and reporting, accounts payable and accounts receivable, HR, IT, and office management. Do you all agree?"

Eileen paused. Looking at the roles, she couldn't find a good reason to say no, but it sure didn't feel right to say yes, either.

"Yes," Eileen answered reluctantly enough for Carol to become agitated. "I think she gets, wants, and has the capacity to do those things."

"Vic?" Alan continued, moving to Eileen's left.

Vic took a deep breath. Like Eileen, Swan's visionary couldn't put a finger on what was bothering him. Carol was reliable and technically proficient. She never missed a deadline or made significant errors. Her problems dealing with people were legendary, but except for LMA, there really wasn't anything in the finance seat that required people skills. He wondered whether to risk yet another confrontation.

"Open and honest, right?" Vic finally asked.

"Please," said Alan.

"I worry about LMA," Vic admitted. "It just doesn't seem to fit your, um, style."

"Why would you say that, Vic?" Carol said through tightly pursed lips. "I've had people reporting to me before, and they were *plenty* accountable."

Vic looked at Alan for help; Carol was seething. Instead of bailing him out, Alan just returned the gaze. With the team watching intently, Vic decided to bite the bullet.

"I'm not saying you're a bad person or doing a bad job," Vic replied. "You work hard and are great at lots of valuable stuff. I just don't get the impression that you like managing people very much, so I have a question about whether you want that aspect of the job. That's all."

"Fine," Carol said abruptly. "Take my name out of the seat, then!"

"Vic is simply providing some honest feedback, Carol," replied Alan calmly. "You don't have to agree; you just have to hear it. Before we do anything rash, let's hear from everyone else."

"Whatever," said Carol with a snort.

Sitting to Vic's left, Sue slowly answered with three yeses. She agreed with Vic's concerns on some level, but having never seen Carol manage people, she couldn't say no with conviction.

Art tried to pass, pleading a lack of experience with Carol. When Alan insisted that he weigh in based on the experience that he did have, Art agreed that Carol was the best person for the seat. Finally, Alan turned to Evan.

The VP of ops looked like he was going to be sick. Carol leaned forward and began tapping her fingers on the conference table.

"Well," Evan began slowly, "this almost never happens, but I agree with Vic."

Everyone except Carol chuckled nervously.

"She's the best person for the job, but her name ought to be on the Issues List. I don't think she likes LMA any better than I do."

"To be clear," Alan asked, "do you all believe that Carol is the right person for the finance seat, but LMA might be an issue?"

The team agreed, and Alan recorded "Carol—LMA?" on the Issues List. Carol was still livid about what she perceived as a lack of support from Vic, Sue, and Evan. However, the other leaders were thrilled to have the tense discussion resolved—at least for the moment. Now eager to complete the Accountability Chart, they quickly dropped Eileen into the integrator seat and unanimously supported Vic as Swan's visionary. In both cases, the leaders earned all yeses to GWC as they went around the table.

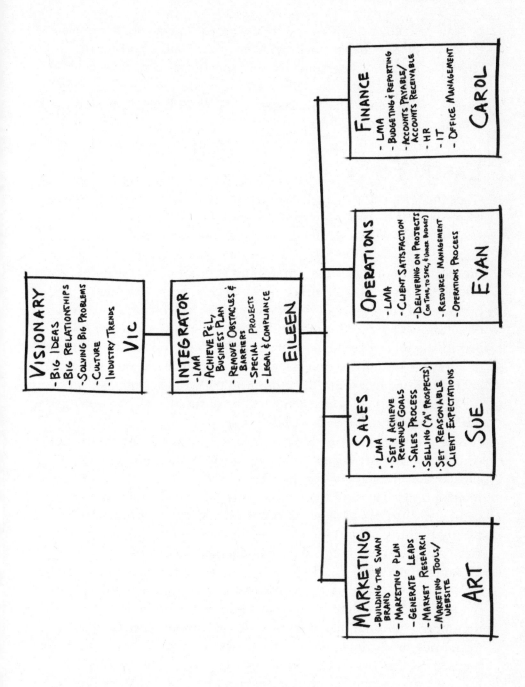

Alan concluded the exercise by assigning homework: a complete build-out of each department, with functions, roles, and names entered for each seat, combined into a one-page, organization-wide Accountability Chart before the team's next session. (See leadership team Accountability Chart on page 71.) At 1:15 P.M., he dismissed the team for another quick break.

LASER FOCUS

Once the team had returned, Alan reintroduced the concept of Rocks by recounting a point from Al Reis's book *Focus*.

"The sun," Alan explained, "showers the earth with billions of kilowatts of energy every day. Because all that energy is diffused by the earth's atmosphere, the worst thing that happens is that you get a little sunburn. On the other hand, a laser beam uses just a few kilowatts of energy. Because that energy is tightly focused in a single direction, it can cut through steel. That is the power of focus. Swan Services is more like the laser than the sun. You don't have billions of kilowatts—you have only a few. If you can get every ounce of that energy focused in a single direction, you truly can accomplish amazing things. If not, all your energy will be diffused, and you won't get much of anything done very well."

Alan brought them to his next point. "In most entrepreneurial companies, the urgent is the enemy of the important. Leaders get sucked into the day-to-day, distracted by daily tasks and countless interruptions. The stuff that really matters to the organization keeps getting pushed off. Ultimately, you're all staring at a growing list of twenty to thirty priorities and falling further and further behind."

Vic laughed out loud, and everyone joined in.

"Sound familiar?" asked Alan. The team nodded its response, and he continued. "Today we're going to force you to focus. We're going to whittle that giant list of priorities down to three to seven lead dominoes—the stuff that matters most this quarter. Then we're going to put our heads down and charge forward for ninety days, staying focused on that handful of priorities where our effort will have the highest possible impact on the organization. After that we'll come up for air, see how everyone did, and set new priorities for the *next* ninety days. We'll create a ninety-day world for you, and ultimately for everyone in the company, because it's human nature that we all lose focus and begin to fray about every ninety days. This is long-term predicting, and when you master this leadership ability, you'll get far better at breaking through the ceiling."

Alan asked the leaders to spend five minutes writing down their own lists of "hot issues," or potential Rocks. He further described them as "the things that must get done in the business in the next ninety days, both big and small."

"All right," he said from the whiteboard when the team had finished. "Who wants to read me their entire list of potential Rocks?"

"I'll start," said Evan.

Alan recorded Evan's list as fast as he could write it. "Carol, you're next," he continued.

Carol began reading her list, and soon Alan moved to a second column. As Eileen, Vic, Sue, and Art followed suit, the list grew to a total of thirty-seven potential Rocks.

"Not to worry," Alan reassured the group. "My record for a Focus Day is seventy-two issues that filled two complete whiteboards. This is *nothing*! We're going to whittle this down to a more manageable list with a process of elimination I call 'Keep, Kill, and Combine.' We may take two or three passes, and we may argue passionately for the greater good of the organization, but I promise we'll get there."

Starting at the top of the list, Alan then read each potential Rock just as it was written, asking the team to do one of three things:

- Keep it—meaning someone on the team believed it was one of the top three to seven priorities *for the company* this quarter
- Kill it—meaning it was *not* a top priority for this quarter
- Combine it—meaning it was similar to something else already on the list and could therefore be combined with the other item into a single Rock

Alan kept the debate to a minimum by invoking an interesting rule: he left on the list any potential Rock that even a single member of the team wanted to Keep. He placed a thin line through any items that the whole team agreed to Kill, and a few times he Combined two similar items into one potential Rock. This process narrowed the list to fifteen.

"Okay, team," said Alan. "Let's take a second pass, and this time we're going to let the debates begin and ultimately make some tough decisions. None of these issues are going away—we're just trying to agree on the three to seven top priorities for the organization this quarter."

The second pass resulted in more discussion and some passionate debate. When it was done, eight potential Rocks were left on the list:

- SALES TOOLS/WEBSITE REDESIGN

- REVISE ANNUAL BUDGET

- IMPROVE CLIENT SATISFACTION/RETENTION

- HIRE NEW PROGRAMMER/CONSULTANT

- CLOSE TWO "A" PIPELINE DEALS

- KEY ACCOUNT PLAN

- ACQUIRE NEW PROJECT MANAGEMENT SOFTWARE

- IMPROVE PROFITABILITY/ADJUST OPS STAFFING MODEL

"Let's take one last pass," Alan said, again starting at the top. "Sales tools/web redesign. Is this truly one of the three to seven most important things you must get done *this quarter*?"

"Keep," said Art, Sue, and Vic at once. Eileen and Evan nodded their approval, so Alan circled the Rock.

"Revise annual budget," Alan continued. "Is that a life-or-death priority for the next ninety days?"

"Kill it," said Vic. "Why spend time revising our forecast for the year downward? Let's just focus our energies on getting the company back on track!"

"Hear, hear," said Sue. The rest of the team agreed, and Alan drew a line through "Revise Annual Budget."

"Improve client satisfaction/retention," continued Alan.

"Kill," said Evan. "I know that's going to fall to me, and I'm too busy to tackle that bear right now."

"Keep!" replied Eileen emphatically. "Evan, I can't think of anything more important right now than holding on to our best clients. Alan didn't ask us to think about what we have time to do; he asked us to prioritize the most important stuff on the list. This is definitely one of them!"

"So we have one vote to Kill and one to Keep," interjected Alan. "Does anyone else have a strong opinion about this Rock?"

"I'm with the boss," said Art. "Keep."

When Carol, Sue, and Vic agreed, Alan looked to Evan. He looked trapped.

"Can't we table this?" Evan asked. "I agree that it's important, but we don't have a consensus, so can't we come back to it?"

"By consensus, do you mean getting everyone on the team to completely agree?" asked Alan.

"Yeah, pretty much," Evan responded. "I mean, it just doesn't seem fair..."

Alan waited for Evan to finish, but his voice trailed off.

"I hear what you're saying," Alan said. "But in all my work with entrepreneurial companies, I've found that consensus management *does not work*. It'll put you out of business faster than anything else. What *does* work is giving everyone the chance to express his or her opinion. If the team can't agree, the integrator makes the final call."

"But I'm the one who has to get the Rock done," said Evan, trying not to sound too whiny.

"Perhaps," said Alan. "We'll talk about that in a minute when we define the Rocks. We may have to shuffle resources if the team believes it's important. All we're deciding right now is whether it's a priority. So, do you feel like the team has heard your views on the matter?"

"Yes," he replied reluctantly.

"Eileen, as integrator, we need you to make the call. Have you heard what each of your leadership team members have to say on this issue?" Alan asked.

"Yes," Eileen replied, quietly calculating the hours she'd save not waiting until the team developed a clear consensus on every single issue. "I have, and I think we should Keep it."

Alan helped the team tackle each remaining item on the list, ultimately settling on the following five priorities for its first set of company Rocks:

- SALES TOOLS/WEBSITE REDESIGN
- IMPROVE CLIENT SATISFACTION/RETENTION
- CLOSE TWO "A" PIPELINE DEALS
- ACQUIRE NEW PROJECT MANAGEMENT SOFTWARE
- IMPROVE PROFITABILITY/ADJUST OPS STAFFING MODEL

With the list complete, Alan illustrated how to clearly define the Rocks by making them "SMART—specific, measurable, attainable, realistic, and timely." As they worked through the list, he also asked the team to assign an "owner" for each Rock—someone who would accept accountability for driving the Rock to completion. He explained that, just like with a seat on the Accountability Chart, only one person could be accountable for a Rock.

"We need one person to lead the charge," he said. "That person is going to need help, and he or she is going to rely on other people around this table. But we still need one set of eyeballs we can look into at the end of the quarter—one person who says the Rock is done or not done."

It was agreed that this first set of Rocks—something of a "practice round"— would be due at or before Swan's third meeting with Alan, about sixty days after the Focus Day. When the exercise was completed, the Rocks were written as follows:

1. TRIFOLD BROCHURE AND WEBSITE DRAFT COMPLETE	ART
2. SURVEY CURRENT CLIENTS AND IMPLEMENT CLIENT RETENTION PLAN	EVAN
3. CLOSE TWO "A" DEALS AND COMPLETE TEN KEY ACCOUNT PLANS	SUE
4. DECIDE ON PROJECT MANAGEMENT SOFTWARE	CAROL
5. IMPLEMENT OPS STAFFING CHANGES TO IMPROVE PROFITABILITY	EILEEN

"Wow," said Vic, staring at the complete list of company Rocks. "If we can get those five things done, it'll be our most productive quarter in a long time—maybe ever. And for once I think we can actually do it!"

"You're just saying that because you don't have a Rock," teased Sue.

Alan cleaned up the original list of thirty-seven potential Rocks by erasing anything that had been Kept or Combined into a company Rock, leaving twenty-two items on the list. He then introduced the concept of individual Rocks.

"Less is more," he reminded the team, "but including the company Rocks you own, each of you can leave here with up to seven Rocks. So if something near and dear to your heart didn't make the cut as a company Rock, you're empowered to add it to your list of individual Rocks for this quarter."

Carol began writing immediately.

"Now before you get started," warned Alan, "setting and completing Rocks requires you to be good long-term predictors. You have to believe you can get each Rock done. These are not suggestions, and this isn't a wish list. You're *predicting* what needs to be done this quarter, and we're counting on you to get it done. So if you have time to complete one or more of the items on this list, please write down each of them as a SMART individual Rock. We'll share them with your teammates in a moment."

Once everyone finished, Alan went around the table asking each executive to share his or her individual Rocks. He listened carefully and encouraged the team to provide feedback to one another, which led to some spirited discussions about individual priorities for the coming quarter. Once done, each leader had clearly defined his or her individual Rocks.

Sue volunteered to compile the company Rock Sheet. To conclude the Rock-setting exercise, Alan worked through the list of crossed-off potential Rocks, erasing any items that had become Rocks until only seven remained. He then added those items to Swan's Issues List and dismissed the team for a quick break. (See Rock Sheet on page 78.)

Swan Services Quarterly Rock Sheet

Future Date: April 8, 20XX
Revenue:
Profit:
Measurables:

COMPANY ROCKS

	WHO
1) Trifold brochure, proposal template and website draft complete	Art
2) Survey current clients and draft client satisfaction/retention plan	Evan
3) Close two "A" deals and complete ten key account plans	Sue
4) Make a decision to acquire project management software	Carol
5) Recommend & approve ops staffing changes to improve profitability	Eileen
6)	
7)	

ART

1) Trifold brochure, proposal template and website draft complete
2)
3)
4)
5)
6)
7)

SUE

1) Close two "A" deals and complete ten key account plans
2) Document sales process, get approved by leadership team
3) Develop sales department scorecard
4) Complete at least one joint prospect meeting with each of the three sales reps
5)
6)
7)

EVAN

1) Survey current clients and draft client satisfaction/retention plan
2) Hire new developer/consultant
3) Complete departmental performance reviews
4) Document project management core process
5) Deliver Acme Industries project on time and on budget
6) Coordinate departmental vacation schedules
7) Implement error-tracking system

CAROL

1) Make a decision to acquire project management software
2) Revise annual budget
3) Revise HR policy manual
4) Complete YTD financials thru June
5) Complete eight hours of continuing education
6) Review IT/payroll processing contracts
7)

EILEEN

1) Recommend & approve ops staffing changes to improve profitability
2) Evaluate variable expenses for cost-savings opportunities
3) Meet with three key clients that have reduced or eliminated spending with Swan
4) Initiate credit line renewal process
5) Complete and implement Focus Day tools
6)
7)

VIC

1) Attend industry trade show in search of at least one "big idea"
2) Visit personally with at least two key clients and two key business partners
3)
4)
5)
6)
7)

THE PULSE

"Entrepreneurial leaders typically *hate* meetings," Alan resumed, pointing to the words "Meeting Pulse" on the whiteboard, "because most meetings are just *awful*. Nothing is worse than these endless reporting sessions where people yammer on forever about things that aren't really important to the entire team. At best, lots of stuff gets discussed but very little is accomplished. But imagine for a moment a regular and highly productive 'Meeting Pulse,' one that keeps you efficiently connected to all the important things happening in the business, makes you more effective as individual leaders and as a team, and is focused on *solving* problems rather than just talking about them. Would you dread *that* meeting?"

"Maybe," Vic said, smiling. "I don't sit still well, Alan!"

Alan laughed along with the rest of the team and continued by explaining that his clients engage in a two-part Meeting Pulse.

"The first part is the ninety-day world I described earlier," Alan explained. "For as long as you're working with me, I'll be responsible for helping you with your ninety-day world by running your Annual Planning Sessions and your Quarterlies. *Your* job over the next few weeks is to master the weekly Level 10 Meeting, beginning next week. Because you can't stay properly connected to the business—and to one another—without meeting more regularly than every three months. That's where the weekly Level 10 Meeting comes in. By investing ninety minutes each week and following a very specific agenda, you'll eliminate the need for a bunch of wasteful one-on-one communication. It prevents bottlenecks and train wrecks that happen when the left hand doesn't know what the right hand is doing."

"I'm sorry," interrupted Evan, "but did you say ninety minutes each *week*?"

"Yes, Evan," replied Alan.

"I don't want you to take this the wrong way," replied Evan, "but we already spend *way* too much time in meetings!"

"I get it," replied Alan reassuringly. "In fact, many clients fight the weekly Level 10 Meetings at first. But they all come back to the second or third session having discovered just how valuable they are. So please give me a little blind faith, because I can promise you that the ninety minutes you invest each week will revolutionize the way you work together *and* save each of you at least twice that much wasted time on unproductive communication, lost opportunities, and crisis management each week."

Evan nodded reluctantly. Alan went on to explain the five keys to a productive, healthy Meeting Pulse—holding weekly meetings on the same day at the same time, starting on time, ending on time, and using the same agenda each week. He then walked the team through the Level 10 agenda one item at a time:

• SEGUE (GOOD NEWS)	5 MINS
• SCORECARD	5 MINS
• ROCK REVIEW	5 MINS
• CUSTOMER AND EMPLOYEE HEADLINES	5 MINS
• TO-DO LIST	5 MINS
○ ————	
○ ————	
○ ————	
○ ————	
○ ————	
• IDS (ISSUES LIST)	60 MINS
○ ————	
○ ————	
○ ————	
○ ————	
○ ————	
• CONCLUDE	5 MINS
○ RECAP TO-DOS	
○ CASCADING MESSAGES	
○ RATING 1-10	

"Vince Lombardi said, 'Early is on time; on time is late,'" Alan continued. "So if your meeting is scheduled for 9:00 A.M. each week, starting on time means you're all seated and ready to begin—with everything you need for the meeting—at 8:59."

"Even the visionary?" joked Vic, acknowledging his chronic lateness.

"Even the visionary," responded Alan. "At precisely nine, the person running the meeting will start by asking for personal and professional good news. This will help you segue into the meeting like we did this morning. You'll find that a few minutes focused on the human element each week will help increase team health. That should take no more than five minutes. The next three items on the agenda are reporting only. No discussions, no excuses, no solving. To make sure you're hitting your numbers each week, you'll first quickly report on your Scorecard, which we will create next. Here you simply describe each measurable as either on track or off track. There's no need to discuss those items at this point in the meeting—we just drop any off-track numbers down to the Issues List. You'll then take the same approach with Rocks, reviewing both company and individual Rocks and letting each leader say his or her Rocks are either on track or off track. Anything that's off track simply drops down to the Issues List. The next item on the agenda is customer and employee headlines. This helps you keep tabs each week on whether your customers and employees are happy. Again we're looking for headlines—no commentary. Any bad reports? Just drop them down to the Issues List. This approach helps us avoid getting bogged down before the meeting gets started, stuck in one of those exhausting reporting sessions where you're spending an hour just sharing news, making excuses, and discussing the same things over and over."

"Okay, Alan," said Evan with a rare smile. "I'm still skeptical, but if you can help us do that, I'll take back what I said about too many meetings."

"That's a deal, Evan," he replied, smiling. He continued, "The next agenda item is your To-Do List. A To-Do is a seven-day action item that one of you agrees to get done before next week's meeting. To-Dos will be baked right into your Level 10 Meeting agenda, a dynamic document with everything you need right at your fingertips. When you get to the To-Do List each week, you'll go down the list asking each person with a To-Do whether it was To-Done."

The team laughed.

"This discipline helps you get to the point at which 90 percent of the To-Dos are dropping off every week," Alan continued. "It creates accountability and helps everyone get more done. From there, we go to the real magic of what makes meetings great—solving issues. Setting 'em up, knocking 'em down, and *really* making them go away *forever*. When you master the weekly Level 10 Meeting, you'll spend two-thirds of your meeting each week solving problems with IDS. You'll recall from our Ninety-Minute Meeting that most leadership teams spend all their time discussing the *heck* out of their issues.

Rarely do they ever identify or solve anything. So in a fit of frustration I created IDS to help teams quit spinning their wheels—talking about lots of stuff and never really getting anything done."

Alan then walked the team through IDS. He carefully explained how to begin each week by prioritizing the three most important issues on the list and then jumping right in to IDS for the first one. Next he reminded the team how to identify the root cause of the issue, discuss it briefly (with everyone saying what needs to be said only once, because more than once is politicking), and solve the issue by agreeing on a plan to make it go away forever.

"Once you solve the first issue," Alan continued, "you just add any To-Dos to the To-Do List, and then you go to issue number two. If you solve all three issues, just prioritize the next three most important issues, and repeat until you run out of time. Some weeks you'll solve ten issues; some weeks you'll solve one. As long as you're tackling the most important issues, you'll always be using your time wisely. This discipline will make you all much better at short-term predicting."

No one raised any questions, and Alan went on: "The last item on the Level 10 agenda is to conclude. Wherever you are with five minutes left in the meeting, you conclude by doing three simple things. You first recap your To-Dos. Next is cascading messages. Did something happen in the meeting that needs to be shared with others? If so, you must all agree on who's going to tell them, what you are going to tell them, and how you are going to tell them. Finally, you end by rating the meeting from one to ten, with ten being best. Rating your meetings each week helps you self-correct. It forces you to work together to get better at meeting—to become more open and more productive. It's a much better approach than leaving the meeting grumbling under your breath and complaining about one another later. Remember when you rated your meetings a four in our Ninety-Minute Meeting?"

Several members of the team nodded. Vic chuckled, thinking in retrospect that four might have been a little generous.

"When you work together to self-correct," Alan continued, "you'll soon get to the point where eight is the lowest rating you ever get and nines and tens are commonplace. And with that, the meeting *always* ends on time."

Alan invited and resolved a few questions, comments, and concerns. Then he concluded the exercise by asking for and receiving three decisions. The team decided to meet every Tuesday at 8:00 A.M. Alan asked the team to enter "Level 10 Meeting" into their calendars and "hit repeat forever." Eileen was selected to run the meetings. Sue volunteered to complete the paperwork.

Eileen was surprised and pleased to learn that she wouldn't have to run the meeting *and* manage the paperwork. Sue readily agreed to prepare and bring to each meeting printed copies of the Level 10 Meeting agenda (with updated To-Do and Issues Lists), the Rock Sheet, and the Scorecard. And she agreed to listen carefully throughout the meeting to record To-Dos and issues in their appropriate places.

"One final thought," Alan said to conclude the Meeting Pulse discussion. "These Level 10 Meetings are *vital*. Attending them must become a priority for all of you. There are only two good reasons to miss a Level 10 Meeting—vacation and death. *Your* death."

Vic, Eileen, and Art laughed out loud, but Alan was mostly serious. With everyone on board, Alan concluded the Meeting Pulse discussion and called another break.

DATA

"We're in the home stretch," Alan said when the session resumed at 3:45 P.M. "Now we're going to take a first cut at your company Scorecard."

He reminded the team that a great Scorecard contains a handful of weekly activities-based numbers, offers thirteen weeks of history at a glance, and helps leaders maintain an absolute pulse on the business. It quickly provides real insight that helps leaders become better predictors and make better decisions.

"So imagine yourself on an island," he said. "A server brings you a frosty beverage and a sheet of paper that contains five to fifteen numbers. Cell reception on the island is terrible, and you have no Internet access. What are all the numbers you need to know to get a definitive sense of what's working and not working in the business? You can't call in and talk to six different people to get the real story."

Eileen and Vic smiled. They spoke at least twice daily whenever one of them was out of the office for an extended period of time.

"So," Alan continued, "what are the numbers you want to see on that sheet of paper? Please take three minutes to write down your own list of five to fifteen company numbers. Remember: we're looking for leading indicators that can be measured on a weekly basis."

"Should we be thinking of metrics from our own departments, Alan?" asked Sue.

"Yes," he replied. "But also think about what you'd need to know about marketing, operations, and finance to get an absolute pulse on the *whole* business."

Sue nodded and started writing. Eileen, Carol, and Art seemed to be making progress on a list, but Evan and Vic both looked puzzled. Alan distributed a list of real-life Scorecard measurables from clients in the manufacturing, distribution, retail, and services sectors to help get the team's juices flowing.

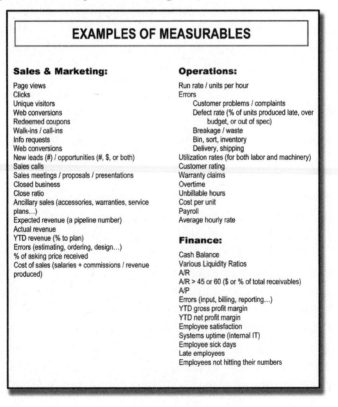

EXAMPLES OF MEASURABLES

Sales & Marketing:

Page views
Clicks
Unique visitors
Web conversions
Redeemed coupons
Walk-ins / call-ins
Info requests
Web conversions
New leads (#) / opportunities (#, $, or both)
Sales calls
Sales meetings / proposals / presentations
Closed business
Close ratio
Ancillary sales (accessories, warranties, service plans...)
Expected revenue (a pipeline number)
Actual revenue
YTD revenue (% to plan)
Errors (estimating, ordering, design...)
% of asking price received
Cost of sales (salaries + commissions / revenue produced)

Operations:

Run rate / units per hour
Errors
    Customer problems / complaints
    Defect rate (% of units produced late, over budget, or out of spec)
    Breakage / waste
    Bin, sort, inventory
    Delivery, shipping
Utilization rates (for both labor and machinery)
Customer rating
Warranty claims
Overtime
Unbillable hours
Cost per unit
Payroll
Average hourly rate

Finance:

Cash Balance
Various Liquidity Ratios
A/R
A/R > 45 or 60 ($ or % of total receivables)
A/P
Errors (input, billing, reporting...)
YTD gross profit margin
YTD net profit margin
Employee satisfaction
Systems uptime (internal IT)
Employee sick days
Late employees
Employees not hitting their numbers

After a few minutes reviewing the handout and compiling their own lists, the leaders were ready to proceed. Carol volunteered to be the "brave one" and read her list.

"Weekly revenues," she said. "WIP—work in process. Utilization rates. Overtime. Customer complaints. Accounts receivable (A/R) forty-five and ninety days past due."

Writing as fast as he could, Alan recorded the numbers and turned to Carol's left. Eileen rattled off a long list of her own suggestions and turned to Vic to await his list.

"Alan," Vic said. "I'm struggling to find leading indicators. Most of the stuff up there is a trailing number—like weekly revenues. I thought we weren't supposed to measure stuff like that."

"Good catch, Vic," replied Alan. "You're right that leading indicators are best, but if you and the rest of the team believe that weekly revenues is one of the numbers that gives you an absolute pulse on the business, it belongs on your Scorecard. That said, let me illustrate what we mean by leading versus trailing indicators."

Alan turned to an open section of whiteboard and began drawing. In just a few seconds, he had completed a diagram that looked like this:

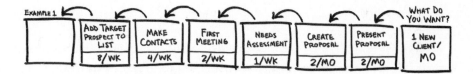

Alan walked the team through his illustration of a typical sales process, identifying "number of new clients" as a trailing indicator and earlier steps in the process as leading indicators.

"I got it," Vic said when the discussion concluded. "In that case I want to measure leads, initial meetings, and proposals."

Sue went next. "Other than what you've already listed," she began, "I'd like to measure new opportunities, thirty-day pipeline, close ratio, and contracts received."

"Number of contracts?" Alan asked. "Or dollars?"

"Both," she replied. "I'm not sure how to say this, but I'd also like to measure near-term resource availability in operations. If they're so busy they can't start a new project for three months, I need to factor that into the way we sell."

Alan recorded "available labor hours" and looked to Sue for approval. She nodded and continued with her list.

"Number of projects behind schedule," she added. "Number of projects over budget. Billing errors. I also had complaints and past due receivables."

Art followed, adding a few marketing numbers and "customer satisfaction survey results."

"Evan?" Alan asked.

"Mine are all up there," said Evan.

"Really?" queried Alan. "Nothing at all to add?"

"Nope," replied Evan. "But is this the right time to talk about whether the numbers up there even make sense?"

"Actually," Alan replied, "we're going to do that next."

He redirected the team to the top of the list of twenty-two potential Scorecard measurables. Beginning with "weekly revenue" at the top of the list, he asked the following questions about each number:

- Is this a number the leadership team wants to see every week?
- Does the number make sense weekly?
- Can we gather this data each week?

Several financial measures were discarded as either meaningless or difficult to compile weekly. Carol seemed to oppose anything that would require a change in the way things were already being done in the accounting department. Alan partially agreed, making it clear that the weekly Scorecard augments but does not replace a team's regular review of its financial picture.

"All of my clients review both a weekly Scorecard *and* monthly or quarterly financial statements," he said, which seemed to placate Carol.

As the exercise unfolded, the team fell into two camps. Some wanted to measure everything and to make each measurable as complex as possible. Others seemed intent on measuring very little, insisting that only numbers that were easy to measure and 100 percent accurate could be meaningful and useful. The complete list was reduced to the following:

- NEW LEADS (#)
- INITIAL SALES MEETINGS (#)
- PROPOSALS (#)
- PROPOSALS ($)
- THIRTY-DAY PIPELINE
- CONTRACTS (#)
- CONTRACTS ($)
- PROJECTS LATE (#)
- PROJECTS OVER BUDGET (#)
- DEFECTS DELIVERED TO CLIENTS (#)
- UTILIZATION RATE (%)
- CASH BALANCE
- A/R > 60 (% OF TOTAL)
- BILLING ERRORS (#)

Throughout the exercise, Evan resisted the team's effort to create a great Scorecard. He was particularly opposed to measuring late projects, dismissing that as a complex and subjective measurable. Working together, Alan and Swan's other leaders helped Evan understand the value of such a number and envision a reliable way to measure late projects. Though not fully convinced, he reluctantly agreed to do so for a quarter before making a decision about whether the measurable was worthwhile.

The discussion was repeated nearly verbatim when the team discussed billing errors, although this time Carol was the one insisting the number wouldn't be accurate.

"Can't the billing clerk and account managers just make a tick mark somewhere whenever a client calls to report an error?" asked Sue.

"But the clients don't know what an error *is*!" exclaimed Carol. "And neither do the account managers."

Ultimately, she agreed to report the number of reissued invoices each week, but she didn't seem happy about it. Once the list was complete, Alan drew a grid around the measurables. Next he helped the team set goals for each number. When discussing the goal for initial sales meetings, Sue's gears were turning hard.

"So, Alan," she said when he asked what the goal should be, "I'm not sure this is right, but I used that diagram you drew earlier, and I think our sales team needs to have twelve initial meetings with qualified prospects each week in order to get a contract from two new customers each month. That doesn't even seem possible!"

"How many of you are there?" Alan asked.

"Four, including me," she replied. "Five if you count Vic, but I don't see him participating in the early stages of the sales process."

"Okay," Alan replied, "so each of your reps have to schedule and hold four meetings each week—three if you sign up for a share of the goal. What would have to happen to make that possible?"

"Well," she replied, "we'd have to get a better list of suspects. And we'd need Art's help to get better leads and to make them more willing to meet with us. And we'd all have to make more time to focus on initial contacts and meetings—especially me."

"So am I hearing you correctly?" Alan asked. "Is the goal twelve? Are you going to clear the decks to make that a priority for you and the sales team?"

"Yes, I have to," she replied with a mixture of worry and determination. "I still don't know whether it's possible, but we'll never hit our new sales numbers if we don't find a way to get it done."

"I'll get involved if you need me to make it work," Vic volunteered.

"Thanks, Vic—I may have to," she replied.

Alan recorded a "twelve" as the weekly goal for initial sales meetings and continued down the list.

He then asked the team to establish accountability for each number. He explained that the name of the single person most responsible for keeping a number on track would be written into the "Who" column. One interesting clash occurred during this discussion.

"Who's responsible for keeping past due accounts in check?" asked Alan.

"Sue or Evan," said Carol quickly.

"Whoa!" came Evan's reply. "How do you figure?"

"Most of the time an account is past due, they're pissed off because their stuff doesn't work or we overcharged them," she replied. "Just because Lisa works for me and makes those collection calls doesn't mean we're responsible for every late account."

A heated argument ensued. Alan helped calm the team by agreeing that responsibility for late accounts was probably often shared between several members of the team. He helped Carol understand that she and her collections person were probably the most likely people to "fix" the number if it veered off track, so she reluctantly agreed to accept accountability for the number.

When the exercise was concluded, the completed template looked like this:

Who	Measurable	Goal	Weeks												
			1	2	3	4	5	6	7	8	9	10	11	12	13
Sue	New leads	36													
Sue	Initial sales meetings	12													
Sue	Proposals (#)	4													
Sue	Proposals ($)	$300K													
Sue	30-day pipeline	$1.5M													
Sue	Contracts (#)	2													
Sue	Contracts ($)	$150K													
Evan	Projects late	1													
Evan	Projects over budget	1													
Evan	Defects to clients	0													
Evan	Utilization rate	80%													
Carol	Cash balance	$75K													
Carol	A/R > 60 days	< $30K													
Carol	Billing errors	0													

Carol was assigned the task of gathering numbers from each leader every week. She made her limits clear.

"I'm putting this spreadsheet on the shared drive," she said flatly. "I'll print the report Monday at 4:00 P.M. If your numbers aren't in the spreadsheet, they won't be there at the meeting the following day. I'm not chasing any of you down."

Alan invited questions and concluded the exercise.

"I know it is late in the day," he said, "but that felt like really good work. Just remember that this is a first cut at your Scorecard. It can take one to three months—even longer—before you get the Scorecard just right. Be patient, stick with it, and let it evolve. Bring your questions and comments back into the next session."

Alan checked his watch and, seeing that it was 4:40, quickly continued. He promised the team that after the two Vision-Building sessions on March 4 and April 8, everyone in the room would be "on the same page" about where Swan was going and *exactly* how it planned to get there. Vic couldn't help but get excited, and as he glanced around the room at his fellow leaders, he could see several of them felt the same way.

"Eileen," Alan continued, "your homework is to create Swan's Accountability Chart as you get department build-outs from Sue, Evan, and Carol. We need to be looking at the whole company on one page at your first Vision-Building Day in thirty days. Carol will complete the company Rock Sheet, but all of you need to email her your SMART individual Rocks by this Friday. *Each of you* needs to stay focused on completing your Rocks throughout the quarter. Start early, plan well, and get them done. Next Tuesday morning at eight, begin holding weekly Level 10 Meetings, with Eileen running them. Sue will bring an agenda for each of you. Carol will create your company Scorecard and bring it to each Level 10 Meeting. She has asked each of you to report data from this week by 4:00 P.M. each Monday."

When everyone agreed, Alan went on, "It's time to conclude. I'd like you each to take two minutes to record three things to share with the team. The first is feedback. Reflect on the day: Where's your head? How are you feeling? The second is a yes or no question: Were your expectations for the day met? The last is a rating, from one to ten, with ten being best. How did we do today?"

After the executives wrote down their answers, he asked for someone to begin.

"I'll go," said Sue. "Feedback—exhausted and a bit overwhelmed. I can't believe how much ground we covered, and I'm a little worried that we bit off more than we can chew. But a really good, focused, productive meeting. This is stuff we've needed to address for a long time. I'm really excited about the clarity around my role and Vic's role. My expectations were actually exceeded. I'd say ten."

"Thank you, Sue," Alan replied. "Art?"

"Well, my head is swimming," Art said. "But overall it was a good meeting. I'm not sure I needed to be here all day—it's a long, expensive day when you're paying for my time hourly, and a lot of what we covered didn't really benefit from my presence. But I learned a lot and think it was a really well-run meeting. Expectations met; I give the meeting a nine."

"Thanks, Art," replied Alan. "Evan?"

"Overwhelmed," came Evan's reply. "Way too much for me to cram into a day. I'm terrified of what's waiting for me back at the office. I thought we did some good stuff—it's just a long day, and I can't yet see how this is going to help me get more done."

"Expectations?" queried Alan.

"Well, other than ending before five, I didn't really have any expectations," he replied. "Since it's not yet five, I'd have to say yes."

"Rating?" asked Alan.

"Oh. Seven," he replied.

"Thanks, Evan." Alan replied. "Carol?"

"I'm tired and frustrated about how much more I have to do before the day is done," replied Carol. "Expectations were met, I guess. Rating? Six. I still can't believe we had to spend the whole day in a room with someone to cover all these basics. There's nothing new here, and frankly I don't understand why we can't do this ourselves."

Carol grabbed her things and made it clear to those who still had to respond that she was ready to go and they should keep it short.

"Thanks, Carol, I appreciate your candor," replied Alan. "Moving left?"

"Great day," began Eileen. "Like Sue, I really can't believe how much we got done. Frankly I'm feeling a little sheepish because if I'd have been running this meeting, we'd have accomplished nothing and killed one another before lunch!"

Everyone laughed heartily, including Alan. He nodded for her to continue.

"My expectations were met, and I give the meeting a nine," she said. "I think we can get better at being open and honest."

"Good feedback, Eileen. Thank you," replied Alan. "Vic?"

"Ten," he began. "My expectations were *vastly* exceeded, Alan."

"Feedback?" Alan asked.

"The day flew by," Vic replied, "but I am definitely worn out. A full day in a conference room is *torture* for me, so the fact that I stayed engaged this long is amazing. We did a lot of heavy lifting, and I think we did it well."

"Thanks, Vic," Alan replied. "And thanks to all of you for making it such an open, productive day. This was a great first step, but remember that this is a journey. We're just getting started, and for a while things aren't going to click the way you'd like them to. Be patient, stay focused, and make progress every day—I promise things will all begin to fall into place very soon. I'll check in with you before our next meeting, but please call me in the meantime if I can help."

CHAPTER 4
VISION PART 1

FOUR WEEKS after their first full-day session, the Swan Services team found itself back in Alan's office for the first of two days of Vision Building. Eileen arrived at 8:45 A.M. and exchanged pleasantries with Alan while she got settled. Carol and Evan arrived together a few minutes later. They made a point to tell Eileen they had been at the office early that morning and decided to ride together because each planned to return to the office to "get caught up" later that day.

Sue and Art followed. Vic was the last to arrive, racing through the door at ten minutes after nine. While Vic settled in, Alan checked his watch, grabbed a green marker, and added the words "Vince Lombardi" to the Issues List. His only response to the curious looks from the leadership team was a wry smile and a nod, as if to assure them he'd explain soon enough.

Once again, Alan began by reviewing the Six Key Components and the proven process the leadership team had begun following to strengthen those Components. He walked the team through an overview of the objectives and agenda that he'd written on the whiteboard:

OBJECTIVES (2 DAYS)

- MASTER FOCUS DAY TOOLS
- CLEAR VISION
- CLEAR PLAN
- ISSUES LIST CLEAR

AGENDA (2 DAYS)

- CHECK-IN
- REVIEW FOCUS DAY TOOLS
- CORE VALUES
- CORE FOCUS
- 10-YEAR TARGET
- MARKETING STRATEGY
- 3-YEAR PICTURE
- 1-YEAR PLAN
- QUARTERLY ROCKS
- ISSUES LIST
- NEXT STEPS
- CONCLUDE

"Our first objective for these two days of Vision Building," he continued, "is to help you master the Focus Day tools that you learned in our last session. In this journey, mastery means two specific things—that you *understand* the tool and that you've *implemented* the tool in your organization. The second and third objectives are to walk out of here in about thirty days—after day two—with a crystal-clear vision and a clear plan to achieve that vision. That means everyone in this room is 100 percent on the same page with where the business is going and exactly how we plan to get there. There can be no exceptions."

Alan pointed at the twelve issues on the board left over from Swan's Focus Day as he went on: "The last objective is to get your Issues List clear and complete. We're going to continue smoking out issues during these next two sessions, and this list is going to grow."

Alan quickly reviewed the agenda, explaining that the team would first thoroughly review the Focus Day tools and then begin working on the eight questions from the V/TO. He then moved to a section of the whiteboard marked "Check-In" and gave the team two quiet minutes to record three things:

1. Bests—your best news from the last thirty days (one personal highlight; one business)
2. Update—a list of what's *working* and what's *not working* at Swan Services
3. Expectations for the session today

Most of the leaders were very upbeat. Sue and Vic both mentioned promising new sales opportunities as "business bests." Eileen's good news was all the work the team had done together on the Accountability Chart. Carol's business best was that all of her Rocks were on track.

The updates were also largely positive. Several leaders said the Level 10 Meetings were "working." They acknowledged that the meetings had been a little rocky at first but had been getting much better. Three leaders mentioned Rocks as working, and both Carol and Eileen identified the Scorecard as a promising tool in progress.

However, Sue thought IDS wasn't working as well as it could in the team's Level 10 Meetings. She also admitted she and the sales team hadn't yet "cleared the decks" and weren't hitting their Scorecard numbers. She mentioned the Accountability Chart as well.

"I can't say it's not working," she explained, "but Vic and I are eager to share the Accountability Chart with the rest of the organization. Until the sales team and others clearly recognize our new structure—with Vic as visionary and me leading sales—it'll be more difficult for Vic to let go and for me to step up into my role."

Sue also mentioned the unresolved marketing seat issue as "not working." Art agreed that not having reached an agreement about his schedule was a disappointment. A few leaders agreed with Sue on IDS, and two others mentioned the incomplete Scorecard as not quite working. Still, these items were mentioned as mere annoyances, not major problems. In general, the team seemed pleased with its progress.

Evan was a different story. His check-in was abrupt and apologetic. He struggled to come up with good news and had a long list of things that didn't seem to be working. He admitted to being off track on most of his Rocks and to have not gotten his team's Accountability Chart completed. He also hadn't consistently reported Scorecard numbers.

"So what's not working," said Evan haltingly, "is either this system . . . or me. I just can't seem to find the time to keep our projects on track, manage my team, and do all this homework. I'm sorry, Eileen, Vic—I feel like I'm letting you guys down."

"Thanks for being so open, Evan," Alan replied. "What you're experiencing is normal at this stage of the process. Don't get me wrong—we *do* need you to regain control, keep your Rocks on track, and complete your To-Dos. We'll work through some of the root causes of those issues when we review the Focus Day tools today."

Evan seemed soothed by Alan's response, but his struggles troubled Eileen.

Alan enjoyed hearing the team's expectations. Each leader expressed real enthusiasm for diving into the company's vision. Alan finished the exercise by also checking in, again expressing his expectations as, simply, "open and honest." He then moved to a whiteboard where he had written the following list:

Focus Day Tools

- Hitting the Ceiling
  - Simplify
  - Delegate
  - Predict
  - Systemize
  - Structure
- Accountability Chart
- Rocks
- Meeting Pulse
- Scorecard

He began by reminding the team that every organization, every department, and every leader hits the ceiling from time to time. He stressed the importance of mastering five leadership abilities: simplify, delegate, predict, systemize, and structure. He then reviewed them one by one, this time identifying specific tools he would be helping the leaders master to strengthen each of the abilities.

"The tool we use to get the right structure for the organization is the Accountability Chart," Alan concluded. "Unless there are any other questions about hitting the ceiling and the five leadership abilities, we'll move on to the Accountability Chart next."

Alan asked Eileen to hand out copies of the updated Accountability Chart to each leader and moved to a simplified version of it that he'd created on the whiteboard. (See updated Accountability Chart on pages 98–99.)

"Alan," Evan said carefully, "I have to confess. I didn't really do my homework. Eileen built out my department on her own."

"Thanks, Evan," replied Alan. "We'll work through what she did here today and try to get you all on the same page, okay?"

"Absolutely," responded Evan.

"Looking at your Accountability Chart," Alan said to the team, "we need to answer three questions. The first question is, 'Is it the right structure?' Without thinking about people, have we accounted for all the critical functions in the organization? Are they connected to one another properly? Do we have the five roles right in each seat? Take a few minutes to review the Accountability Chart. Circle any seat or department where you think we don't have the right structure or you have questions about the structure."

Once Swan's team had reviewed the chart, circling seats and making notes, Vic was the first to speak. "I circled the marketing seat."

"What's the specific issue, Vic?" asked Alan.

"Sue and I believe the marketing seat really isn't a leadership team function," he replied. "We think it's a critical seat, and we think Art owns it, but we feel it should report to Sue."

"You're suggesting the right structure at this stage is to have one person on your leadership team accountable for *both* sales and marketing?" Alan asked.

"That's right," replied Vic. "Nothing against you, Art. But the more we talked about it, the more it made sense to have one leader accountable for growing revenues—generating demand, closing sales, the whole shebang. I was wrong in the last session."

"Art," Alan asked directly, "how does this square with you?"

"I don't know what to think," Art admitted. "This comes as a surprise, so I guess I want to know why they feel this way."

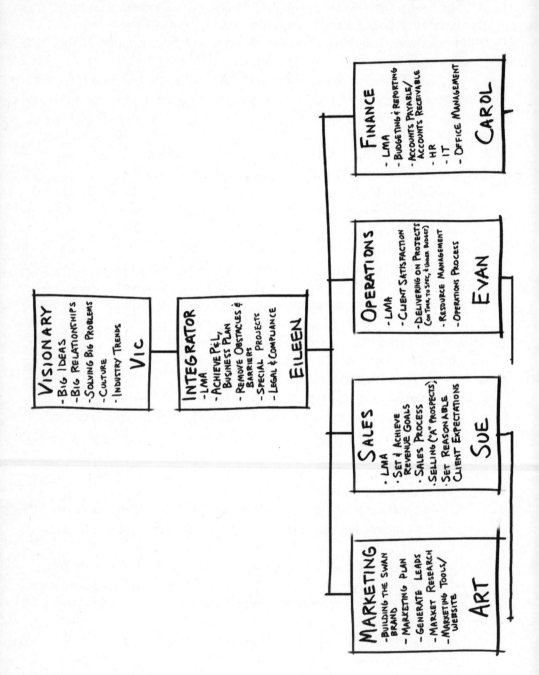

VISIONARY
- Big Ideas
- Big Relationships
- Solving Big Problems
- Culture
- Industry Trends

Vic

INTEGRATOR
- LMA
- Achieve P&L, Business Plan
- Remove Obstacles & Barriers
- Special Projects
- Legal & Compliance

Eileen

MARKETING
- Building the Swan Brand
- Marketing Plan
- Generate Leads
- Market Research
- Marketing Tools/ Website

Art

SALES
- LMA
- Set & Achieve Revenue Goals
- Sales Process
- Selling ("A" Prospects)
- Set Reasonable Client Expectations

Sue

OPERATIONS
- LMA
- Client Satisfaction
- Delivering on Projects (On Time, to Spec, & Under Budget)
- Resource Management
- Operations Process

Evan

FINANCE
- LMA
- Budgeting & Reporting
- Accounts Payable/ Accounts Receivable
- HR
- IT
- Office Management

Carol

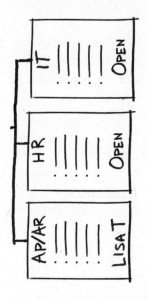

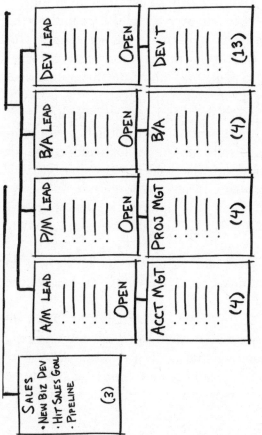

An awkward but controlled discussion followed. Vic and Sue explained their logic and again assured Art that their conclusion was structure-driven and not based on concerns about him as a leader.

Once the dialogue became repetitive, Alan urged the team to conclude. As he moved left around the table, each leader (except Art) quickly agreed to the new structure.

"Art?" Alan asked. "In the wake of everything that's been said, can you support this revised structure?"

"I'm not sure," Art said slowly, avoiding direct eye contact. "I really wish I'd been included in the discussions before today, because this isn't the way I'd do it if it were my company."

"So you'd leave the structure as is?" Alan asked.

"Yes," replied Art. "I believe marketing is a critical function that belongs on the leadership team."

"Thank you, Art," replied Alan sincerely. "That's a valid opinion—exactly what the team needed to know to make a decision for the greater good of the organization. Eileen, the team's been heard. Not everyone agrees, but you'll recall that we don't do consensus management in this system. It's time to make the call. As the integrator, what structure do you believe is best for Swan?"

All eyes turned to Eileen. Swan's integrator had made a lot of decisions in her career, but something about this moment in her own company felt different. She couldn't rally the troops, lobby dissenters, or side with the majority and move on. She needed to decide right now. That's when it hit her. *This* is what I do best and love most—I *decide.*

"At this point in time," she said, "the right structure is to have a single person accountable for marketing and sales represented on the leadership team."

Alan moved to the whiteboard and erased the marketing seat on the left side of the Accountability Chart, redrawing it as part of the sales and marketing department.

"Art," Eileen continued, "I know this surprised you, but I do think it's best for our company right now. You'll continue to play a vital role; you'll just do it as a member of Sue's team. And there was no conspiracy here. It truly just became clear to me as I stared at the Accountability Chart, listened to Vic, and considered all the options."

"I know that," Art admitted. "I'd be lying if I said I wasn't disappointed, but it's your company, and I respect your decision."

"Okay," Alan said after a few moments, "with the marketing seat question resolved, are there any other structure questions?"

"Obviously we've still got some work to do in operations," Eileen volunteered.

"Right," replied Alan, pointing to the ops department he had replicated on the whiteboard. "Does everyone feel that this is the right structure for the next level of the Accountability Chart?"

"Well," Evan began tentatively, "this is different from what we have today."

"It is," Eileen responded carefully. "But the way it's structured today—with you having twenty-five or more direct reports—doesn't seem to be working. So I'm suggesting that inserting mid-level managers accountable for leading the account management, project management, business analysis, and development teams makes more sense than the flat structure that we have now."

Evan had trouble maintaining his composure. It was embarrassing enough that his boss needed to complete his homework for him. Now she was suggesting that the way he had been running the department for years was wrong.

"Who do you see *filling* those seats, Eileen?" he asked.

"Structure first!" shouted Carol and Vic simultaneously.

"Very nice," Alan said, nodding. "They're right, Evan. Let's talk first about structure, and then we'll deal with people."

Evan racked his brain, searching for a good reason to defend his own approach. He began to imagine what life would be like with just four direct reports (instead of the four account managers, four project managers, four business analysts, and thirteen developers who reported to him today).

Eileen knew this structure was better than the one the overwhelmed ops leader had been mired in for years. She'd been worried about stepping on his toes when she built out his department, but he was unable to think strategically and contemplate change. That fact deepened her concern about his fitness for the ops leadership seat.

"Just thinking about structure," Evan finally said, "I can't think of any reason that what Eileen proposed wouldn't work. But I still don't understand where we're going to find the money to hire or promote four new managers. I know that's a people issue, but the reason I never proposed something like this is I don't think it's possible financially. Am I wrong, Eileen?"

"No," Eileen replied. "I agree that we can't pay for four new mid-level managers tomorrow. But if we put our heads together, we can probably figure out how to add those people in a way that will pay dividends for us."

Alan continued around the conference table, soliciting feedback about the newly proposed ops department. With Evan reluctantly on board and the rest of the team supporting Eileen's proposal, Alan was able to quickly fill in the five roles for each of the four new seats. He then helped the team build out the next level of the ops department.

As he watched his Accountability Chart take shape on the whiteboard, Evan gradually became relieved and then excited. He'd expected to be apologizing all day for not getting his work done. Instead, with everyone in the room working together, it had taken the team less than thirty minutes to structure his entire department!

When that was completed, Alan helped the leaders tackle a few minor structural questions in the sales and finance departments. He then moved to the second question.

"Now that we have the right structure," he said to the team, "the next question is, 'Are all the right people in the right seats?'" He reminded the team that Evan, Carol, and Art were already on the Issues List. He asked the leaders to review the Accountability Chart for any additional "people issues," which he defined as seats filled with someone who didn't fit Swan's culture or someone who didn't GWC the roles in his or her seat.

When everyone finished, Alan asked each member of the team to identify Swan's people issues. Now fully engaged in the exercise, Evan spoke first.

"All four of those new seats in my department are empty," he explained. "Does that make them people issues?"

"It does," Alan replied. "Let's take a few minutes to see if we can solve one or more of them today. As you look at the five roles for each seat, is there anyone in the organization today who gets, wants, and has the capacity to own one of the seats?"

This question started a lively discussion. Evan suggested Lisa Erickson, one of the current account managers, as the potential owner of the account management team leader seat. Alan moved left around the table, ultimately getting yeses from everyone, and wrote the name "Lisa E." into the seat.

Similar attempts to fill the other seats were rebuffed—mostly by Evan. Eileen and others suggested candidates only to have Evan explain why none of them really "fit" the seat in question. After spending fifteen minutes on this section of the Accountability Chart, Alan sensed the dialogue getting redundant and helped the team conclude.

"Evan, we've reached an impasse," he explained. "In your department there are three right seats for which there appear to be no right people. So until you fill those seats with someone else, you own them. When you fill them and how you fill them is a matter for the team to decide as you move forward in this process, but for now we have to conclude that this is an issue."

Alan wrote "Open" in the three seats, circled them in green, and then added the three separate issues to Swan's Issues List before the team moved on to other sections of the Accountability Chart. Carol started a tense discussion when she suggested Troy and Natalie—two of Sue's three sales team members—were people issues because they hadn't hit their quotas consistently. Vic reacted strongly, defending the salespeople and taking Carol to task for "attacking people who aren't here to defend themselves."

Alan jumped in quickly. "Carol, Vic," he said calmly, "it sounds like you have strong feelings about Troy and Natalie, and there's nothing wrong with that. But right now it would be a mistake to get bogged down in that debate. This is how the Issues List works. If somebody on the team has a people issue, we get it on the list. In a little while, I'll introduce a simple, objective tool that'll help you resolve these debates without having those endless, emotion-filled arguments about people. Okay?"

Vic was about to argue, but Sue stopped him.

"Vic," she said quietly, "I actually circled Troy and Natalie as well, for the same reason. I'm not saying they should be canned tomorrow or anything, but if they really did GWC the seat, they'd be hitting their quotas more regularly."

Sue's candor rendered Vic speechless, a rare feat. He was conditioned to defend "his" salespeople but accepted her position and let the team move on.

After Evan added two members of the operations team to the list, there were nearly a dozen seats circled in green on Swan's Accountability Chart. Several leaders looked concerned about the number of people issues, but Alan reminded them that issues cannot be solved until they are smoked out. He promised to introduce soon the process for resolving them.

Alan then asked the third question, "Does everybody in the organization have enough time to do his or her job well?"

"Ha!" Evan said out loud. The rest of the team laughed along with him.

"I'll take that as a no?" Alan asked jokingly.

"A *big* no," replied Evan. "I haven't had enough time in as long as I can remember. Isn't that just the nature of the beast when you work at a small company?"

"In most small companies, it is," replied Alan. "But it doesn't have to be that way, and frankly it *shouldn't* be that way. Most of my clients have enough time."

Alan went on to explain that leaders who work beyond their capacity can only endure for about six months before they burn out, leave, or begin consistently underperforming. He helped Evan and the rest of the team understand why not having enough time is a serious issue that should be added to the Issues List, not ignored or accepted as the way things are destined to work forever.

"I guess you should add me to the Issues List—again," suggested Evan, smiling.

Alan added "Evan, enough time" to the list. Carol raised her hand and suggested that she be added as well.

"So Evan, Carol," Alan continued, "when you don't have enough time to do your job well, you need a plan to make that issue go away forever. What do you need to do to make that happen?"

In the discussion that followed, Alan first helped Evan and Carol understand that leaders who have one or more people issues on their team often feel like they don't have enough time. Since both executives had at least one direct report on the Swan Services Issues List, Alan implored each leader to resolve those issues first.

"If you have the wrong people in the wrong seats reporting to you," Alan explained, "you will *never* have enough time because you'll be doing some or all of their work and cleaning up messes they make. So the first step in getting enough time is solving the people issues in your department. Evan, based on our work today, three of the four seats that report to you are open. Until you *permanently* resolve those issues—"

"I'll always be the bottleneck," Evan interjected.

"Exactly," Alan replied, smiling. "If you still don't have enough time after you've resolved the people issues," he continued, "you have to use the Accountability Chart and another tool in my tool-box to permanently resolve the issue." Alan quickly mentioned the "Delegate and Elevate" tool, a simple way for leaders to figure out exactly what they should delegate and what they should continue doing themselves. He promised to illustrate that tool more fully in the next session. He answered a few questions and then dismissed the group for a five-minute break.

DISCIPLINE

Alan moved on to review the next Focus Day tool, Rocks. He asked Eileen to distribute copies of Swan Services' Rock Sheet (see page 106) and led the team through a Rock review, one leader at a time. After instructing each Rock owner to respond "on track" or "off track," Alan read each Rock exactly as it was written.

"Art, trifold brochure and website draft complete," read Alan. "Is that on track or off track?"

"Well," Art replied, "the brochure's looking goo—"

"All we need to know is on track or off track, Art," said Alan kindly.

"Oh, um, on track," Art replied. Alan recorded the note and moved to the next leader on the Rock Sheet.

"Sue," Alan said. "Close two 'A' deals and complete ten key account plans."

"On track," she replied quickly. She was also on track with her other three Rocks.

"Survey current clients and implement client retention plan," read Alan. "On track or off track, Evan?"

Swan Services Quarterly Rock Sheet

Future Date: April 8, 20XX
Revenue:
Profit:
Measurables:

COMPANY ROCKS	WHO
1) Trifold brochure, proposal template and website draft complete	Art
2) Survey current clients and draft client satisfaction/retention plan	Evan
3) Close two "A" deals and complete ten key account plans	Sue
4) Make a decision to acquire project management software	Carol
5) Recommend & approve ops staffing changes to improve profitability	Eileen
6)	
7)	

ART
1) Trifold brochure, proposal template and website draft complete
2)
3)
4)
5)
6)
7)

SUE
1) Close two "A" deals and complete ten key account plans
2) Document sales process, get approved by leadership team
3) Develop sales department scorecard
4) Complete at least one joint prospect meeting with each of the three sales reps
5)
6)
7)

EVAN
1) Survey current clients and draft client satisfaction/retention plan
2) Hire new developer/consultant
3) Complete departmental performance reviews
4) Document project management core process
5) Deliver Acme Industries project on time and on budget
6) Coordinate departmental vacation schedules
7) Implement error-tracking system

CAROL
1) Make a decision to acquire project management software
2) Revise annual budget
3) Revise HR policy manual
4) Complete YTD financials thru June
5) Complete eight hours of continuing education
6) Review IT/payroll processing contracts
7)

EILEEN
1) Recommend & approve ops staffing changes to improve profitability
2) Evaluate variable expenses for cost-savings opportunities
3) Meet with three key clients that have reduced or eliminated spending with Swan
4) Initiate credit line renewal process
5) Complete and implement Focus Day tools
6)
7)

VIC
1) Attend industry trade show in search of at least one "big idea"
2) Visit personally with at least two key clients and two key business partners
3)
4)
5)
6)
7)

"Off track," replied Evan glumly.

"Hire new developer/consultant," Alan continued.

"On track," replied Evan with a halfhearted smile.

All of Evan's five additional Rocks were off track. Alan made a few notes on the Rock Sheet and moved on to Carol's list.

"Decide on project management software," read Alan.

"That's off track but not because—" said Carol quickly in a failed attempt to explain herself.

"Sorry, Carol," Alan cut in gently. "Let's finish the review first and then discuss the Rocks, okay?"

She nodded reluctantly and let Alan continue, saying "on track" rather proudly to the other five Rocks on her list.

"Eileen," Alan continued. "Implement ops staffing changes to improve profitability."

"Off track," she replied. Her other four Rocks were on track.

Vic was last.

"Attend industry trade show in search of at least one 'big idea'?" Alan asked.

"Looking good," replied Vic.

"On track?" clarified Alan.

"Somehow I knew you were going to ask me that," replied Vic, laughing. "Yes, that's on track."

"Visit personally with at least two key clients and two key business partners?" Alan continued.

"On track."

Alan quickly reviewed his notes on the Rock Sheet and appeared to be doing a few calculations.

"Great progress thus far," he said with a smile. "You're on track to complete seventeen of twenty-five Rocks—just under 70 percent, which isn't far from the completion rate goal of 80 percent. Have you learned anything yet about Rocks?"

"Well," said Eileen, smiling. "I just learned that I need to cut people off so we don't spend twenty minutes on the Rock review in our Level 10 Meeting. I'm letting people ask questions and explain things too much."

"Music to my ears," replied Alan. "The better you get at reporting, the more time you have to solve issues each week."

"What do we do when someone wants to explain something about their own Rock or ask a question about someone else's?" Eileen asked.

"You drop it down to the Issues List," Alan explained. "Use that very phrase—'drop it down'—whenever someone on the team starts to explain or defend an off-track reporting item or goes off on a tangent. Shout it if you have to. That'll help you quickly get the meeting back on track and drop questions, issues, and concerns to your Issues List. And remember, any off-track Scorecard numbers automatically go to the Issues List as well. Does that make sense?"

"It seems a little inefficient," Carol offered. "I mean, if we drop something down to the Issues List, it might get lost. We might forget about it or not get to it for a couple of weeks. If we have a quick question or comment, why can't we just spit it out right then?"

"Because the questions and comments about Rocks are not always the highest priority issues," Alan explained. "When you 'drop it down' and use the Issues List, you'll spend time on only the issues that are most important each week."

Alan turned to the others. "Any other issues or questions about the Rocks?"

"How do you get or provide status updates?" asked Evan.

"What do you mean, Evan?" asked Alan.

"Well," he replied, "some people on the team seem to want evidence that each Rock is on track before they believe it. And they also like to share a bunch of detail about what they've accomplished."

Alan was formulating a response when Carol broke in loudly.

"Oh, come on, Evan," she huffed. "I asked about your Rocks because you're *always* behind and you kept saying 'on track.' You're just pissed that I called you out."

"Why don't you get off your high horse for once, Carol," Evan replied, red-faced. "You're right, as always, but that's no excuse for crowing about the progress you've made each week. You're not the only one around here that works hard, you know."

"Hold on, guys," Alan jumped in. "I appreciate your passion, but debate and conflict can only be healthy and productive when we stay focused on the greater good of the business and avoid getting personal. We're dangerously close to breaking that rule. So let's take a step back and get clear on the specific issue we're IDSing right now."

Neither Carol nor Evan let go of the fight easily, but they both sat back and stopped talking.

"Thank you," replied Alan. "Now if I remember correctly, the original question was, 'How do we provide and receive status updates?'"

"That's right," Eileen agreed.

"The simple answer is this," replied Alan, making direct eye contact with the two angry executives. "When you say 'on track' or 'off track' at a Level 10 Meeting, you're providing the only status update a healthy leadership team needs. Capable, hardworking leaders need to trust one another to get stuff done. When you have a legitimate question or need for information, drop it down to the Issues List and IDS it later. If you need to get or provide more information than that because you don't trust one another, there's an accountability issue or a team health issue—or both."

The team sat quietly, digesting what had been said. When they thought about it later, both Vic and Eileen would describe this as a defining moment. Vic realized Alan had just described an environment that could be created only through a massive cultural shift. Eileen realized she couldn't let petty bickering slow her or the team down. And both owners instantly understood—very clearly—that some of the people in the room weren't cut out for what lay ahead.

Alan proceeded on to discuss the Meeting Pulse. "I loved hearing several of you mention in your check-ins that the Level 10 Meetings are starting to come together," he said with enthusiasm. "You also said some things don't feel quite right, which is completely normal. It'll take you a while to master all the ins and outs of the Level 10 Meeting and IDS. What I've found is that the quickest way to help you get there is to walk through the Level 10 agenda exactly as it should be run."

Alan asked Eileen to pass out copies of the team's most recent Level 10 agenda and walked the team through a Level 10 Meeting in its purest form.

"Please follow along and take notes about the things that sound different from the way things work in *your* meetings. If you'll hold your observations, questions, and issues until the end, we'll tackle them all at once. Does that work?"

After verifying that the team's meetings were still occurring on Tuesdays at 8:00 A.M. and were being run by Eileen with Sue managing the paperwork, Alan walked through the agenda step by step, just as he had done at the Focus Day.

"At *precisely* eight o'clock," he began, looking at Vic as the other leaders glanced nervously around the room, "you begin with a segue. Eileen invites the brave one to start with personal and business good news from the previous week and then moves left around the table. The next three items on the agenda are reporting only. When reporting numbers on the Scorecard and Rocks, the owner of each measurable and Rock simply says 'on track' or 'off track.' No explanations, no excuses, no defensiveness. When a number or Rock is off track or there's a question or comment, you drop it down to the Issues List. Customer and employee headlines are quick-hitting comments about customers and employees. Bad reports automatically drop to the Issues List. Good reports are occasionally worthy of further discussion and can be added to the list as well."

Alan moved to the To-Do List, drawing a few symbolic To-Dos on the list and checking them off as he explained how to conduct the review. He reminded the team that 90 percent of these To-Dos should be "To-Done" and dropped off the list each week.

"The next item on the agenda is the essence of what makes for a great meeting," Alan continued. "Resolving issues. When you master the Level 10 Meeting, you'll be spending sixty minutes each week prioritizing and solving issues—setting 'em up, knocking 'em down, and making 'em go away forever."

"This is where we really struggle," admitted Vic. "Our Issues List seems to get longer and longer each week."

"That's normal at this stage," replied Alan. "So let's go through IDS one more time, and I'll answer all your questions about how to make it work for you."

Alan reminded Eileen to first invite everyone to add new issues and then ask Sue to read through every issue on the list—new and old. Next he explained how to quickly invite the team to prioritize the three most important issues.

"That should take about thirty seconds each week," he explained to surprised looks from several leaders.

Alan then reminded the team to start with issue number one and IDS it. He explained how to first identify the root cause(s) of the issue, discuss it without grandstanding or politicking, and solve the issue by agreeing on a To-Do or a plan of attack to make the issue go away forever. Several leaders recorded thoughts and questions as he spoke.

"Once you've solved issue number one," Alan explained, "just move to issue number two and IDS it. If you solve all three and there's time left, simply reprioritize the next top three and start again with number one. Some weeks you'll tackle some low-hanging fruit and solve a handful of issues; others you'll spend the whole time on one big issue. As long as you're prioritizing properly and working hard to really solve each issue, you're using your time well. Wherever you are at 9:25, Eileen makes sure you stop working through issues and move to conclude the meeting."

Alan wrote three items on the whiteboard: "Recap To-Dos," "Cascading Messages," and "Rating (1–10)." He completed the walk-through by explaining each of the items. He reminded the team to help improve the quality of the meetings by rating them and, when helpful or necessary, providing constructive feedback for a low rating.

"And with that, your meeting always ends on time," he continued. "So meetings don't run over, collapse on top of other meetings and commitments, and force everything to run late. Questions?"

Virtually everyone on the team had something to say. To focus the discussion, he asked the team to start at the top of the agenda and work through the list. "Are you starting every meeting on time?" he asked, already knowing the answer.

There was a brief, awkward silence, which Eileen decided to break. "No," she answered matter-of-factly. "But it's a lot better than it used to be. We've never started later than 8:10."

"It's completely my fault," blurted Vic. "I've been late to every single meeting."

"And how does the rest of the team feel about that?" Alan asked.

"They've been very patient," he replied. "I've struggled with this my whole career, and I'm working harder than ever to get it right. Let's move on."

Alan surveyed the room. Several of Swan's leaders looked at him with a mixture of doubt and hope. This was clearly a hot-button issue.

"Point taken," he replied carefully. "But if you could see the facial expressions I'm seeing, you wouldn't want to move on. I put 'Vince Lombardi' on the Issues List because my clients and I subscribe to *his* approach to being on time. He said, 'Early is on time, and on time is late.' So when a meeting starts at nine, we're expecting you to be in your seat at nine, ready to go. That didn't happen this morning, and it's not happening consistently in your Level 10 Meetings. So for the good of the company, can we dig a little deeper?"

Sue couldn't believe Alan had tackled the issue head-on like that. She seized the opportunity to give Vic some heartfelt feedback.

"It really bothers me," Sue admitted. "It's clear that you're trying harder than ever, Vic, but I'm so busy that wasting ten minutes at the start of a meeting seems *excruciating*! And when you do that for fifty to a hundred meetings a year, we're all wasting a week of productivity, sitting around ticked off, twiddling our thumbs."

Alan thanked Sue for being open and honest and then got similar input from Evan and Art. Clearly the team was frustrated. To his credit, Vic listened carefully, contemplating the time he'd wasted and frustration he'd caused.

"So, Vic, would starting the Level 10 Meetings at 8:15 make it easier for you to arrive on time?" Alan asked.

"No," said Vic flatly. "I get it, and all I can say is I'm sorry. I honestly never knew I was frustrating everyone—it's always just seemed like five harmless minutes. I can get better at this without us changing the meeting time."

With the on-time discussion resolved, Alan answered a few additional questions about the reporting-only section of the meeting. All in all, the team was doing a good job reviewing the Scorecard, Rocks, and headlines, so they moved on to the To-Do List.

"We're nowhere near a 90 percent completion rate," muttered Carol.

Alan asked a few clarifying questions and learned that the team had been using the To-Do List as a holding area, a common problem. He reminded them that a To-Do is a seven-day action item and urged the leaders to stop signing up for To-Dos that couldn't possibly be done in seven days. A quick discussion helped them understand how to use To-Dos and the Issues List to avoid repeating that mistake.

"You'll naturally get better at capturing and completing your To-Dos as you master the Level 10 Meeting and the rest of the Focus Day tools," Alan said.

When the team moved on to discuss the Issues List, the focus turned immediately to prioritization. The Swan team had been taking five minutes or longer in an effort to reach agreement about what to IDS first. When Alan said the exercise should take no longer than thirty seconds, Sue was perplexed.

"How's that possible when there are fifteen or twenty issues on your list?" she asked.

"When Eileen asks you to prioritize the issues," Alan replied, "be ready to suggest at least one issue as the top priority. Some weeks you'll have an off-track Rock or Scorecard measurable that you're burning to IDS. Others you'll have a customer or employee issue that requires immediate attention. And occasionally you'll all know exactly what needs to be tackled first. But whatever the reason for your preference, be quick and vocal when Eileen asks for priorities. And Eileen, when the team is stuck, be ready to make the call and prioritize the top three issues on your own. After all, if it's taking you five minutes, that's one more issue you could solve each week!"

"We discuss things more than we identify or solve things," Carol admitted.

"Eileen," Alan said, "your job is to help the team IDS properly. When someone just wants to *discuss* an issue, make sure the team first identifies the root cause. That will help you discuss and solve the *right thing*. When you don't identify the root cause, you end up discussing one or more symptoms or stuck in an endless dialogue about everything. Once you've identified the real issue, keep the discussion focused and free from politicking. Help the team *conclude* by making a decision and agreeing to a plan of action. Remember, when the team is divided and everyone's been heard, you have to make the call. Once you solve the issue, make sure that whatever the conclusion, it's crystal clear and fully supported by everyone in the room."

"Understood," replied Eileen. "I have to say, we've been getting pretty good ratings, and I'm amazed at how many issues we *have* solved. We can certainly get better, but I think we've come a long way in the last month."

The rest of the team agreed with Eileen. Alan made sure everyone's questions had been answered and called for a break before moving on to review the Scorecard. On his way out, Art approached Eileen and asked her to step down the hall with him.

"Yes?" she said when they were out of sight.

"Should I still be here?" he asked awkwardly.

"What do you mean?" she asked, a little surprised.

"Well, I was removed from the so-called leadership team about forty-five minutes ago," he explained. "I report to Sue now, so . . ."

"Oh!" Eileen exclaimed. "I'm not sure."

Eileen thought for a moment and then suggested they bring Alan into the conversation to get his perspective. Art reluctantly agreed— he'd hoped to avoid further embarrassment by handling this issue privately with Eileen.

Alan listened carefully and, to Art's dismay, suggested he ask the question again after the session had reconvened. At the very least, Sue needed to be included in the discussion, and he believed this was an issue best IDSed by the whole team. The impromptu huddle broke up, and the leaders began reassembling in the meeting room.

"Before we review your Scorecard," Alan said as the session resumed, "Art's asked a good question that only the team can help him answer. Art?"

"Well, the question was," Art began, "should I still be here?"

Swan's leaders let Art's question sink in. Vic was the first to speak.

"Are you saying that maybe you shouldn't be here because your seat on the Accountability Chart got moved off the leadership team?"

"That's what I'm asking, yes," Art replied, feeling better now that the question was out of his head and on the table.

"For what it's worth," Sue said, "I still think you add tremendous value here. We're about to start defining our vision, and you'll be a real asset during that process."

"Thank you, Sue," Art replied, genuinely touched. "That means a lot."

Vic chimed in to support Sue's position. Neither Carol nor Evan offered a strong opinion.

"So can we conclude?" Alan asked.

"Yes," Eileen replied. "It sounds like having Art continue to participate in these sessions through Vision-Building Day Two is the right call. Agreed?"

Eileen got agreement from everyone on the team. Art and Sue in particular seemed genuinely pleased with both the decision and the way it was made. Eileen smiled, starting to see more clearly how IDS worked best.

With that delicate issue resolved, Alan moved on to review the final Focus Day tool, the company Scorecard. He started by asking Eileen to distribute copies.

Who	Measurable	Goal	Weeks													
			1	2	3	4	5	6	7	8	9	10	11	12	13
Sue	New leads	36	11	4	47	17									
Sue	Initial sales meetings	12	8	9	4	14									
Sue	Proposals (#)	4	2	1	3	4									
Sue	Proposals ($)	$300K	$175K	$70K	$275K	$350K									
Sue	30-day pipeline	$1.5M	$1.15M	$1.05M	$1.10M	$1.25M									
Sue	Contracts (#)	2	2	1	1	2									
Sue	Contracts ($)	$150K	$161K	$135K	$75K	$170K									
Evan	Projects late	1			4	4									
Evan	Projects over budget	1													
Evan	Defects to clients	0		1		1									
Evan	Utilization rate	80%													
Carol	Cash balance	$75K	$55K	$85K	$70K	$61K									
Carol	A/R > 60 days	< $30K	$42.5	$42.5	$31.0	$26.1									
Carol	Billing errors	0	0	1	1	0									

"Is this Scorecard giving you all an absolute pulse on the business?" Alan asked.

"Well, this is becoming a recurring theme," admitted Evan, "but it's my fault nobody has even a faint pulse on the ops department. I just haven't been able to build the right system for measuring this stuff."

Alan asked the team to confirm that it still wanted to see all four of Evan's numbers, and everyone did. One measurable at a time, he asked Evan to verify that it was possible to measure each number weekly. In each case Evan agreed, so Alan walked to the Issues List and wrote "Ops Scorecard Numbers" in green marker.

The team quickly reviewed each of the other departments' numbers. Concerns were expressed about several measurables, but eventually the team decided to track those numbers for the rest of the quarter before making any changes.

Lunch was delivered just as the Scorecard discussion drew to a close. The team took another quick break and settled in for a working lunch. Alan cleared the whiteboard and prepared for the transition to Vision Building.

TRANSITION TO VISION

Fifteen minutes later, Alan began by explaining the logic of traction first and vision second. By implementing the Focus Day tools *before* working on the company vision, he explained, Swan Services would be far better able to execute its vision.

"I often say vision without traction is hallucination," Alan began, getting a few laughs. "With clear accountability and discipline in place, your discussions about the future and the decisions you're about to make become more real, more attainable. You aren't just hoping or wishing for something to happen. You're *predicting the future* with people who will take ownership and then working hard together to achieve your vision."

His words drew a few smiles, and he continued: "We'll take a simple approach to defining Swan's vision. The reason we can is that it already exists in your heads. Unfortunately, there are six different variations, and we can only have one. We're going to get you all 100 percent on the same page with the answers to the eight questions on the V/TO."

He then pointed to the middle of the agenda on the whiteboard, where the following items were listed:

- CORE VALUES
- CORE FOCUS
- 10-YEAR TARGET
- MARKETING STRATEGY
- 3-YEAR PICTURE
- 1-YEAR PLAN
- QUARTERLY ROCKS
- ISSUES LIST

"Let's take these one question at a time, beginning with Core Values," Alan said. "Core Values are a small set of essential, enduring principles that define your culture. Three to seven is the rule of thumb, hopefully closer to three because less is more. When we're done with this exercise, we will have defined the culture of this organization—what makes Swan and its people unique. This is who you are. These Core Values will become useful, indispensable—the rules you play by. You *must* live by them yourselves and use them to hire, fire, review, reward, and recognize your people. When these Core Values live and breathe in the organization, you'll attract more of the right people to the company. The wrong people will stick out like a sore thumb, feel out of place, and more comfortably exit."

Following a process he'd used to help many organizations discover their own Core Values, Alan asked the leaders to write down the names of three people at Swan who were true superstars.

"These are people you love. They fit the culture, and it fits them. They're people you'd like to clone, because if you had a thousand of 'em, you could conquer the world," he explained. "Ideally, pick three people who are currently in the organization but not here at this table."

After a few minutes, Alan asked each leader to read his or her list, and he recorded the names on the whiteboard. There were several duplicates, which he recognized by placing a tick mark next to the name.

MATT |

MARY C.

HENRY ||||

BELLA ||

RACHEL |||

RICHARD

STEPHANIE

MARK

"Thinking of these people," Alan continued, "please make a list of the characteristics, attributes, or traits that make them so valuable."

When everyone had finished, Alan started recording the characteristics one leader at a time, resulting in a list of forty-one words or phrases on the whiteboard.

"Are you sure less is more, Alan?" asked Vic, laughing.

"This is nothing," replied Alan, laughing. "I promise we'll walk out of here with three to seven."

He led the team through the first cut of the lengthy list by using the "Keep, Kill, and Combine" process of elimination. Again during this first pass, there could be no debates. If anyone wanted to keep a potential Core Value, it stayed on the list. At the conclusion of that first cut, fifteen items remained.

POSITIVE/CAN-DO ATTITUDE
THIRST FOR KNOWLEDGE
PASSIONATE
INTEGRITY
INNOVATIVE/CREATIVE
HARDWORKING
DETAIL ORIENTED
DOES THE RIGHT THING
GETS THINGS DONE
NEVER SATISFIED
COMPETITIVE
HUMBLE
RELIABLE
CONFIDENT
HELPFUL

Before making the second pass, Alan shared the contents of a *Harvard Business Review* article by Patrick Lencioni titled "Make Your Values Mean Something." Lencioni cited three "values traps"—mistakes companies make when defining Core Values that make it hard to use them to build and maintain an enduring company culture.

"*Aspirational* Core Values," Alan summarized, "are characteristics that sound great but don't define the culture that exists in your organization today. If the people who fit at Swan today are a bunch of workaholics, turning in sixty-five-hour weeks and having no life out-side the office, the value 'work-life balance' would be an aspirational Core Value. If it's not true of the company today, you can't use it to hold people accountable tomorrow. It'll be a joke. *Permission-to-play* Core Values are traits essential to this organization. You will never hire someone without these traits, and you'll ask people to leave the organization when you learn they don't possess them. But these Core Values don't define what's unique about *your* culture. Every company requires them; they're table stakes. And if they don't describe *Swan's* unique culture, it's not necessary to call them Core Values. Honesty and professionalism are two Core Values that might be described as permission-to-play values. *Accidental* Core Values are character-istics that may have gotten you to where you are today but won't be required of everyone in the company forever. An example of an acci-dental Core Value is something like entrepreneurial spirit. For most of my clients, that's been an important factor in the early success of their organization. But I ask them to imagine their company in ten years—maybe when they have 250 people. There are 12 people in the accounting department alone. Is it still going to be important for each of them to possess an entrepreneurial spirit? If the answer is no, we have to kill it. It's not a timeless, essential guiding principle."

Eileen grinned. She had participated in her fair share of Core Values exercises while at Anodyne, and virtually every one of her clients had fallen into one or more of Lencioni's values traps.

On the second pass through the Core Values, Alan encouraged rigorous debate. Things got interesting right away.

"Kill it," Carol said loudly when Alan read the first item on the list—positive/can-do attitude.

"Keep it," replied Vic and Sue in unison.

"That defines our best people, Carol," Vic continued. "Things may have gotten tough lately, but this business has been built on the backs of positive, confident, can-do people. I won't let you Kill it."

"Fine," Carol said dismissively. "I think it's fluffy, that's all. You don't need to jump down my throat."

Alan polled the rest of the team; each of them said "Keep." The next two items on the list were nearly unanimous Keeps. Integrity was quickly Killed as a permission-to-play Core Value, innovative was Killed as accidental, and Alan drew a line through hardworking when the team concluded it was also a permission-to-play value.

They moved down the list, Keeping, Killing, and Combining, until another battle occurred while discussing "competitive." Evan wanted to Kill it as an undesirable trait. Vic insisted it had been key to Swan's success and should continue to be a required characteristic. Ultimately, it was Killed as not essential for every employee.

After an interesting discussion, the team decided to Combine humble and confident into a single Core Value. Eileen and Evan had been concerned that confident would be misconstrued as arrogant. Having suggested both potential values for the list, Sue assured the team that she didn't mean arrogant at all. It dawned on her that she recorded both characteristics to make precisely this point.

"What if we Combined these two into a single Core Value?" she asked. "We make the point that we're people who believe in ourselves and our solutions but don't come off as cocky or arrogant. Would that work?"

"I love it," replied Vic. "Keep."

"Agreed," said Eileen. Art agreed as well, Carol shrugged, and Evan flashed the thumbs-up sign, so Alan Combined the two Core Values.

The team made one last pass through the following list:

> POSITIVE/CAN-DO ATTITUDE
> THIRST FOR KNOWLEDGE/NEVER SATISFIED
> PASSIONATE
> DOES THE RIGHT THING
> GETS THINGS DONE/RELIABLE
> HUMBLE/CONFIDENT
> HELPFUL

When Alan reminded the leaders that "less is more," two quick discussions resulted. First, Sue suggested that the team Combine positive attitude with helpful, arguing that the attitude alone wasn't as important as a genuine desire to dig in and help others get the results they needed. And although Vic held on to "passionate" until the bitter end, Eileen helped him understand that an employee who really fit Swan's culture as defined by the other five Core Values would be, by default, passionate about Swan and his or her role in the organization.

As the discussion concluded, Alan congratulated the team on a job well done. During a quick break, he set up the next part of the Core Values exercise. When the team returned, he handed each of them blank copies of a grid, a tool he called the "People Analyzer." Alan asked the leaders to record Swan's five Core Values in the diagonal columns at the top of the People Analyzer and the names of each leader in the rows down the left side.

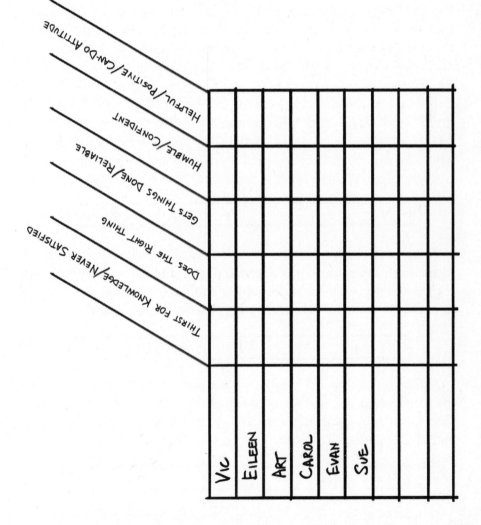

"To test your Core Values," Alan explained, "we're going to people-analyze everyone in the room—one Core Value at a time—using one of three scores: Plus (+) means the person exhibits this Core Value *most* of the time—nobody's perfect. Minus (−) means most of the time the person does *not* exhibit the Core Value. Plus/minus (+/−) means some of the time the person does and some of the time he or she doesn't."

Alan then asked the team to rate everyone in the room for each Core Value. The leaders became very still, and a couple of them hunched over their grids. Carol covered her responses with her hand. Tension mounted as everyone realized where this exercise was going.

"Let's start at the top by rating Vic," Alan suggested. "We'll go rapid-fire around the room, one Core Value at a time, starting to Vic's left."

For "thirst for knowledge/never satisfied," Eileen said "plus," Art said "plus," Carol said "plus/minus," and Evan and Sue each said "plus." Alan recorded a "+" in the diagram and explained that he would be recording the average of what was said. When the exercise was complete, Vic was rated as follows:

Although Vic hadn't gotten a vote in Alan's tally, he admitted rating himself a "plus/minus" in the "gets things done/reliable" category, and the team moved on to rate Eileen. Evan and Vic rated her a "plus/minus" for "positive attitude," but her average scores were all pluses.

EILEEN	+	+	+	+	+

Sitting to Eileen's left was Art, who was growing apprehensive as his turn neared. He began to relax when he made it through the first three Core Values with all pluses. His average score was "plus/minus" in "humble/confident" (the same way he rated himself).

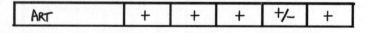

Carol was up next. The pressure in the room had become intense, but Alan noticed a strange half-smile on Eileen's face. She seemed almost eager to begin the discussion. The Core Values exercise had crystallized Eileen's feelings about Carol. Staring at her scores, she thought back to her struggles rating the controller's GWC in the Focus Day. She realized competence for the roles in her seat hadn't been the issue. Carol was clearly a *wrong person* in the *right seat.*

Starting with Evan, Alan asked each leader to give his or her rating for Carol in "thirst for knowledge/never satisfied."

"Plus/minus?" Evan said weakly.

"Plus/minus," repeated Sue.

Carol shot both a withering look; each leader worked hard to avoid eye contact. Vic, Eileen, and Art all chimed in with "plus/minus" in rapid succession, and Alan recorded the score. Carol calmed slightly when she earned an average rating of "plus" for "does the right thing" and "gets things done/reliable." Alan moved on to "humble/confident."

"Plus/minus," Evan began.

"Plus/minus," said Sue.

"Minus," said Vic.

"Minus," said Eileen immediately afterward. Someone gasped. Carol turned a bright shade of red.

"Plus/minus," said Art. Alan recorded the rating and continued unfazed.

"Helpful/positive/can-do attitude?" Alan said to Evan.

"Minus," he said more confidently in the wake of Vic's and Eileen's earlier ratings.

"Minus," said Sue and Vic in succession.

Eileen had been watching Carol carefully. She was visibly angry and looked to be contemplating either an outburst or a hasty exit. Undeterred, Eileen read the rating she had recorded.

"Minus," she said coolly.

"Plus/minus," Art said gently. Alan recorded a minus and stepped away to let Carol's marks sink in.

CAROL	+/-	+	+	+/-	−

After a brief pause Alan continued, "Okay, now rating Evan."

"Hold *on*!" Carol blurted. "We're not just moving on without talking about this, are we? You're acting like nothing happened."

"I'm sorry, Carol," Alan said kindly. "Are you surprised or frustrated by the ratings?"

"Yes!" she shouted. "I'm flat-out pissed! Don't I get a chance to defend myself?"

"Well," said Alan slowly, "it would be best if we deal with any frustrations about the way any of you were rated after the exercise. I realize that might be difficult, but right now we're just focused on testing your Core Values. Is that okay with you?"

Carol was flabbergasted. She hadn't anticipated Alan saying no, so she wasn't able to respond. She just sat back in her chair, angry and defeated. Relieved to be done rating Carol, the team moved quickly and painlessly through Evan's and Sue's scores. Alan ultimately recorded the following ratings for each leader:

EVAN	+	+	+/-	+	+
SUE	+	+	+	+	+

With the entire team rated, Alan added another row at the bottom of the People Analyzer and entered "THE BAR" in the left-hand column.

"Next we need to set the bar," Alan explained. "In other words, what's the minimum rating that would make you feel an employee shares your Core Values? Once that's defined, someone who is at or above the bar is a 'right person.' Where we should set the bar is completely up to you, but the rule of thumb when you have five Core Values is any combination of three pluses and two plus/minuses. Somebody with a minus can never be above the bar."

The team asked questions and discussed its options, ultimately defining the bar as Alan suggested. Carol remained visibly agitated throughout and didn't say a word.

"We're almost done," Alan promised. "But I'd like to test your Core Values one more time. Can somebody give me the name of one of Swan's shining stars?"

Evan pointed to the employee names Alan had written on the whiteboard earlier and said, "How about Henry? He got five votes." The team quickly agreed.

"So Henry's one of the best people in your organization," Alan continued, recording his name on the People Analyzer. "Can you give me one of the worst? Is there somebody in this organization that clearly doesn't fit the culture?"

"Jerry," said Evan right away. Eileen nodded. The two of them had been discussing Jerry Ryan's performance issues and personal problems for months. He was a relatively capable developer but seemed to need constant attention and often got into scrapes with other employees.

Alan added Jerry's name to the list and asked each leader to rate Henry and Jerry according to the Core Values. As Alan began gathering scores from each leader, Art looked perplexed.

"I don't know Jerry at all," explained Art. "Should I pass?"

"Yes, if you have no relevant experience with him," Alan answered.

Alan compiled the ratings, recording averages on the whiteboard as follows:

THE BAR	+	+	+	+/-	+/-
HENRY	+	+	+	+	+
JERRY	+/-	+/-	+	+/-	+/-

"Wow," said Vic. "That certainly makes me feel like we got these right."

Alan let Vic's comment settle, watching as the team processed the data reflected in the People Analyzer. "Congratulations. *Very* well done," he said sincerely. "You've clearly defined what it means to be a 'right person' at Swan Services. Before we move on, I also want to explain how the People Analyzer helps you define the right seats."

Alan reminded the team that GWC stands for gets it, wants it, and has the capacity to do it." He explained that the bar for GWC is three yeses—a nonnegotiable. He recorded that on the whiteboard. (See page 126.)

"To determine whether someone is in the right seat using the People Analyzer," he continued, "you look at the person's seat on the Accountability Chart and the roles in that seat. Just as we did for each of you earlier, you then rate that person a yes or a no in each of the three columns—G, W, C. If you can't comfortably say yes, that's a no. There's

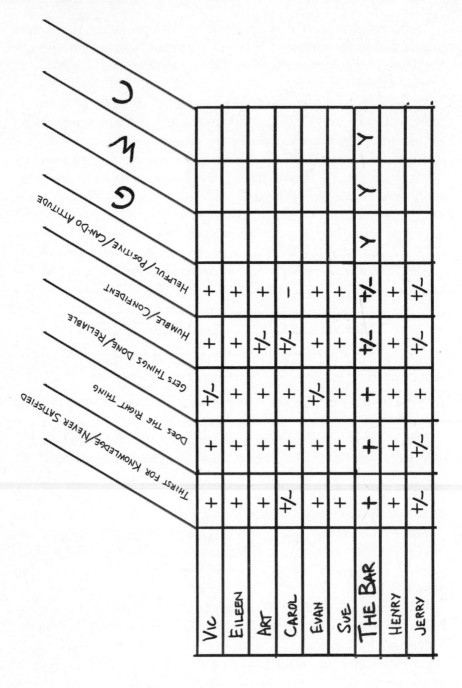

no such thing as a yes/minus or a maybe. You must have all yeses to be in the right seat—a single no is a deal killer. Got it?"

This discussion helped the team begin to see exactly how it would soon be using the People Analyzer to clearly identify people issues. Alan further explained that some employees who learn they're "below the bar" are able to elevate themselves by more consistently exhibiting one or more of the Core Values or more clearly showing that they GWC the roles in their seat on the Accountability Chart.

"In fact," he explained, "*most* of your people will respond well once you make your expectations more clear. Remember that you're introducing these clearly defined standards for the first time. Up to now you've actually failed your employees, not the other way around. When you begin using your Core Values, Accountability Chart, and the People Analyzer to hire, fire, review, reward, and recognize people in your organization, you'll be amazed at how clear-cut your people issues become. When something doesn't feel right, you simply pull out the People Analyzer and use it to determine whether the employee is the right person in the right seat."

Vic was thrilled. He'd always described the company's culture—or vibe—as something that could be felt and sensed but not quantified. As a result, he and Eileen had wasted weeks and months discussing and debating swings in morale, attitude problems, and other confounding people issues without ever resolving any of them. On the rare occasion that they *had* made decisions to terminate people, both leaders had laid awake at night agonizing about making the right call—sometimes for weeks on end. In fact, they often did the same thing about *hiring* decisions! In the People Analyzer, Vic saw a tool that would end all that agony.

"What do you do when someone is below the bar?" asked Sue.

"Great question," Alan replied. "Most of my clients use a three-strike rule. You sit down with that person for the first of three meetings and explain exactly why he or she doesn't fit your culture, doesn't GWC his or her seat, or both. Provide specific examples of what's not working, and set a deadline for correcting those problems—say, thirty or sixty days. If the person hasn't risen above the bar by then, it's the second strike, and it means a second meeting and a written warning with another deadline. Strike three means termination."

The leaders remained quiet as they contemplated this approach.

"These five Core Values are your handful of rules," Alan explained. "But before they start working for you, there are two things you need to do. The first is repeat yourselves often; I'll explain exactly how in a moment. The second is be consistent—walk the talk. If you don't exhibit the Core Values yourselves, you can't expect your people to follow the rules. In other words, lead by example. To help you repeat these Core Values often, we need someone to write a Core Values speech that can be used consistently by everyone. This is homework that needs to be completed by the next session. Do I have a volunteer?"

"I'll do it," said Vic. "It's right in my wheelhouse."

The rest of the team nodded its agreement, so Alan continued by explaining the assignment. Vic was to first "wordsmith" the five Core Values—to settle on a word or a short phrase that most clearly defined each of them. He then needed to provide two or three examples, stories, or analogies for each of them. Vic was expected to bring a one-page summary of the Core Values speech to the next session.

Although ready to move on, Alan decided to deal with what had become a noticeable distraction. Since receiving her Core Values ratings, Carol had been visibly agitated. She had reluctantly offered a rating or opinion when pressed but otherwise had remained seated with her arms crossed tightly across her chest and a determined grimace on her face.

"It's clear we have an elephant in the room," Alan said. "I think we need to deal with it right now. Obviously Carol is below the bar."

This blunt statement got everyone's attention.

"Carol," Alan went on, "as I said earlier, these Core Values have never been defined before. They represent a new set of standards, and in my experience most leaders and employees who find themselves below the bar respond well and elevate themselves above the bar. However, you're clearly upset by what's happened here. So I'm asking you and the rest of the team, how do you want to handle this issue?"

Carol was speechless. She was accustomed to stewing about issues like this for weeks and subtly exacting revenge on those leaders she felt had wronged her. A late report here, a snide remark there—she'd have the last word eventually. But confronted with this opportunity to deal openly with her frustration, she fell suddenly silent.

Eileen jumped in. "I'd like to meet with Carol to discuss this in depth tomorrow. Let's compare calendars at the break and find time away from the office. Okay?"

"Okay," Carol replied grimly.

Alan dismissed the team for another break and cleared the white-board to prepare for the Core Focus exercise.

SWEET SPOT

"One thing is certain in business," began Alan when everyone was seated. "We're all going to lose focus."

"I'm sorry, Alan," interrupted Vic. "What were you saying?"

Once again, the team erupted with laughter.

"Sometimes we lose focus because things are slow and we're desperate for that next big deal," Alan continued, smiling. "Sometimes we get overconfident, thinking that because we've succeeded in one business, we can automatically succeed in another. And sometimes we just get bored, become distracted, and start chasing what one of my clients calls 'shiny stuff.'"

He went on to explain the importance of focus—of channeling the energy a small, entrepreneurial company has in a single direction.

"To do that, we need to define and stick to Swan's Core Focus," he continued. "Your sweet spot as an organization. This has been called many things—'mission statement,' Stephen Covey calls it 'voice,' Jim Collins calls it the 'hedgehog concept,' Dan Sullivan calls it 'unique ability.' We call it 'Core Focus' because it comes from your core and you must stay focused on it to avoid getting distracted. As with Core Values, your Core Focus already exists; we just need to discover and define it."

Alan then set up the exercise by drawing a diagram on the board:

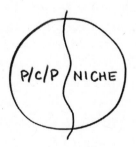

He explained that Swan's Core Focus exists at the intersection of its "purpose, cause, or passion" and its "niche," that thing the company is genetically encoded to do. He asked the leaders to record their thoughts about the company's purpose, cause, or passion—"the thing that gets you out of bed every morning." He made it clear that Swan's "reason for being" must be bigger than money; bigger than its industry, products, or services; and bigger than a goal.

Next, Alan asked the team members to record their thoughts about Swan's niche, including a description of the company's "superior skill—the thing you do better than anyone else with whom you compete."

Sue and Evan had been looking forward to this exercise since Alan mentioned the Core Focus in the Ninety-Minute Meeting. They had clashed regularly about what kind of work Swan's sales team should be selling. Art was also excited. The company's website and collateral material suffered from a lack of focus and clarity—in Art's humble and previously unspoken opinion—because Vic and Eileen wanted the company to seem more broadly capable than it really was.

"Let's start with the purpose, cause, or passion," Alan said when everyone had finished. "Who'd like to begin?"

"Helping clients get the most from the latest technology," read Evan right away.

"Terrific. Thanks, Evan," replied Alan while he wrote Evan's point on a legal pad. "Sue?"

"Doing great work with and for great people," she said.

"Just to be clear, Sue," asked Alan, "when you say 'great people,' are you referring to clients, fellow employees, or both?"

"Both—and more," replied Sue. "I'm passionate about working closely with genuine, interesting, highly capable people. I'm here because of Vic and Eileen. I love being surrounded by the talented, hardworking people at Swan. I get excited about competing for and winning business when the prospective client is a *real person* with a *real problem* and is looking to form a *real partnership* with us."

"Got it. Thanks, Sue," replied Alan.

"Making the world better, one lifelong client at a time," Vic said. "It's all about winning the deal and doing great work for the clients in my book."

Eileen went next. "Creating the best technology solutions company in the world, with great employees and happy clients."

"Carol?"

"This may not be what you're looking for," she said, "but passion is not really my thing. I wrote down, 'Making this company more stable and profitable.'"

"That's just fine. Thanks, Carol."

Alan then asked the team to review two things to stir the pot, a list of real-world examples and a checklist describing essential attributes of a clear, effective purpose, cause, or passion statement.

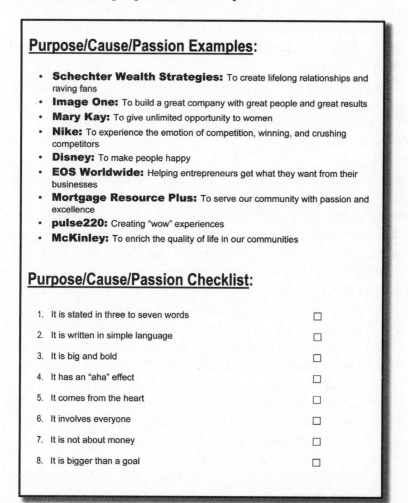

Purpose/Cause/Passion Examples:

- **Schechter Wealth Strategies:** To create lifelong relationships and raving fans
- **Image One:** To build a great company with great people and great results
- **Mary Kay:** To give unlimited opportunity to women
- **Nike:** To experience the emotion of competition, winning, and crushing competitors
- **Disney:** To make people happy
- **EOS Worldwide:** Helping entrepreneurs get what they want from their businesses
- **Mortgage Resource Plus:** To serve our community with passion and excellence
- **pulse220:** Creating "wow" experiences
- **McKinley:** To enrich the quality of life in our communities

Purpose/Cause/Passion Checklist:

1. It is stated in three to seven words ☐
2. It is written in simple language ☐
3. It is big and bold ☐
4. It has an "aha" effect ☐
5. It comes from the heart ☐
6. It involves everyone ☐
7. It is not about money ☐
8. It is bigger than a goal ☐

That helped the team further narrow the list, so Alan recorded what remained on the whiteboard near the side of the diagram marked "P/C/P":

- HELPING PEOPLE
- SOLVING PROBLEMS
- CREATING THE BEST COMPANY

Alan moved on to the niche. This time Eileen went first.

"Designing and deploying the best, most appropriate technology solutions," she said.

Sitting to Eileen's left, Art said, "Comprehensive solutions that leverage the latest technology."

"Enterprise technology solutions," Carol said quickly.

"Custom integration of enterprise technology," said Evan. Alan looked at Sue.

"I took a different approach," she said. "What we do better than anyone else is *listen*. We get to know our clients, we come to understand their issues and challenges, and we speak their language. Because we act like real people instead of technology geeks—no offense, Evan—we recommend only stuff that makes sense for them."

The rest of the team was listening intently.

"So I wrote down, 'Solving real problems with the right technology,'" she said with a shy smile. "That's what we do better than anyone else. We dig in and help our prospective clients figure out what they really need, and then we figure out how best to solve that problem or build the right solution. And if they don't really need something we do well—*we tell them*. Most of our competitors just throw solutions at their prospects, hoping something will stick."

"Holy cow," said Vic. "That's *much* better than what I wrote down."

"I really like that, too," agreed Eileen. "How does everyone else feel?"

"This 'geek' thinks Sue got it just right," said Evan, chuckling. "I mean, it sounds less mundane than the industry jargon a lot of us used."

The other two agreed, so Alan wrote, "Solving real problems with the right technology" in the "Niche" section of his diagram. He then pointed back to the side of the diagram marked "P/C/P" (for purpose/cause/passion) and continued.

"You know, Alan," said Vic. "I think we can strike 'solving problems' from the list because we've already got them covered in the niche."

"Right," Alan said while erasing.

From there, the team quickly agreed that its passion was a combination of helping people and building a great company. They spent a few minutes experimenting with different ways of saying it before settling on "Building a great company with great people." That left the team with the following conclusions on the whiteboard:

"Love it," said Vic immediately.

Sue, Art, and Evan nodded enthusiastically as well. Alan then asked the first of two questions: "Is there enough business within your Core Focus to meet your revenue and profit goals?"

"Yes, of course," Vic answered right away. "Everybody *wants* to solve real problems with the right technology. Some may not even know the difference between that and what they actually buy. We just have to do a better job of telling our story so more prospects know they ought to be working with Swan Services."

"I agree," Sue said, and the rest of the team nodded.

Alan continued with question number two: "Are you doing any work today that's outside your Core Focus?"

"You know," Sue thought aloud, "if we're really going to use this Core Focus as a filter, we'll have to stop doing business with Dynatrend Industries—"

"Why?" exclaimed Carol, suddenly fully engaged. "They account for almost 5 percent of our revenues!"

"Because it's staff-aug work," Evan jumped in to explain, catching on quickly.

"I'm sorry, Evan," injected Alan. "I'm sure everybody here knows what you mean when you say 'staff-aug,' but I don't. Would you mind explaining it to me briefly?"

"Sure," replied Evan. "Normally we're hired to design, build, and implement a technology solution that solves a specific problem. In 'staff-augmentation' work our clients don't buy a solution; they buy one or more people. They just want affordable, capable developers to complete a short-term project they can't staff with their own employees. It's not our sweet spot; we're not helping them solve real problems, and we don't have any control over what technology they use. It might be padding our revenue totals, but it causes all kinds of resource-allocation problems for my team and me."

"I get it," Alan replied. "Thank you, Evan."

Ever the financial analyst, Eileen listened intently. On the one hand, she wasn't thrilled about the idea of *choosing* to strip away revenues the company had been struggling to hold on to. On the other hand, she immediately grasped the value of focus and discipline.

"So do we just fire all the clients that don't fit?" Vic asked.

"That's up to you," Alan replied. "As you live with your Core Focus over the next thirty days, you'll have some tough decisions to make about what fits and what doesn't. Some of my clients have shut down entire divisions after clearly defining their Core Focus. Others have taken their time—grandfathered existing clients, focused on building new business within the Core Focus, and let the old business die of attrition. What's important is that you use this Core Focus to IDS those issues and make those decisions—and the ones you'll encounter in the future—as a team."

Eileen slowly wrapped her mind around the picture Alan had just painted. She realized that, with this system at work throughout the organization and a team of committed, focused leaders around her, the integrator role would consist primarily of strategic decisions like those he had just described. "*That's* what I love to do and am best at," she thought again.

"Alan's right," Eileen offered. "There are some tough decisions ahead. But clearly defining our sweet spot and staying focused on it is going to pay some huge dividends. We'll win more of the right kind of business. We'll make more money and have more fun doing the work. Like Carol, I'm a little afraid of the risks, but I'm *way* more excited about the opportunities."

The Core Focus exercise closed with Alan writing "Staff-Aug within Core Focus?" on the Issues List. He then asked for a volunteer to "wordsmith" the work the team had done; Sue quickly raised her hand. Alan checked his watch and continued.

"It's 3:45," he noted. "Let's take a break and then tackle the next item on the agenda—10-Year Target. Then we'll move to next steps and conclude by five."

THE GOAL

The team quickly freshened up, checked in at the office, and returned to their seats.

"Core Values define *who* you are, Core Focus defines *what* you are," Alan began, "and your 10-Year Target is *where* you're going. It's a long-range, energizing goal that everyone at Swan will rally around. While you will have many goals on your journey, the 10-Year Target is *the* goal. Ten years is most common, but any long-range target from five to twenty years out will do. Whatever you choose, you all have to agree to want it and to work hard to make it happen."

Alan explained the importance of making the target SMART to help everyone in the organization know precisely where the organization was headed. Many 10-Year Targets were both quantitative and qualitative in nature. He shared a few real-life examples to get the team's juices flowing: Henry Ford's goal to "democratize the automobile," Apple's goal to "democratize technology," and two of his clients' 10-Year Targets—"To build a great $50 million company" and "A referral from every client; every client from a referral."

Alan then asked each leader to jot down a description of the Swan Services he or she wanted to create over the next five to twenty years. After a few minutes, he invited the brave one to begin.

"$100 million," blurted Vic. "The go-to technology solutions company in the upper Midwest."

Alan recorded those thoughts on the whiteboard and, moving to Vic's left, asked for Eileen's target.

"I said $40 million," she said. "Same time frame."

"Now who's the sandbagger?" asked Vic, joking with his conservative partner.

"I also wrote down 15 percent net profit," she responded without skipping a beat, "roughly double what we were doing in a good year before we hit the ceiling."

"$40 million works for me," Art said when Alan turned to him. "I'd also like Swan to be top of mind in every market into which it sells."

Alan recorded those thoughts and turned to Carol, who claimed to have written down simply "more profitable."

"I had $30 million in ten years," Evan said next. "I also wrote 'more stable.' To me that includes improved profitability. But it also means more proactive, predictable workflows. Fewer crises, late nights, and missed deadlines."

Alan recorded Evan's thoughts and looked to Sue.

"$50 million," Sue said. "I also had 'top of mind in our markets,' Art. I look forward to the day that every one of our best prospects just automatically includes us on their bid list."

"Got it," replied Alan. "So you all see significant growth on the horizon, ranging from $30 million to $100 million. Let's see if we can narrow that down. Vic, explain your thinking on the $100 million."

"Well, Alan," he replied, "I just think we can get there. I agree with Eileen—profit is key. But once we get this system in place..."

"I don't disagree, Vic," responded Eileen as her partner's voice trailed off. "I just think we need to be careful about pursuing growth for growth's sake."

Sue chimed in. "I agree with Eileen," she said. "I think if we can generate stable, profitable growth to $40 million, we'll have the people and the structure and the *capital* to scale from there to $100 million and beyond. Plus, I can only imagine that a $100 million company is way more complex."

Alan solicited feedback from everyone around the table, and the team quickly settled on the following 10-Year Target, which Alan recorded on the whiteboard:

10-YEAR TARGET —$40 MILLION IN REVENUE, 15% NET PROFIT

"Gosh," Evan said. "Now that I see just the numbers on the whiteboard, it seems so *cold*. Shouldn't we add something qualitative? Maybe something about being a great company or a leading provider or something?"

"That's the team's call, Evan," Alan replied. "I have clients who do it both ways. Remember that this is just a long-range, energizing goal. The purpose of this exercise is to get you all 100 percent on the same page with where you're going and help everyone in the organization understand that things have to start being done differently *today* if you're going to make this happen."

"Evan," interjected Vic, "I also worried about it being too matter-of-fact, but I think this'll work. I mean, $40 million and crazy profitable is going to do *more* than fire people up. It'll freak 'em out—in a good way. You with me?"

"Sure," said Evan, shrugging his shoulders. "If you think it doesn't sound like we're overly focused on the money, I'm good."

The clock read 4:40. Alan concluded the exercise and segued directly into the "next steps" segment by inviting someone to capture the 10-Year Target and add it to the V/TO. Sue readily volunteered. He then made sure everyone on the team left with a clear sense of what needed to happen for Swan Services to stay on track between sessions.

"Any questions on your next steps?" Alan asked. When there were no questions, he said, "I'll see you all back here for Vision-Building Day Two in about thirty days."

He walked to the whiteboard, grabbed a red marker, and recorded the following:

- FEEDBACK?
- EXPECTATIONS?
- RATING - 1- 10?

Again he asked the team to compose its answers to those three questions. When everyone seemed to have finished, Evan raised his hand right away.

"Feedback," he began. "Being open and honest, I was *dreading* this meeting. Best case, I thought it would be a waste of a precious eight-hour day. Plus I expected to be drilled—and deservedly so—for not doing my homework. I still feel lousy about that, but it actually felt like we stayed focused on the task at hand today and made some real progress. Amazingly, there's probably less on my plate as a result of the meeting today. I can't ever remember feeling that way after a meeting before. The meeting *exceeded* my expectations. I'll give it a nine."

"Thank you, Evan," Alan replied. He looked to Evan's left. "Sue?"

"I'm exhausted but really pleased with the quality and quantity of the work we got done today," she replied. "Expectations were met—I was really looking forward to establishing Core Values and a Core Focus, and I think we nailed those. I give the meeting a ten."

"Vic?"

"Nine," Vic said quickly, "solely because I was late. Other than that, this was an astoundingly positive day. We got a ton of stuff done, and that Core Values exercise was super cool. I loved the way it all came together, and I can really see us using these Core Values to manage people and run the business. That's tremendously exciting. My expectations were met, and then some."

"Eileen?" Alan continued.

"Extremely pleased," she said, "and especially after hearing Evan's feedback. I think the way we focus on the future and avoid getting caught in a cycle of blame and frustration is a really important lesson for me. I also learned a lot from the review of the Focus Day tools. I'm thrilled with the work we did on the V/TO and excited about where it can lead us. My expectations were easily met; ten."

Alan thanked Eileen and turned to Art.

"This was a tough day for me," he began slowly, "and it affected my ability to contribute. I'm sorry for that. But I really thought the team did great work. The three questions we answered from the V/TO were rock solid. So while I'd rate my own participation as a seven, I'd rate the entire meeting a nine."

"Interesting perspective, Art. Thank you," Alan replied before asking Carol to finish the exercise. As usual, she looked ready to leave.

"Feedback?" she blurted. "Obviously, I didn't like the way that whole People Analyzer was handled. It's not fair to criticize someone like that and then not deal with it right away. I didn't really have any expectations, and I'd give the meeting a six."

Alan thanked Carol and congratulated the team for another open, honest, and productive day. He urged them to stay focused over the coming month, call with questions or challenges, and come to the next session ready to continue mastering the Focus Day tools and finalize Swan's vision and plan. With that, he dismissed the team.

As Alan said good-bye to each departing leader, he asked Eileen to stay behind for a few moments. He hoped to help prepare her for the conversation she'd scheduled with Carol. The two discussed Carol's demeanor in the session, the kinds of behavior she exhibited that resulted in her being below the bar, and the right approach to a tough People Analyzer conversation.

"Whenever you're dealing with a people issue," he explained, "whether you're discussing a problem with one or more Core Values, GWC—really anything—always bring three data points. One example the person can rationalize, two she can wiggle out of, but three is a flat-out epidemic!"

Eileen laughed and then resolved to take the time to assemble specific examples of Carol's behavior before their meeting the following day. Although worn out by the day's events and relieved to have survived some of the conflict, she was exceptionally pleased with what the team had already accomplished and eager for what lay ahead.

CHAPTER 5
VISION PART 2

E ACH MEMBER of the Swan Services team left Alan's office with the strong feeling that something significant had begun happening. It manifested itself differently in the mind of each leader, but they all seemed to know that a line had been crossed, and there was no going back.

Vic was thrilled about the work the team had done on the V/TO. After years of trying to focus Eileen and others on what he called the company's "soul," he'd seen the team settle on Core Values and a Core Focus in a half-day's work. More important, he'd begun to understand how to use those tools to rebuild the company culture, and the rest of the team seemed genuinely excited.

To her credit, Eileen was prepared for the tough journey ahead. She expected a colossal battle with Carol but welcomed it as an opportunity to begin permanently resolving a longtime source of pain and frustration. She wondered what Evan's real role should be; he clearly wasn't getting it done as the leader of the ops department. Though unsure how the situation with Art would play out, she knew the company and her friendship would survive.

In fact, Sue and Eileen would meet later that day to resolve any ambiguity over their decision to remove Art from the leadership team. They agreed that he'd stop attending the weekly Level 10 Meetings but, as discussed during the session, would attend the next Vision-Building Day. Eileen was happy that Sue and Art were able to comfortably resolve the issue without tension.

Last, Eileen was positively *delighted* that Alan had taken Vic to task for being late. She hoped (against her better judgment) that Vic would self-correct but was also intent on holding her partner accountable if he needed a nudge from time to time.

Both Eileen and Carol spent the next morning preparing for a difficult discussion. Swan's controller researched Core Values on the Internet, hoping to discredit the concept, and compiled a mountain of evidence to support her years of hard work. At 11:45 A.M., Carol entered Eileen's office carrying a thick file full of spreadsheets and other documents.

"Hi, Carol," said Eileen. "Thanks for making time today."

"Sure," replied Carol uneasily. "Should we ride together?"

"I'll drive," Eileen replied. "That way we can start working through this right away." She reached for the file in Carol's hands. "Did you bring this by for me to review later?"

Reflexively, Carol clutched the folder to her chest. "No," she blurted, "I brought this along to share with you *during* our discussion, if that's all right."

"Oh," Eileen replied, furrowing her brow. She didn't expect to be poring over numbers. "Sure, I guess, if you think it might be helpful."

With that awkward exchange setting the stage, the two leaders left for lunch. Never one for small talk, Eileen started in as soon as Carol's car door closed.

"Carol," she said, "let me start by making two things crystal clear. The first is that you're very good at your job and work really, really hard. Nobody questions your skills as a controller or your work ethic, so we aren't going to discuss that today."

"But...," said Carol, staring at the folder.

"The second," Eileen said firmly, "is that you being below the bar is *our* issue, not yours. I want to fix it just as badly as you do, so let's start solving the issue right now—together. Okay?"

"But...I don't really think I'm below the bar," Carol protested weakly. "That's what I thought we'd talk about today. Plus I think there are a lot of other people—"

"Carol," Eileen said commandingly, "I'm not willing to go there right now. We have an hour together, and I intend to spend that time helping you understand why the team feels you don't consistently exhibit the Core Values we settled on yesterday and looking for ways to get you back above the bar."

To Eileen's surprise, Carol didn't protest. When they arrived at the restaurant, she exited the vehicle without her file folder and walked dutifully alongside her boss.

"Okay, Eileen," Carol finally said, "what do I need to do?"

For the first time, Eileen saw a look of earnest vulnerability etched into Carol's face. It wasn't complete surrender, but it wasn't her typical fighting stance, either.

"You know," replied Eileen gratefully, "the first thing you needed to do was ask that question. Because if you don't want to accept the standards we set yesterday or work to meet them, we're really wasting our time here. So thank you."

Eileen pulled out a sheet of notepaper and placed it on the table. (See People Analyzer on page 143.) On it she had copied the Core Values and Carol's ratings from the session with Alan.

Eileen used the People Analyzer as a guide, carefully reviewing each Core Value. One at a time she defined each of them in her own words and then illustrated the things someone might do regularly to earn a plus for that value.

"Someone with a thirst for knowledge constantly looks for ways to improve herself and others," she explained. "She joins professional associations, reads books, takes classes, conducts research, refines processes—she never stands still."

"But I *do* take classes," Carol protested. "My continuing ed—"

"I agree, Carol, but I don't see you doing it *most* of the time. Some of the time you show a thirst for knowledge. Other times you appear satisfied with the status quo. In fact, you're positively rigid. That's why I rated you a plus/minus. And while I can't speak for everyone else on the team, I think that's what they'd tell you as well."

Recalling Alan's advice, Eileen then cited three specific events to help Carol understand exactly what she was doing to earn that rating. Carol was able to dismiss the first and second examples but grudgingly accepted Eileen's viewpoint when confronted with three concrete data points.

"But I'm just so busy," Carol began to explain. "How will I ever—"

"I don't know," interjected Eileen. "But if you want to get yourself to a plus for this Core Value, you have to make it happen. I'm willing

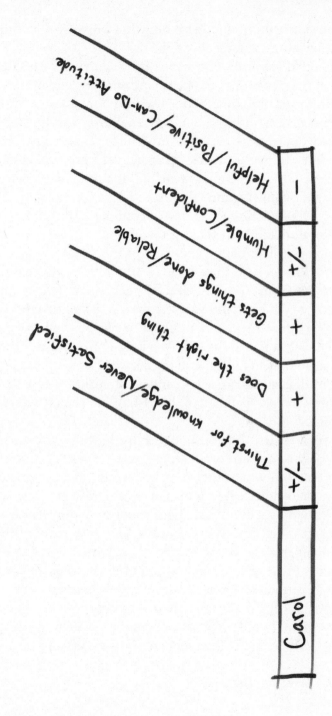

Carol

| − | +/− | + | + | +/− |

Helpful / Positive / Can-Do Attitude

Humble / Confident

Gets things done / Reliable

Does the right thing

Thirst for knowledge / Never Satisfied

to help you figure it out and get it done but only if you're fully committed to elevating yourself above the bar."

Carol nodded carefully. She wasn't fully agreeing with Eileen's assessment of the situation, but she wasn't rejecting the notion either.

Eileen followed the same pattern with the next two Core Values, defining them, illustrating them, and finally providing three examples. Even when Carol's ratings were pluses, Eileen gave examples and provided positive feedback. That helped Carol understand that Core Values could work in her favor, and it also helped pave the way for the tougher conversation to come.

"You were a plus/minus for humble/confident," began Eileen, "but I'm sure you noticed that I rated you a minus."

"Yes," said Carol sullenly, "and so did Vic."

"Right," acknowledged Eileen. "So clearly we have a little work to do here. I can't speak for Vic, but here's my perspective. To get a plus here you have to be confident, but you can't be arrogant or overbearing. We want people to know their stuff, be happy to take on challenges, and sincerely feel they can rise to the task. What we don't want is for everyone to parade around like they have all the answers. None of us are perfect, Carol. We're all just human beings, and we all make mistakes."

"You think I make people feel like I have all the answers?" Carol asked sincerely.

"Well, yes," replied Eileen thoughtfully. "I think you enter into a lot of conversations certain you're right. As a result, you seem unwilling to listen to what other people have to say and quick to dismiss those who don't agree with you as inferior in some way. For example, yesterday when Evan asked about providing status updates and asking detailed questions about Rocks, you really jumped on him. I remember your words vividly—you started the sentence with 'Oh, *come on*, Evan.' There was the sound of *contempt* in your voice, even though you know Evan's working just as hard as you are. That's the kind of stuff that makes me say minus to humble/confident."

Eileen went on to offer two other examples, watching Carol's resistance fade as she realized Eileen's perspective was valid.

"I see," said Carol, still glum but beginning to process what Eileen was saying. "And the last one?"

"Yes—helpful/positive/can-do attitude," Eileen read aloud. "Carol, how would you rate *yourself* on this Core Value?"

Carol stared silently at the notepaper. When she looked up, her eyes were moist.

"Minus," she said. "But isn't it okay to get frustrated with people when they don't do what they're supposed to do? How many times do I have to help Vic fill out a contract properly or Evan's people turn in time sheets before I'm allowed to get a little negative? All I'm trying to do is hold people accountable to our standards. When people don't seem to care, I get mad, and when that happens, I am certainly not positive and helpful."

"It's not a question of motives for me, Carol," replied Eileen gently. "It's *how* you go about helping people and enforcing standards that needs to change. It's never okay to get angry or frustrated with another employee in public. When you take Vic or Evan or me to task in a Level 10 Meeting, even when we've made a mistake, it's just not helpful or productive. There's no need to act like you've caught us screwing up and are somehow proud of that; it's not about you winning and us losing. Open and honest is okay; critical and condescending is not. Understand?"

"Yes," Carol said.

"Okay," replied Eileen. "The tougher, more important question is are you committed to changing? Will you work hard at being more positive and helpful? Will you control your impulse to jump on someone when you're feeling frustrated or angry? Will you ask the rest of the team to help you when you're falling into your old habits?"

"Geez, Eileen," Carol exclaimed, "you're making this seem like an intervention!"

"Perhaps it is," Eileen replied immediately. "Perhaps it is. But if you and I work hard at this together, I hope and believe we can get you above the bar. And remember that you don't have to be perfect; none of us will be. You can have two plus/minuses and still be above the bar. That's what I want if that's what *you* want."

"That's what I want," Carol affirmed. "It's going to be hard, but I'll do it."

In the four weeks that followed, Swan's leaders worked hard to master the Focus Day tools. As they finalized the Accountability Chart, completed Rocks, reviewed the Scorecard each week, and used the Level 10 Meetings to solve pressing issues, a new vibe developed. The team became more open and more optimistic. Things weren't perfect, but nearly everyone could feel Swan Services starting to gain traction.

The one exception was Carol. Instead of attacking everyone, however, she retreated into a shell and gradually withdrew from the team. While she dutifully attended the Level 10 Meetings, Carol rarely said a word and never pressed for conflict. She came in early, went home late, and made sure to remind people of her presence by loading their inboxes with work she had done.

LAYING THE FOUNDATION

When the Swan Services team returned to Alan's office four weeks later, Carol's status on the People Analyzer was no longer an elephant in the room. She had clearly been making an effort, but everyone could see that consistently exhibiting Swan's Core Values was going to be a stretch. When Carol *did* behave in a way that didn't match Swan's Core Values, Eileen simply pulled her aside later to privately discuss the incident.

At 8:48, Vic walked into Alan's office and extended his hand. He gazed at the clock in an exaggerated fashion and shook Alan's hand, beaming proudly.

"Vince Lombardi," he said loudly. "Darn glad to meet you!"

Alan laughed and patted Vic on the shoulder. The rest of the team filtered in slowly, each expressing surprise to find Vic settled comfortably at the table, ready to begin. Always a good sport, Swan's visionary happily endured some good-natured ribbing until just before 9:00, when the entire team was ready to begin.

After welcoming the group, Alan began the session reviewing the Six Key Components and his Proven Process. He then walked through the objectives and agenda for the two days of Vision Building:

OBJECTIVES (2 DAYS)

- MASTER FOCUS DAY TOOLS
- CLEAR VISION
- CLEAR PLAN
- ISSUES LIST CLEAR

AGENDA (2 DAYS)

- CHECK-IN
- REVIEW FOCUS DAY TOOLS
- CORE VALUES
- CORE FOCUS
- 10-YEAR TARGET
- MARKETING STRATEGY
- 3-YEAR PICTURE
- 1-YEAR PLAN
- QUARTERLY ROCKS
- ISSUES LIST
- NEXT STEPS
- CONCLUDE

Alan made it clear that he expected the team to fully achieve the four objectives by the end of the day. He also promised to review all the work that had been done on the Core Values, Core Focus, and 10-Year Target before moving on to answer the remaining questions on the V/TO. Finally, he again asked the team to check in by providing three pieces of information: bests, an update, and expectations. After a few quiet minutes, Alan asked the "brave one" to begin.

"Had a great weekend up at the cabin with my girls a few weeks back," Art volunteered. "My professional best is being here. What happened last time was hard, but I want you all to know I'm at peace with it and completely focused on helping Sue and the rest of the team take Swan to the next level."

Eileen and Sue nodded to affirm that they'd been working productively with Art since the last session. Art shared his update and expectations, and then Alan moved left and asked Carol to check in.

Her response was muted but relatively positive, given the events of the last month. Her professional best was completing five of six Rocks. She mentioned Rocks and the Level 10 Meetings as working, explaining that both tools seemed to help improve accountability. As for expectations, a rare display of self-deprecating humor elicited a healthy laugh from the team.

"I just hope this session goes better than the last one," she said, smiling faintly.

Alan then invited Evan to check in. Looking customarily frazzled and distracted, Evan dutifully went down his list. He couldn't think of a personal best. His professional best was "making progress on a lot of my Rocks."

"Not working?" Evan continued. "Completing Rocks and finding time to get everything done. As for expectations, I just hope we set more attainable Rocks."

Sue was next. "Professional best was *definitely* getting the sales Rock done," she said with a big smile. "Everybody contributed, Vic and I worked really hard together, and it went right down to the wire, but we got our two 'A' deals and ten account plans done."

Sue mentioned Rocks, the Meeting Pulse, and the Accountability Chart as tools that were working and completing all her Rocks and hitting Scorecard numbers as not working. She had two expectations—that the team complete the V/TO and put a solid plan in place to roll out the tools to the rest of the organization.

Vic followed Sue; it was clear the two sales leaders had been working closely together because his check-in almost exactly matched Sue's. Vic also mentioned the Core Values as working. Eileen followed Vic and agreed, identifying the Core Values Speech and the effort Vic and Sue had put in with the sales team as professional bests. Like Sue, she also expected to complete the V/TO and agree on a rollout plan before leaving that day.

Alan finished recording Eileen's comments and reviewed the Focus Day tools for a second time. He quickly walked the team through the concept of hitting the ceiling and the five leadership abilities. He helped the team connect each of those abilities—simplify, delegate, predict, systemize, and structure—to one or more of the tools in his system. Once again the message was clear—implementing the tools would help the executives become their best as leaders. After concluding the review of the five leadership abilities, Alan asked Eileen to distribute copies of the Accountability Chart. (See pages 150–151.) He moved to an updated version he had re-created on the whiteboard.

"As you may recall," Alan began, "we need to answer three questions about your Accountability Chart—and get three affirmative answers—before our work is complete. The first question is 'Do we have the *right structure* for the organization?' Remember, don't think about people—we have to focus on structure first."

The one structure question involved the operations department. Eileen and Evan had put the finishing touches on that part of the Accountability Chart late the previous evening, so the rest of the team was seeing it for the first time. To Eileen's disappointment, Evan asked her to explain.

"We still believe the group should include four functions," she said. "Account management, project management, business analysis, and development. At the last session, we had a team leader for each of those functions reporting to the ops leader. But today there just aren't enough people in that department for so many managers. So instead of four mid-level managers, the AMs, PMs, and BAs will continue to report to Evan—I mean the ops leader—and we'll have just one mid-level manager for the twelve developers."

"Two structure questions," Sue said. "Will that help enough? Can we afford it?"

"Yes, it'll help," Eileen replied. "With more than twenty direct reports, Evan feels like he's not able to LMA effectively. No one could. The whole team is reactive, operating in crisis mode too often. None of them are at their best. This new structure—with the right people in the right seats throughout the department—will make us far more efficient and productive. It will vastly reduce waste, late projects, and client dissatisfaction. I'd love to move right to four managers, and as we grow, that's the way we'll probably scale this department, but we can't afford that right now. So this breaks up the department into two more manageable teams."

"Can we even afford the development team leader?" Carol asked matter-of-factly.

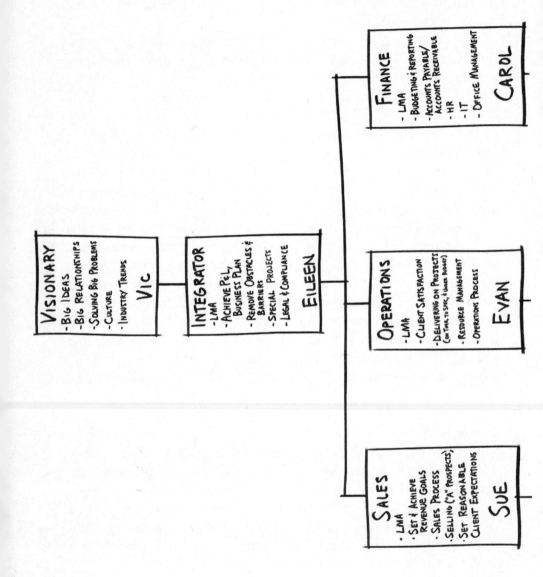

VISIONARY
- Big Ideas
- Big Relationships
- Solving Big Problems
- Culture
- Industry Trends

VIC

INTEGRATOR
- LMA
- Achieve P&L, Business Plan
- Remove Obstacles & Barriers
- Special Projects
- Legal & Compliance

EILEEN

SALES
- LMA
- Set & Achieve Revenue Goals
- Sales Process
- Selling ("A" Prospects)
- Set Reasonable Client Expectations

SUE

OPERATIONS
- LMA
- Client Satisfaction
- Delivering on Projects (on time, to spec, & under budget)
- Resource Management
- Operations Process

EVAN

FINANCE
- LMA
- Budgeting & Reporting
- Accounts Payable/ Accounts Receivable
- HR
- IT
- Office Management

CAROL

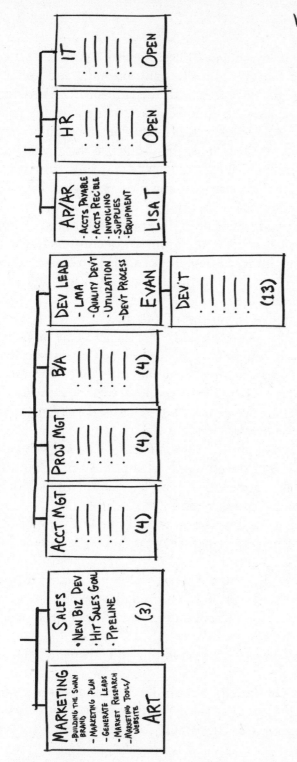

"Yes, that'll be a great investment," Eileen replied. "We'll get better at understanding what our clients really want, planning and executing projects, and managing resources in the department. The research I've done for my Rock suggests that unnecessary overtime, highly paid emergency contractors, and project waste account for almost 30 percent of our total operations cost! That's more than $600,000 this year alone. If we can reduce that number to 20 percent next year, we'll *easily* pay for this new resource and anything else we might need as we grow."

Eileen now had the complete attention of everyone in the room, including Evan. He agreed with Eileen's findings and proposals but was disappointed that he hadn't come to these conclusions himself. He began to realize how hungry Swan Services was for something he wasn't able to provide. For the first time, Evan began to think that not having enough time wasn't the only reason he had been over-promising and under delivering as the VP of ops.

"The reduced costs are great," Vic said, "but Sue and I are more excited about the impact this might have on client retention. It's a heck of a lot easier to sell to a happy existing client than to go find a new one."

The team quickly agreed that Eileen's proposal was the right structure for operations. There were no other structure issues, so Alan dismissed the team for a break.

"Now that you've agreed on the right structure," he began when they returned, "the second question we have to answer before the Accountability Chart is complete is, 'Do we have all the right people in the right seats?' You have to have both."

Alan again defined those two terms with a quick review of the tool designed to help determine whether the right people were in the right seats—the People Analyzer.

"Right people share your Core Values," he explained. "They fit Swan Services' culture. Last session you agreed that anyone receiving at least three pluses and two plus/minuses would be considered a right person. Is that still accurate?"

"Yes," replied Eileen, with others nodding in agreement. "That's exactly right."

"In addition," Alan continued, "a person in the right seat is someone who gets it, wants it, and has the capacity to do it. That person's score on the GWC section of the People Analyzer is yes, yes, yes.

Anyone who doesn't share your Core Values *and* GWC his or her seat on the Accountability Chart is below the bar on the People Analyzer. *Those* are your people issues. Does that make sense?"

The leaders nodded, and Alan asked them to review the Accountability Chart for people issues. When everyone had finished, Sue volunteered to go first.

"I wrote down two names that are already on the Issues List," she explained. "Troy and Natalie, from the sales team. Natalie is still a people issue. She isn't on track to hit her quota. Worse, she hasn't responded to the challenge Vic and I laid out for the sales team two months ago—to clear the decks and focus on making more calls, getting more meetings, and generating more proposals. She's off track with those numbers as well. So frankly, I don't think she's in the right seat."

Alan used a green marker to circle Natalie's seat (Sales) and confirmed her name's presence on the Issues List.

"On the other hand," Sue continued, "Troy should come *off* the list. He's been like a different person since Vic and I spoke with the team. His activity levels are way up, his attitude has improved, and he's largely responsible for one of the two 'A' deals we just got. If he keeps this up, he'll not only hit his quota for the rest of the year, but he'll make up the deficiency from the first two quarters."

Alan removed Troy's name from the Issues List.

"Any people issues, Vic?" Alan asked next.

"Everything I circled is already on the Issues List," he said.

"Eileen?" Alan queried.

"Well, I circled the open development leader seat in operations," she said. "And based on my conversations with Evan, there are two developers—Bill and Terry—and one account manager—Jennifer—that I have questions about."

Alan circled each seat in green and added those names to the Issues List. Art and Carol had no people issues to add, so Alan turned to Evan.

"Well," Evan said haltingly, "circle my seat. I don't GWC the ops leader seat."

This got everyone's attention.

"These last two months have been hard," Evan continued, "but they've helped me see things more clearly. I'm ready to admit that being *too busy* isn't the only reason I'm struggling to run that department. If I really belonged in that seat, I would have recommended changes to the way the department was structured long ago. As it happened, I needed Eileen to do it for me. If not for her and this process, I'd still just be grinding away, doing the same old stuff and hoping something would change. Bottom line: we're never going to get to $40 million in ten years with me running operations."

"Team?" Alan said gently. "What do you think about Evan's open and honest assessment?"

"Evan, you're definitely being hard on yourself," Vic said. "But there's some truth to what you say, and I'm impressed by how you put the company's needs first. That's just another indication for me that you're a right person we have to make sure is in the right seat."

"Evan," Eileen said slowly and with real emotion, "I'm with Vic 100 percent. You exude Swan's culture, and you've been instrumental in getting us where we are today. I can't imagine running the business without you in a vital role; we just need to figure out what that right seat is."

"Thank you," Evan replied, struggling with powerful emotions.

"Come to think of it, Evan," Eileen went on, "what would you think about filling the development leader seat?"

"That's exactly what I was thinking," replied Evan. "I started here as a developer. I still spend most of my time leading the developers. I can do that job well in my sleep, and I think I'd really enjoy it—as long as we find the right ops leader."

"What about the LMA role in that seat?" Carol asked pointedly.

"I feel better about leading a team of developers than I do about running the whole department," he answered, unfazed by Carol's insinuation. "It's a whole lot easier for me to manage people when I know what they do and how they think."

"Fair enough, Evan," replied Alan. "So team, whose name should we put in the ops leader seat for the time being?"

"Can't we just put the word 'open' in the seat?" asked Evan innocently.

"I understand why you might say that," Alan replied, "but the simple answer is no. You've agreed ops leader is a major function. By default, that means the company can't function properly without someone accountable for that seat. So we need to decide who's going to own the seat until we're able to fill it with the right person."

"Does this happen a lot?" asked Vic.

"Absolutely," replied Alan. "It's quite common to have a leadership team seat with no ideal person in the company to fill it. Often a leader has to own two or three seats until the company can fill them with the right person. That's not ideal, and it's an issue, but it's better than having an important seat vacant for an extended period of time. Who's going to step up and own the ops leader seat in the short term? Is it still Evan?"

"Yes," said Eileen. "Until we fill it, Evan's *far* more than capable of running the department than anyone else here. I'll continue to help where I can. Okay?"

Evan nodded; Alan circled the ops leader seat. He adjusted the Issues List by removing "Development Seat Open" and adding "Evan in 2 Seats," leaving a total of nine people issues.

"As you may recall," he continued, "the third question about the Accountability Chart is, 'Does everyone have *enough time* to do his or her job well?' Who doesn't have enough time?"

Vic and Carol were the only ones who didn't raise their hands. Given the events of the last meeting, Carol wasn't about to complain about working too hard.

"We won't solve that problem today," Alan admitted, "but you should walk out of here knowing exactly what needs to happen for you to *get* enough time. Does anyone recall from our last session the first step to solving an 'enough time' issue?"

"Solve your people issues," Sue said quickly, "or you'll *never* have enough time."

"Exactly," Alan agreed. "If the people in your department don't share the Core Values or don't GWC the roles in their seat, they're consuming precious time of yours each week. Keeping them around means you have to do some of their work. You have to deal with mistakes, personality conflicts, and management issues. So when I ask if you have enough time, you'll never say yes until you permanently resolve those issues."

Eileen stared at the Accountability Chart on the whiteboard. Over 20 percent of the seats on the chart were circled in green, including two of her three direct reports—the ops leader and finance leader seats. She set her jaw, becoming more resolute about the people moves that would be required to help Swan achieve its vision and return some semblance of control to her life.

Alan continued by walking the team through the three steps to using his Delegate and Elevate tool.

"Step one is deciding what 'full time' means to you," he explained. "Are you at your best when you're putting in forty hours each week, or seventy? I see successful people and companies who work both ways, and neither is good or bad. You just have to agree what kind of culture you have at Swan."

"I gotta tell ya," replied Vic, "this is *never* going to be a nine-to-five shop."

"It doesn't have to be," Alan responded. "Your team gets to decide what Swan's culture demands. But if you're a fifty-hour culture and you're consistently putting in seventy-hour weeks, something is going to give. You must delegate and elevate twenty hours, or you will eventually burn out."

"Fair enough," agreed Vic.

"When you're over capacity," Alan continued, "step two is listing everything you do during a typical week on a blank legal pad. Record everything you do and how much time it takes. Step three is putting everything you do into one of four quadrants on this simple diagram." Alan illustrated the tool.

"The upper left quadrant is for the stuff you love to do and are great at. The stuff you like to do and are good at goes into the upper right. Everything you don't like to do but are good at goes in the lower left quadrant. Most entrepreneurial leaders spend *lots* of time in this quadrant. You've trained or forced yourself to do things that the business requires because, frankly, there's nobody else here to do them. The lower right-hand quadrant is where you put stuff you don't like to do and aren't very good at. Lots of people could do those things better than you, and some of them are already employed at Swan Services and earning far less per hour than you. If you're trying to delegate twenty hours worth of work each week, delegate it from the lower two quadrants. If there's nobody on your Accountability Chart who will love to do and be great at that stuff, you occasionally need to create a new seat. Either way, when everybody spends most of each week doing work they love and are great at, they'll have more energy, be more effective, and *get more done*. And the company will make more money. That's good for you, good for your people, and good for Swan Services."

"It seems like such a simple concept," admitted Sue, "and I am definitely spending time each week doing stuff someone else can do better and more affordably. But whenever I try to delegate something, I think of ten reasons that we can't solve the problem. It'll cost too much. I don't have time to train anyone. They'll screw it up."

"I've heard that many times," Alan acknowledged as Eileen and Evan nodded knowingly. "But this system and these tools are designed to help you see that you're not stuck. Keep working together to run Swan on this system and resolve your issues. Soon enough you will each be able to say you consistently have enough time to do your job well."

Alan concluded the Accountability Chart exercise by asking four questions: "Are we done with the Accountability Chart? Do you feel good about it? Have we captured all your people issues? Are you all clear on how to get enough time?"

When everyone agreed, Alan asked Eileen to distribute copies of the Rock Sheet. (See page 158.)

"As we review Rocks today," he explained, "you'll notice a change. Until now you've been saying whether Rocks are on track or off track. Today is the moment of truth: it's done or not done—and 95 percent done is not done. Are you ready?"

Swan Services Quarterly Rock Sheet

Future Date: April 8, 20XX

Revenue:

Profit:

Measurables:

COMPANY ROCKS

	WHO	
1) Trifold brochure, proposal template and website draft complete	Art	ND
2) Survey current clients and draft client satisfaction/retention plan	Evan	ND
3) Close two "A" deals and complete ten key account plans	Sue	Done
4) Make a decision to acquire project management software	Carol	ND
5) Recommend & approve ops staffing changes to improve profitability	Eileen	Done
6)		
7)		

ART

1) Trifold brochure, proposal template and website draft complete	ND
2)	
3)	
4)	
5)	
6)	
7)	

SUE

1) Close two "A" deals and complete ten key account plans	Done
2) Document sales process, get approved by leadership team	ND
3) Develop sales department scorecard	Done
4) Complete at least one joint prospect meeting with each of the three sales reps	ND
5)	
6)	
7)	

EVAN

1) Survey current clients and draft client satisfaction/retention plan	ND
2) Hire new developer/consultant	ND
3) Complete departmental performance reviews	ND
4) Document project management core process	ND
5) Deliver Acme Industries project on time and on budget	Done
6) Coordinate departmental vacation schedules	ND
7) Implement error-tracking system	Done

CAROL

1) Make a decision to acquire project management software	ND
2) Revise annual budget	Done
3) Revise HR policy manual	Done
4) Complete YTD financials thru June	Done
5) Complete eight hours of continuing education	Done
6) Review IT/payroll processing contracts	Done
7)	

EILEEN

1) Recommend & approve ops staffing changes to improve profitability	Done
2) Evaluate variable expenses for cost-savings opportunities	Done
3) Meet with three key clients that have reduced or eliminated spending with Swan	ND
4) Initiate credit line renewal process	Done
5) Complete and implement Focus Day tools	Done
6)	
7)	

VIC

1) Attend industry trade show in search of at least one "big idea"	ND
2) Visit personally with at least two key clients and two key business partners	ND
3)	
4)	
5)	
6)	
7)	

One leader at a time, Alan read through each Rock in five minutes, asking the leader to say only "done" or "not done." On several occasions he reminded the leaders that 95 percent done is not done.

"Accountable means doing *exactly* what you say you'll do," Alan explained. "If your Rock says 'hire someone,' and they're not on board, saying 'done' because you tried hard or almost made it is just rationalizing—not completing it. When getting close counts as done, you will never feel like you've held each other completely accountable. And you're not going to gain traction."

Alan recorded notes as he went along. When the Rock review was finished, he worked through the ratios and informed the team that it had completed thirteen of twenty-five Rocks for a completion rate of 52 percent.

"The goal for Rock completion is 80 percent," Alan explained. "The good news is that this first set of Rocks is kind of a practice round. My clients average around 50 percent for this first set, so you're normal. Now, let's talk about what you learned."

"Setting attainable Rocks would help," admitted Vic. "It turns out there were zero industry trade shows to attend between our first session and this meeting. I'll never live *that* down."

Alan smiled and moved left around the table, soliciting feedback from everyone. The leaders all felt that their first set of Rocks wasn't very SMART—specific, measurable, attainable, realistic, and timely. Evan and Eileen said they needed to sign up for fewer Rocks. Sue admitted she didn't get started early enough to get her Rocks done. Carol said she'd never sign up for a Rock that required her to rely on somebody else. That drew a sharp look from Evan and a comment from Alan.

"I understand why you'd say that," Alan responded, "but if you're on a team, it's inevitable that you'll have to rely on others to get Rocks done. Sometimes you'll do everything humanly possible to complete a Rock, and something outside your control gets in the way. That's what leaders do, Carol. They set aggressive goals, assume some risk, and work hard to get everything done. When they own Rocks that involve other people, they call the meetings, kick the butts, and get the important stuff done. And the more people you're relying on to get your Rock done, the more you have to factor in lost time when you're making a plan to complete your Rock. You have to think three steps ahead and plan for delays, because busy people aren't always going to be available when you need them. If you plan for that, people can occasionally let you down and you'll *still* complete your Rocks."

Alan addressed all the leaders: "I realize my goal-setting philosophy is different from the way it works in many companies. When we set a goal or a Rock, we're setting it to hit it. We don't aim for the stars and walk away happy when we hit the mountaintops. We set 'em to hit 'em. So when you leave here today with goals for your 1-Year Plan and Rocks for next quarter, walk out believing you can hit them all. When life happens and you miss a goal, you'll look at why you missed it, learn from it, get better, and move on. That's the reason that the Rock completion rate goal is 80 percent, not 100 percent. And congratulations to Carol and Eileen for achieving it."

Once the Rock discussion ended, Alan moved on to a quick review of the Level 10 Meeting. He began by acknowledging the progress the team had referenced in their check-ins. As he had a month earlier, Alan walked through the agenda one item at a time, clearly explaining how to properly conduct each facet of the meeting. There were fewer questions; the team was clearly getting the hang of the Level 10 Meeting.

However, Art asked a good question about the team's low To-Do completion rate. "Alan," he said, "you said that the goal is to complete 90 percent of the To-Dos each week, and I don't think we're even close. Is that unusual?"

"Not at all," replied Alan, "but we have to solve the issue. So let's IDS."

After a few minutes of identifying, it became clear that the team was confusing Rocks, To-Dos, and issues. Alan created the following diagram on a clean section of whiteboard:

COMPARTMENTALIZING

GOALS	ROCKS	TO-DOS	ISSUES
1 YEAR	90 DAYS	7 DAYS	LONG-TERM – V/TO SHORT-TERM – L10

"In business," Alan explained, "you're constantly being bombarded by *stuff*. Your website needs a face-lift, a client calls, there's a people issue, you have the opportunity to acquire a competitor, the toilet's backed up—somehow it lands on your desk all at once. If you don't put that stuff in the right place, you're probably frazzled, focused on the wrong stuff, and wasting time."

Several members of the team chuckled, acknowledging Alan's accuracy.

"In this system," he continued, "there's a place for all that *stuff*. Everything falls neatly into one of the four compartments: The first compartment—goals from your 1-Year Plan—is for your twelve-month priorities. We'll set these three to seven important long-term goals for the year today. The second compartment is for quarterly Rocks. The third compartment is To-Dos—where you capture and commit to seven-day action items. The fourth compartment is filled with your issues—everything that's left unresolved. Issues fall into two categories—long-term and short-term. Long-term issues go on your V/TO; they're big issues that you don't want to be distracted by right now. We'll solve as many of those as we can at your next Quarterly. Short-term issues go on your Level 10 Meeting agenda; they're the issues you must solve or want to solve this quarter.

Compartmentalizing takes a while to master. But once you do, it'll help you manage all the moving parts of this business as part of a single, coherent system. It'll help make everyone in the organization more focused, disciplined, and accountable. Your To-Do List will get filled purely with seven-day action items, and you'll be turning that list over each week."

With Art and the others satisfied, they cleaned up their To-Do List, leaving only pure To-Dos. Alan answered a few more questions about the Level 10 Meeting and concluded by making sure each leader felt confident in his or her mastery of the concept. He then asked Eileen to hand out copies of the company Scorecard.

Who	Measurable	Goal	Weeks												
			1	2	3	4	5	6	7	8	9	10	11	12	13
Sue	New leads	36	11	4	47	17	29	24	35	41					
Sue	Initial sales meetings	12	8	9	4	14	11	15	16	13					
Sue	Proposals (#)	4	2	1	3	4	2	4	5	4					
Sue	Proposals ($)	$300K	$175K	$70K	$275K	$350K	$150K	$370K	$410K	$325K					
Sue	30-day pipeline	$1.5M	$1.15M	$1.05M	$1.10M	$1.25M	$1.15M	$1.05M	$1.10M	$1.25M					
Sue	Contracts (#)	2	2	1	1	2	3	1	3	4					
Sue	Contracts ($)	$150K	$161K	$135K	$75K	$170K	$201K	$41K	$170K	$320K					
Evan	Projects late	1			4	4	4	3	3	4					
Evan	Projects over budget	1							2	2					
Evan	Defects to clients	0		1		1	0	2	1	1					
Evan	Utilization rate	80%													
Carol	Cash balance	$75K	$55K	$85K	$70K	$61K	$52K	$91K	$77K	$68K					
Carol	A/R > 60 days	< $30K	$42.5	$42.5	$31.0	$26.1	$35.5	$40.5	$34.0	$36.4					
Carol	Billing errors	0	0	1	1	0	0	1	1	0					

Alan led a quick Scorecard review. The leaders saw a few opportunities to improve things, but the feedback was uniformly positive. Everyone felt the Scorecard had started giving the team an absolute pulse on the business. Sue and Vic both believed the sales team's performance had improved largely because their activities and outcomes were being measured weekly. Eileen enjoyed watching trends and patterns develop over the quarter. Carol claimed to "love" the Scorecard because it connected each leader to specific goals and forced everyone to report his or her numbers each week.

"That concludes our review of the Focus Day tools," Alan explained. "Let's take a quick break."

When the team returned, Alan had cleaned up the whiteboard and was now standing next to a section titled "Focus Day Tools."

"We've reached a major milestone on our journey together," he announced. "You've now mastered the Focus Day tools, and it's time to talk about introducing them into the organization. There's no hurry; soon you will decide as a team when it's time to roll out this system to the rest of the company and how best to do it. Right now I just want to help you understand everything that's involved in a system rollout. What were once the Focus Day tools now become the foundational tools." Alan erased the words "Focus Day" and replaced them with the word "Foundational." He explained that "hitting the ceiling" would now become a common term for the organization, erased it from the list, and replaced it with "V/TO."

FOUNDATIONAL TOOLS
- V/TO
- ACCOUNTABILITY CHART
- MEETING PULSE
- ROCKS
- SCORECARD

"I call these foundational tools," Alan explained, "because mastering them yourselves and rolling them out to the rest of the organization lays the foundation for this system becoming the Swan Services way of operating. It's 80 percent of the work that will result in you strengthening the Six Key Components. When you're truly running the company on this system, everyone will be using the foundational tools. They'll all know where you're going and how you plan to get there, as described in your V/TO. Everyone's roles and responsibilities will be crystal clear, thanks to your Accountability Chart. Level 10 Meetings, Scorecards, and Rocks will be in place throughout the organization, helping keep everyone focused, disciplined, and accountable for doing his or her part to help Swan Services achieve its vision. We'll decide how much of that future state you want to bite off later today when we set Rocks. For now, I just wanted you to understand that these five foundational tools will ultimately be used by every person in the company."

After inviting questions, Alan asked Eileen to distribute updated copies of the V/TO and Vic to distribute copies of the Core Values speech.

VISION AND PLAN

"Now that we're done reviewing the tools that help create traction," Alan explained, "we'll spend the rest of the day focused on clarifying Swan Services' vision by finishing the eight questions on the V/TO. We're going to move through the V/TO one question at a time, signing off on our work from last session to make sure everyone has bought in. Let's begin by reviewing your Core Values. Please read through Vic's Core Values speech, and be prepared to share your thoughts with the team when you're done."

THE SPEECH

Be humbly confident

- don't be arrogant
- know your stuff
- be vulnerable; you're not perfect

Grow or die

- be more uncomfortable with the status quo than the prospect of change
- be a maximizer (take something strong and make it superb)

Help first

- you must provide value before receiving anything
- you get out of life what you want if you help enough people get what *they* want
- genuinely get a high from helping people

Do the right thing

- enter the danger
- no amount of money is worth betraying a trust
- think, "If Mom were watching…"

Do what you say

- fully deliver, on time
- it's okay to say "no"
- take the responsibility; blame no one
- finish what you start

The team quietly reviewed the speech, a single-page document with the five Core Values listed in bold and each further described by a few bullet points. Vic shifted nervously in his seat. He had hoped to get feedback from the team long before this meeting but hadn't completed his homework assignment until late the previous evening.

When the team seemed to have finished reading, Alan said, "The first question is do you all believe these Core Values define Swan Services' culture?"

Moving left around the table, Alan got a yes from each member of the leadership team before asking his second question: "Are you prepared to use these Core Values to hire, fire, review, reward, and recognize people in this organization?"

"I should point out," added Vic, "why this homework assignment was so hard. I had to define each Core Value in a way that we'd all feel comfortable terminating someone who was below the bar. That's a lot harder than it sounds!"

Several members of Swan's leadership team nodded appreciatively and resumed their review of the Core Values speech. When everyone was done, Alan again went around the conference table, receiving yeses from each member of the team.

"Last question," he continued. "How do you feel about the Core Values speech?"

Everyone seemed genuinely pleased with the slight changes Vic had made to the wording of the Core Values. A few leaders made suggestions to change or clarify the examples Vic had selected to clearly illustrate each value. Vic took notes, eager to get the speech right.

"Nice job, Vic. Do you have everything you need to finalize the speech?" Alan asked after each leader had provided feedback.

"Absolutely," he replied. "I can have this ready to roll by early next week."

Vic had been making notes on his own copy of the speech. He was so excited to roll out the Core Values that he presented a completed outline to the leadership team within days.

"Remember to repeat yourselves often," Alan explained. "Give this speech frequently. When you catch an employee doing something worth recognizing, praise him or her in public for exhibiting one or more of the Core Values. If you see someone behaving in a way that doesn't match your Core Values, counsel him or her privately. When you repeat yourselves often about these rules to play by, your team will respond, and you'll create an amazing culture."

He went on to make another point: "Start using these core values in the hiring process. Once you think you've identified a right person for a right seat, give the core values speech with real passion so that person knows what he's about to get himself into. Make it clear that people who don't fit the culture will stick out like a sore thumb. If you do this properly, you'll usually scare away candidates who can't consistently exhibit these core values."

With the Core Values discussion concluded and the energy level high, Alan asked the team to review the Core Focus on the V/TO Eileen had passed out.

"Does everyone feel your sweet spot is clear?" Alan asked.

"It feels right," Eileen replied, "but we've had some difficult conversations about some of the work we're doing today."

Alan dug a little deeper to identify the real issue. Evan and Sue had become increasingly vocal about the need to stop doing staff-augmentation work. Vic was warming to the idea, but Carol was adamantly opposed to anything that would reduce revenues. Eileen saw both sides of the debate clearly and wasn't ready yet to make the call.

CORE FOCUS	Passion: Building a great company with great people
	Niche: Solving real problems with the right technology

Alan quickly helped the team confirm its Core Focus; each of the leaders felt they had nailed Swan's sweet spot. And after a brief and passionate debate, Eileen suggested that the question of what to do about staff augmentation belonged on the long-term Issues List. The team quickly agreed.

With the Core Focus discussion concluded, Alan directed the team's attention to the 10-Year Target on the V/TO.

10-YEAR TARGET	$40 million in revenue with 15% net profit

In the weeks since the last session, Evan had become more comfortable with the company's potential. With his vocal support, the team agreed that it remained committed to achieving its long-range, energizing goal. Food had been delivered a few moments earlier, so Alan dismissed the team for a quick break, and then they returned for a working lunch. He added the following items to a clean section of whiteboard:

TARGET MARKET:

    DEMOGRAPHIC:

    GEOGRAPHIC:

    PSYCHOGRAPHIC:

THREE UNIQUES:

    1.

    2.

    3.

PROVEN PROCESS: Y/N

GUARANTEE: Y/N

The session resumed with the next question on the V/TO: "What is your Marketing Strategy?"

"Really nailing your Marketing Strategy," Alan began, "will help this team overcome the number-one problem faced by small businesses: trying to reach a huge audience with few resources. This will create laser focus for your sales and marketing efforts and help you win more of the right kind of business. You'll spend all your time connecting with the right potential clients or customers, and you'll communicate with them in a consistent, effective way."

Alan introduced the four parts of the Marketing Strategy. The first part, the target market, was a clear definition of Swan's ideal prospects—those companies most likely to become the best long-term, highly valued clients. The last three items—three uniques, the proven process, and the guarantee—would make up Swan's marketing message to those ideal prospects.

"Today we're going to complete the first two parts of your Marketing Strategy," Alan explained, "the target market and three uniques. With both the proven process and the guarantee, we just need a yes or no. If you believe creating them will help you win more business, we'll add them to your Issues List, and—at some point—they'll make for great quarterly Rocks."

Alan pointed to the first term on the whiteboard. "Let's start with your target market, or what we call 'The List,'" he said. "To define your ideal *prospects*, think about your best *customers*. *Who* are they, *where* are they, and *what* are they, or *how* do they think? Please take three quiet minutes to jot down the demographic, geographic, and psychographic profile of those ideal customers."

As the leaders began jotting notes, Carol looked puzzled. She asked for the specific definition of a demographic profile.

"The type and size of the companies that you want to work with, and sometimes the people within those companies," Alan replied.

"How's that different from the psychographic profile, Alan?" asked Evan.

"Psychographic is how the right clients think and act and what they appreciate," Alan explained.

"For example," Vic chimed in, "we work best with people who are looking for true technology *partners*. If someone puts a project out to bid and is just going to choose the lowest price without evaluating who is most likely to understand and resolve their business problem—well, that's not someone with the right psychographic profile."

"Exactly," Alan agreed. "Did that make it clear, Evan?"

"Perfectly," Evan replied.

Soon everyone looked ready to proceed.

"I'll start," said Sue. "For 'who,' I wrote down IT directors or CFOs at large, technology-dependent companies. Insurance companies, banks, hospital systems, med-tech firms, universities, and even government agencies. 'Where' is the U.S. How they think? Well, they have to be comfortable outsourcing key technology initiatives. They have to *really* want a strategic partner—not the lowest bidder who just comes in and does the work."

Alan moved left around the room, soliciting input from each of the other leaders. Most felt Sue had largely nailed it, but a few additional descriptors were added. Art took issue with Sue's geographic profile.

"The U.S. seems a little too broad for you and three salespeople to cover. Shouldn't we focus on a smaller market?" he said.

"No," Sue responded immediately. "If somebody from Maine wants to do business with us, I'm all for that!"

"But that doesn't mean we should spend time marketing or cold-calling in Maine," Eileen chimed in. "Remember, the target market is about where we spend our *proactive* sales and marketing energy. Right, Alan?"

"That's right," replied Alan. "If you focus your proactive marketing and sales efforts within this market and you get a lead from outside, win the business if it fits."

"Right," Eileen agreed. "I'd rather see you and your team connect with all the ideal prospects in Minnesota and the upper Midwest before we waste time elsewhere."

Sue thought for a moment, contemplating Art and Eileen's point.

"What does the upper Midwest mean to you, Eileen?" Alan asked.

"Minnesota and the five contiguous states," she replied. "Plus the northern half of Illinois—we've done enough business in Chicago to focus some energy there."

"Are there enough ideal prospects in those seven states to keep Art and your sales teams busy for a while, Sue?" asked Alan.

"Yes," she said. "We could easily hit $40 million in those seven states. Plus, focusing on this market will reduce the breadth and complexity of our sales and marketing efforts. It'll eliminate time zone issues, long flights, and big expense reports. We have a better chance of developing long-term relationships close to home. Maybe we can even stop attending trade shows—they're so expensive and disruptive."

With the geographic profile resolved, Alan answered a few more questions before asking the team to weigh in on the target market defined on the whiteboard:

TARGET MARKET:

DEMOGRAPHIC: IT DIRECTORS OR CFOs AT TECHNOLOGY-DEPENDENT COMPANIES (HEALTH CARE, FINANCIAL SERVICES, EDUCATION) WITH REVENUE > $100 MILLION

GEOGRAPHIC: HEADQUARTERED IN UPPER MIDWEST

PSYCHOGRAPHIC: COMFORTABLE LOOKING OUTSIDE THE COMPANY TO SOLVE TECHNOLOGY PROBLEMS, WANT A LONG-TERM RELATIONSHIP WITH A STRATEGIC PARTNER, NOT A LOW-COST VENDOR

"Now that you've defined your ideal customer and you're clear on your target market," Alan continued, "you can run the whole world through this filter, and out will pop the name, phone number, and email address of all your ideal prospects. Of course, it's more complicated than that, but with this tool you can begin building 'The List' and then focus *all* of your marketing and sales efforts on it. Everyone clear?"

With the target market properly defined, Alan asked Eileen to capture the work on the V/TO and moved on to the three uniques.

"Imagine Swan Services lined up against ten of your competitors," he said. "You're speaking with someone from your target market—an ideal prospect that wants to know exactly why you're different and better than those other companies. You need to come up with three things you're doing that—together—make you the best choice for your ideal prospect. Perhaps all ten of your competitors can say they're doing one of them, and a small handful can claim to be doing two, but nobody else can say they're doing all three. These are qualities that make you uniquely valuable to your target market."

Alan gave the team three quiet minutes to list potential uniques, invited the leaders to read their lists, and recorded them on the whiteboard:

REAL PEOPLE
PROBLEM SOLVERS
EASY TO WORK WITH
DO WHAT WE SAY
TECHNOLOGY EXPERTS
FOCUSED ON LONG-TERM RELATIONSHIPS
WE UNDERSTAND BUSINESS AND TECHNOLOGY
RESPONSIVE
GREAT LISTENERS

With another Keep, Kill, and Combine exercise and some healthy debate, the team pared down the list and agreed on three items:

1. WE'RE REAL PEOPLE WHO CARE

2. WE'RE EXPERTS IN USING TECHNOLOGY
   TO SOLVE BUSINESS PROBLEMS

3. WE DO WHAT WE SAY

Alan went around the table. Each leader agreed that these three uniques perfectly described the reasons Swan was different from and better than the competition and why they'd been able to retain their best clients. That prompted Vic to wonder aloud about the reason Swan had begun losing clients.

"Maybe we're struggling because we've gotten away from the delivering on these three uniques," he suggested.

The team agreed, acknowledging how much more difficult that had become as they'd grown. Sue volunteered to own the homework assignment—wordsmithing the three uniques—and asked Art for his help.

"Now that your three uniques are defined," Alan continued, "they should become the common thread running through all your sales and marketing efforts. Your sales team should use them *every single time* they're asked, 'Why Swan Services?' The three uniques should appear on your website, your sales collateral—you name it."

"I can really see this helping," said Art enthusiastically. "It'll help us produce clearer, more powerful stuff. And with fewer questions to ask about the message, it'll happen more quickly and affordably as well."

With that settled, Alan defined the next part of Marketing Strategy.

"Your proven process is a one-page visual that illustrates the life of the relationship you have with your clients," he explained, "from the moment they start speaking with you about doing business through the time they're a longtime, satisfied client. This will help prospective clients understand that you have a carefully defined, replicable way of taking care of them. By illustrating your proven process on a single page rather than a wordy brochure or a twenty-slide PowerPoint presentation, you *show* them how things work rather than *telling* them how they work. It'll quickly and clearly differentiate you as a company that has a proven way of taking care of its clients and give potential clients peace of mind. They'll feel like they're in good hands if they decide to work with you, *and* it'll ensure that new clients know exactly what to expect."

Alan illustrated the concept by distributing copies of his own proven process (see page 173), along with other client examples.

"So the question is," he continued, "do you feel defining the Swan Services client experience using a one-page visual would help you win more business?"

"Absolutely," Sue said immediately. "I love this. Right now the sales team is all over the board when a prospect asks us how things work. If we can all tell the same story, quickly and clearly, we'll sell more *and* make Evan's job a little easier."

"I'm all for that," said Evan, smiling. "This will really help us behind the scenes in operations. If we know there's a consistent process our clients are expecting, we can create and follow internal processes that match those expectations."

The rest of the team agreed, and Alan added "Proven Process" to the Issues List. He explained that creating and publishing this document would likely be someone's Rock in a subsequent quarter.

"It's already on my list as a potential Rock for this quarter, Alan," Sue interjected.

Alan concluded the Marketing Strategy discussion by defining the guarantee.

"The last part of your marketing message," Alan said, "eliminates a common fear in the minds of your potential clients that is preventing them from doing business with you. Sue, Vic, picture yourself in a selling situation with someone from your target market. You've just explained why you're different and better than the competition by sharing your three uniques. You've illustrated the proven process you'll follow to take care of the potential client. The guarantee now helps you explain what'll happen if, for some reason, things don't go as planned. So is there a common fear, concern, or worry in the minds of your ideal prospects when they're making the buying decision? If there is, can you turn that fear into an asset by wrapping a compelling guarantee around it?"

Alan offered up his own guarantee as an example: "If you don't get value from one of these sessions, you won't pay." He also mentioned several well-known guarantees offered by nationally recognized

THE EOS PROCESS™

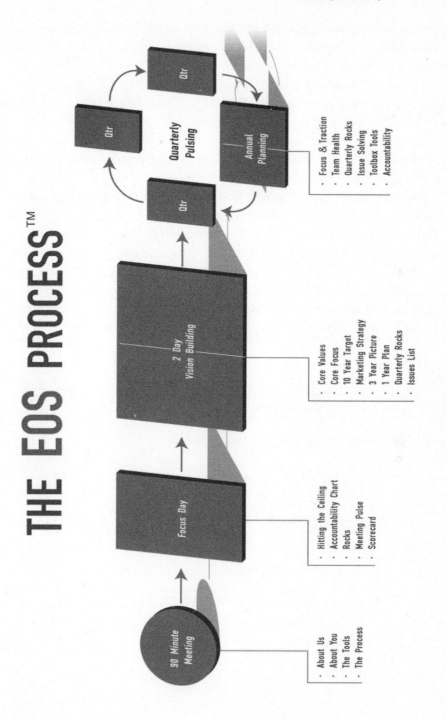

companies: "delivered in thirty minutes or it's free" from pizza restaurants, "free loaners" at collision shops, and "no waiting" in a hospital emergency room.

A quick debate ensued. Evan and Carol strongly opposed a guarantee, citing the financial risk and uncertainty inherent in managing technology projects. Vic and Sue loved it.

"One of our three uniques is 'we do what we say,'" Vic explained. "Without a guarantee to explain what happens when we don't, that's a pretty hollow claim."

In the end, Eileen admitted she wasn't fully committed to a guarantee and didn't know exactly what it would be if Swan had one. But she agreed the idea was a good one and suggested "Guarantee?" be added to the Issues List and decided on another day.

With all the questions answered, Alan wrapped up the Marketing Strategy exercise by making sure that Sue and Vic were clear on their homework assignments and dismissed the group for another five-minute break. The whiteboard summed up the discussion:

TARGET MARKET:

DEMOGRAPHIC: IT DIRECTORS OR CFOs AT TECHNOLOGY-DEPENDENT COMPANIES (HEALTH CARE, FINANCIAL SERVICES, EDUCATION) WITH REVENUE > $100 MILLION

GEOGRAPHIC: HEADQUARTERED IN UPPER MIDWEST

PSYCHOGRAPHIC: COMFORTABLE LOOKING OUTSIDE THE COMPANY TO SOLVE TECHNOLOGY PROBLEMS, WANT A LONG-TERM RELATIONSHIP WITH A STRATEGIC PARTNER, NOT A LOW-COST VENDOR

THREE UNIQUES:

1. WE'RE REAL PEOPLE WHO CARE
2. WE'RE EXPERTS IN USING TECHNOLOGY TO SOLVE BUSINESS PROBLEMS
3. WE DO WHAT WE SAY

PROVEN PROCESS: YES

GUARANTEE:

MAKING IT REAL

"Now it's time to bring your vision down to the ground," Alan said when the team returned. "We've defined *who you are* with your Core Values, *what you are* with your Core Focus, and *where you're going* with your 10-Year Target, and we've begun defining *how you're going to get there* through your Marketing Strategy. Now we have to make this long-term vision real with your 3-Year Picture. With your vision in mind, we paint a clear picture of the organization in three short years and get you all 100 percent on the same page. Until you can see it clearly with your mind's eye, you can't achieve it. This is a simplified approach that flies in the face of detailed three- to five-year strategic plans. We just want to agree—at a high level—on what the organization will look like in three years. It'll help you lay the foundation to achieve your 10-Year Target, resolve the big issues, and do much better one-year planning. You will leave here fully prepared and committed to creating the change necessary to achieve your vision. We'll start by getting on the same page about the future date."

Alan suggested the date be tied to the calendar year, and the team agreed. He wrote "Future Date: 12/31/20XX"—which was actually two years and nine months away—on the whiteboard. He then asked the team to agree on a revenue number for that year.

"What are we going to do this year, Carol?" asked Vic.

"Don't ask me," Carol said with a shrug. "Our goal was $8 million, but we're way off track. Maybe you should ask the head of sales."

Sue bristled at Carol's remark.

"We've got financials only through March," Eileen replied, easing the rising tension, "so this is a guess. I'd put the number between $7 million and $7.25 million."

The team continued thinking and readied its revenue predictions.

"Someone take a shot over the bow," Alan said after a few moments. "Where do you think Swan needs to be with regard to annual revenues in just under three years to put you in position to achieve your 10-Year Target of $40 million?"

"$15 million," said Vic.

"That's more than *double* our current revenues!" Carol exclaimed.

"I think we can get there," Vic said calmly. "After all, isn't that why we're going through this process? To execute better so we can grow and increase profits? We've had 50 percent growth in previous years, and we weren't anywhere near as aligned as we are now."

Carol just shook her head. Eileen smiled, logically siding with Carol but loving Vic's confidence and passion.

"Eileen?" Alan prompted.

"$10 million," she suggested. "That may be a little conservative, but I think we'll need to be careful about what kind of revenues we grow in order to stay within our Core Focus and lay the foundation for the journey ahead. We're going to have to devote energy to infrastructure, leadership, and profitability over the next two years. It can't be an all-hands-on-deck drive for revenues."

Art agreed with Eileen. Carol and Evan were at $9 million, and Sue said $12 million.

"Remember," Alan said, "in this system we're *predicting the future*. We're not forecasting; we're not hoping or wishing for something to happen. We set goals to hit them. These aren't stretch goals or pie-in-the-sky numbers. Whatever we record as your three-year revenue target, we're *going* to hit it. So in that context, let's conclude on a number somewhere between $9 million and $15 million."

Alan facilitated a short discussion to help the team agree on a number, ultimately recording "$11 million." He then asked the team to jot down a profit goal.

"I put down 10 percent," Eileen said to open the discussion. "It's aggressive, especially since we'll have to invest heavily as we build toward $40 million. But I think we can get there, and we *need* to get there."

Art agreed quickly, and Alan looked to his left at Carol.

"15 percent," Carol said quickly. "That's in our 10-Year Target, and the sooner we get there, the better."

"I put down 10 percent," Evan admitted.

"Me, too," said Sue. "That's a healthy improvement over where we are today."

With everyone chiming in, Alan led a brief discussion before the team settled on 10 percent. He recorded the goal and pointed to the next word he had written on the board: "measurable."

He explained that the measurable from the 3-Year Picture and other sections of the V/TO represented the team's goal for scope or size other than revenues. He illustrated the concept by explaining that a widget maker would count number of widgets, a registered investment adviser might measure assets under management, and a property management company might measure number of units or square feet.

After a brief discussion, the team decided it should measure the number of "major projects" it completed in a year. Alan helped the team define "major projects" as those accounting for $100,000 or more in revenue, and the leaders agreed that, with a goal of $11 million, it ought to complete fifty major projects.

"That's crazy!" Evan exclaimed. "We'll do twenty this year if we're lucky!"

"Crazy is too strong a word," said Eileen, smiling confidently. "But we *are* talking about a major change. We're here because we all know that we'll *never* achieve our vision by doing things the way we've always done them. Today's the day all of us must commit to driving that change—to creating a vastly different company in three short years. You have to believe we *will* be marketing to new prospects, we *will* be selling differently, we *will* be executing better in operations, and we *will* be running a better business, or we'll never get there. If you're all on board with achieving this vision—including you, Evan—I *know* we can get there."

Alan nodded, indicating that he agreed with Eileen's description of the journey that lay ahead. He then pointed to the details recorded on the board.

3-YEAR PICTURE:

FUTURE DATE:	12/31/20XX
REVENUE:	$11M
PROFIT:	10% ($1.1M)
MEASURABLE:	50 PROJECTS @ $100K+

"With these goals in mind," Alan explained, "it's time to paint a clear picture of what Swan Services will look like in three years. How many employees do you have? Are there any changes on the leadership team? Have you opened up a new territory or new lines of business? Do you have new technology tools, new offices, or a new brand? Take five minutes to record your thoughts."

When everyone finished, Sue volunteered to go first.

"Thanks, Sue," Alan said. "Please start with the number of right people in the right seats. How many people do you see in the organization at $11 million?"

"Oh," Sue said tentatively, scanning her list, "I wrote down sixty-five people."

Alan recorded her response as "65 RPRS" and motioned for the young sales leader to continue.

"Sales office in Chicago," she said. "Swan running on this system, full-time marketing person, Core Processes implemented."

"The way I typically write that," Alan interrupted, "is 'all Core Processes documented, simplified and followed by all'—FBA for short. Is that okay with you, Sue?"

Sue quickly agreed and read the few remaining items on her list. Vic went next, reading through seven items, which included new corporate offices. Alan then moved left around the table, recording new items from Eileen, Art, Carol, and Evan until there were seventeen on the board.

"Ideally," he explained, "we'll get this list down to five to fifteen things that clearly describe this organization in just under three short years. Remember, these are things you're all committed to making happen. They're essential, and they're things you want to share with everyone in the organization. If there's anything on this list you're not sure about or committed to, it's got to come off the list."

With that context having been set, Alan went through and cleaned up the list one item at a time. There were some debates along the way. For example, Vic and Carol weren't sure both the IT and HR seats needed to be filled within three years. In the end the team decided both positions would be critical components of the plan to reach $40 million and kept them on the list. Soon all the issues were resolved. More quickly than most of the leaders had expected, Alan pointed at the whiteboard and moved to conclude the 3-Year Picture discussion.

3-YEAR PICTURE:

FUTURE DATE: 12/31/20XX
REVENUE: $11M
PROFIT: 10% ($1.1M)
MEASURABLE: 50 PROJECTS @ $100K+

- 60 RPRS
- THRIVING CULTURE
- STRONG SALES TEAM OF 8 PEOPLE
- NEW SALES OFFICE IN 1 OR MORE MAJOR MARKETS
- ALL CORE PROCESSES DOCUMENTED, SIMPLIFIED AND FBA
- NEW COMPANY HQ
- INTERNAL IT SEAT
- HR SEAT
- DEVELOPER/BA/PM/RECRUITING PROCESS WORKING
- 40% RECURRING REVENUES

"What I ask you to do next may feel a little silly, but there *is* a method to my madness. Please sit back in your chairs, get comfortable, and close your eyes," he began, waiting for everyone to reluctantly comply. "Fast-forward two years and nine months. You've just finished a terrific year, achieving $11 million in revenues with a 10 percent net profit. You completed fifty $100,000 projects. You have sixty right people in the right seats..." Alan read the rest of the list aloud and finished with an important question: "Do you see it? I need a verbal 'yes' from all of you. If there's something on the list you don't really see, speak up now. Don't just say yes to agree. So, do you see it? Because you are the team that needs to make it happen."

"Ab-so-lutely!" exclaimed Vic in an exaggerated fashion. "It's so clear I can taste it!"

Alan smiled and turned to Eileen.

"Well, I can't quite *taste* it," she replied in jest. "But I do want it, and I think it's doable if we work together. For the first time, I actually think we *can* work together to achieve a common vision. So yes, I can see it."

"I'm excited," added Art, sitting to Eileen's left. "It's cool to see this team really come together. I think we can do it, and I'm eager to be part of it."

"I see it," said Carol quietly. "I'm not all misty-eyed about it, but I can see it."

Evan and Sue also agreed, each of them professing excitement and optimism. Alan concluded the exercise by asking Eileen to capture the details from the whiteboard and transfer them to Swan's V/TO. He then moved to the next item on the agenda, the 1-Year Plan.

"With your 3-Year Picture in clear focus," Alan continued, "we can now do much better one-year planning. I realize there are only nine months left in the year, but your future date ought to be tied to your calendar or fiscal year. It's the cleanest, simplest way to think about your year and your quarters as a team and as a company. Let's begin by agreeing on our revenue goal for the year. We talked about this earlier. Is someone ready to predict revenues through December 31?"

"Eileen said it was somewhere between $7 million and $7.25 million," said Evan. "I'm inclined to pick one of those numbers."

"Agreed," said Eileen. "I'd leave it up to Sue. Can we get to seven and a quarter?"

If Sue had been asked this question a month ago, the answer would have been no. But she'd been hitting her stride as the leader of the sales team; Vic had started letting go while being helpful and very productive in his own right; and, with the exception of Natalie, the sales team seemed to be picking up steam.

"I think we can," she replied. "It won't be easy, but unless Vic thinks I'm overconfident or crazy, I'll commit to making it happen."

"You think I'm going to talk you *out* of a big number?" Vic asked incredulously.

Sue laughed, and the rest of the team joined in. Alan recorded the revenue prediction on the whiteboard and walked the team through the remaining numbers, quickly agreeing on the following totals for the year:

1-YEAR PLAN:

FUTURE DATE: 12/31/20XX
REVENUE: $7.25 M
PROFIT: 5%
MEASURABLE: 20 PROJECTS @ $100K+

"When we build out our 1-Year Plan," Alan went on, "we'll get even more specific than we did with our 3-Year Picture. If we're going to achieve our long-term vision, we have to resolve the key issues and start making tangible progress right now. The way we do that is setting goals—three to seven priorities the company must get done this year, hopefully closer to three. Please make a list. Looking at your 3-Year Picture, your Issues List, and your Accountability Chart, what must you accomplish as a company by December 31?"

Eileen was deep in thought. She'd written down "hire ops leader" immediately. She had also been tempted to write down "Carol—RPRS?" Despite the progress her testy controller had made the last few months, something in Eileen's gut told her Carol would need to be replaced sometime soon. In the end, though, she decided that adding that to her list of potential goals would simply be pouring gasoline on a smoldering fire. She decided to share her concerns with Vic and quietly work on a contingency plan.

After five minutes Alan addressed the team. "We're going to prioritize your one-year goals a little differently," he explained. "Rather than using Keep, Kill, and Combine, I'd just like you all to look at your lists and get ready to take a one-at-a-time approach. Is there something on your list that you're reasonably certain everyone else wrote down or will agree on? Give me your best shots first. What's goal number one?"

"Implement this system in the business," Vic blurted out. "Sue and I are *dying* to roll out the Accountability Chart and the People Analyzer alone. If we can also get the V/TO out there and start implementing some of these other tools..."

"It's on my list, too," said Evan. Art, Sue, and Eileen all nodded to indicate they had written down something similar.

"Carol?" Alan asked.

"I didn't write it down," Carol said, "but if everyone else thinks it's a priority, I guess it's a priority."

"Say, Alan, what do you *call* this system?" Vic asked as Alan turned to record the goal. "I've been calling it the 'Entrepreneurial Operating System'—EOS for short. Does that work?"

"Whatever works for you," Alan replied. "This is *your* way of operating this business."

"Well EOS gets my vote," said Vic. The other leaders agreed, and Alan recorded "Implement EOS" on the whiteboard as the first goal. He then asked for another "slam-dunk" priority.

"Sales team: right people in the right seats," Sue said immediately. "If we're going to hit this year's revenue goal and get the pipeline filled with opportunities for next year, we can't afford any people issues. I'm thinking mostly about Natalie, but every seat is critical. We need more and better leads from Art; maybe one more salesperson; and Vic's magic as a relationship builder, closer, and mentor to the young sales team."

"Hear, hear," said Eileen enthusiastically.

Alan went around the table to gather feedback, getting support from everyone to include this as a one-year goal. He recorded "Sales Team: RPRS" on the board.

"While we're on the subject of sales and revenue, I also wrote down 'implement Marketing Strategy,'" Sue volunteered. "I'd really like us to focus on the target market that we defined today, and I'd like to begin using at least the three uniques and the proven process as key parts of our message right away."

When the others all agreed, Alan recorded the third goal.

"Any other goals?" he asked. The room was silent for a moment until Evan spoke up.

"I wrote down 'hire ops leader,'" he said. "It feels a little weird to say that, but it has to happen. It's our biggest barrier to growth, and I'm actually looking forward to focusing on the developers."

Eileen and the other leaders felt a huge sense of relief.

"Team?" Alan asked. "Is filling the ops leader seat a priority for the year?"

"It was on my list, too," Sue admitted.

"If Evan thinks it's a priority, I do, too," said Vic.

"Me, too," Eileen said, surprised that she was becoming a little emotional. "And thank you, Evan, for demonstrating exactly what it means to put the greater good of the business before your personal interests. I'm humbled and inspired by what you just did and what you mean to this company."

When Art and Carol agreed, Alan added the fourth priority to the list.

"I'd like us to document the Core Processes," Carol suggested next.

Evan, Sue, and Eileen acknowledged having the same item on their lists, so the team quickly agreed to add a fifth priority. Several other suggestions were made, but the team concluded that accomplishing those five priorities would make for a very full and productive nine months. Alan concluded the exercise by reviewing the work and securing a verbal commitment to the 1-Year Plan from each leader.

1-Year Plan:

FUTURE DATE: 12/31/20XX
REVENUE: $7.25M
PROFIT: 5%
MEASURABLE: 20 PROJECTS @ $100K+

- IMPLEMENT EOS
- SALES TEAM RPRS
- IMPLEMENT MARKETING STRATEGY
- HIRE OPS LEADER (RPRS)
- CORE PROCESSES DOCUMENTED, SIMPLIFIED AND FBA

"With your 1-Year Plan complete," Alan began after a quick break, "we can now move to the next section of the V/TO—quarterly Rocks. Looking at your 1-Year Plan and the Issues List, write down what you believe are the company's priorities for the next ninety days. What roadblocks do you want to eliminate? What ideas and opportunities must you pursue? Rack your brains, get it all on paper, and we'll build the list."

When everyone had finished, Alan again led the team through the pure approach to setting Rocks. He recorded each potential Rock on the whiteboard as each leader read through his or her list. To the team's surprise, today's list was appreciably shorter than the one compiled on the Focus Day. This time there were only eighteen potential Rocks.

Once again, Alan led them through Keep, Kill, and Combine. After the first pass, the team had narrowed the list to ten potential company Rocks:

- FOCUS ON TARGET MARKET
- PUBLISH PROVEN PROCESS
- NATALIE: RPRS?
- MORE/BETTER LEADS
- CLOSE THREE "A" DEALS
- INTRODUCE OPERATING SYSTEM
- DOCUMENT CORE PROCESSES
- FILL OPS LEADER SEAT
- DEFINE HR/IT SEATS
- ACQUIRE PROJECT MANAGEMENT SOFTWARE

"Time to get laser-focused," Alan urged the leaders. "Let's take another pass. If we come to something that's not a life-or-death priority for the quarter, we have to Kill it. Remember, it's not going away—it's either going to be someone's individual Rock or we'll transfer it to the Issues List and tackle it in a later quarter."

With those words of guidance and encouragement, the team was quickly able to trim the list to six company Rocks. Before helping the team make them SMART, Alan reminded everyone that Rocks are always due at Quarterly Sessions. He then helped establish Swan's quarterly Meeting Pulse.

"As you see from my proven process," he explained, "we'll meet four times each year—three times for one-day Quarterly Sessions and once for a two-day Annual Planning Session. I'll help you run those meetings for as long as you need me, and then you'll graduate and run them on your own. So for today the question is when does this team want to complete its 1-Year Plan for next year?"

After a brief discussion, the team decided to conduct its Annual Planning Session each December so that Swan's plan for the next year could be rolled out to the company before January 1. From there, the leaders drew the natural conclusion that its Quarterly Sessions should occur in March, June, and September each year.

"That means we should schedule your next session for sometime in mid- to late June," he concluded. "Does that sound right?"

The team quickly agreed, compared calendars, and settled on June 24 for its first Quarterly. Alan recorded the date on the whiteboard and continued.

"Next we have to decide where we need to be at the end of this next quarter to be on track to achieve our financial goals for the year," he said. "So Carol, Eileen, where do we need to be on June 30 to make the two of you feel like we're on target to achieve $7.25 million in revenue with a 5 percent net profit?"

After some quick math, the two leaders agreed that achieving YTD revenues of $3.5 million with a 5 percent net would put them on track to achieve their prediction for the year. Alan recorded those numbers and asked for some input about the key measurable. The team settled on eight projects over $100K each.

Moving down the list one item at a time, he then helped the team write SMART Rocks and assign owners for each of the six company Rocks. To write a SMART rollout Rock, Alan directed the team's attention to the list of foundational tools and explained that process in detail.

"Most of my clients introduce the foundational tools in an all-company meeting," he explained. "That meeting typically begins by sharing your vision. Move through the V/TO one section at a time, beginning with the Core Values speech. This tells your people who you are, where you're going, and how you plan to get there. Follow that by presenting your Accountability Chart, which clearly defines the right structure for the organization and crystallizes everyone's role in helping achieve your vision."

"What about the other tools?" asked Eileen.

"Level 10 Meetings, Rocks, and Scorecards are typically implemented one level at a time into the organization," Alan replied. "You've been learning how to use these tools over the last sixty days. When each of you is ready to begin holding departmental Level 10 Meetings with your direct reports, you'll start doing that. Those meetings may be a little shorter than your leadership Level 10 Meetings, and the agenda may differ slightly, but it's important that you maintain the psychology and discipline of a pure Level 10 Meeting."

"So we can start holding those whenever we feel we're ready?" Sue asked.

"Yes," responded Alan. "What we don't want is the blind leading the blind; that will do more harm than good. You have to be confident leading these meetings."

"What about Rocks and Scorecards for our departments?" Sue inquired further. "Do we set those ourselves and bring them to the first meeting?"

"What my other clients have found works best," Alan replied, "is working *with* the people who report to you to set departmental Rocks and create a departmental Scorecard. This typically works just like it did during our Focus Day. You ask your team members to come to a Level 10 Meeting with a list of key issues they feel the department needs to solve in the next ninety days. Get all those issues on the board, and then go through the Keep, Kill, and Combine exercise until you agree on departmental priorities for the quarter. Write SMART Rocks, put them on a departmental Rock Sheet, and review those departmental and individual Rocks on a weekly basis, just as you've been doing."

"What about the Scorecard?" Sue prompted.

"Same deal," replied Alan. "When you think the team is ready, ask each member to come to a meeting with a list of numbers that will give you all an absolute pulse on the department. Get everyone's suggestions up on the board, and take a first cut at your departmental Scorecard."

"Got it," said Sue. "So, I'm ready to do that, like, tomorrow. Is that okay?"

"That's up to the team," Alan replied. "What's important is that we're all on the same page with how and when we're going to roll out these tools."

Alan answered a few questions and worked through the options. Ultimately, the leaders decided to roll out the V/TO and Accountability Chart at an all-company meeting. They planned to begin holding departmental Level 10 Meetings immediately afterward but elected to hold off on departmental Rocks and Scorecards.

With the company Rocks complete, Alan instructed Sue, Eileen, and Evan to record their company Rocks on a clean sheet of paper.

QUARTERLY ROCKS:

FUTURE DATE: 6/24/xx
REVENUE: $3.5M
PROFIT: 5%
MEASURABLE: 8 PROJECTS @ $100K+

1. Focus Sales and Marketing on Target Market	Sue
2. Sales Rep. RPRS (Natalie or Hire New?)	Sue
3. Close Three "A" Deals	Sue
4. Roll Out EOS Foundational Tools	Eileen
5. Fill Ops Leader Seat	Eileen
6. Implement Project Management Software	Evan

"Once you've defined your company Rocks," Alan explained, "you can add individual Rocks. Remember, three to seven Rocks is the rule—ideally closer to three. So what are the most important things you must get done—as an individual—this quarter? Look through this list of Killed potential Rocks and the Issues List, and record your own SMART Rocks for the quarter."

Sue ended up with five Rocks, picking up "publish proven process" and "complete account plans for twenty clients." Vic agreed to help Sue with her Rocks and complete two of his own Rocks: "build a 'key relationship' list and a plan to strengthen them" and "create an industry event plan for next year."

Eileen agreed to finish one of her Rocks from the Focus Day—"complete credit line renewals."

Still stung by Evan's failure to help her complete her company Rock from the Focus Day, Carol had resisted ownership of the "project management software" Rock so strenuously that Evan ended up taking it. However, when asked for her individual Rocks, she quickly read down a list of departmental objectives—"produce monthly income statements within two weeks, reduce invoice defects to zero, and draft capital expenditure budget for next fiscal year."

"I'll just take the one Rock," Evan said when Alan turned his way. He had clearly learned his lesson from the last quarter.

"What about the Rocks you didn't get done last quarter?" Carol asked him immediately. "Did you want to finish any of those?"

Evan could feel himself getting angry but managed to keep his composure. He was about to defend himself when Eileen jumped in.

"I think Carol makes a good point, Evan," she said calmly. "I'd sure like to see you finalize and implement the error-tracking system and document the project management process. If you need help, I'll pitch in."

"Fine," replied Evan, soothed by Eileen's listing of only two additional Rocks and by her offer of help. "I suppose we can just carry the wording of those over onto the new Rock Sheet?"

"That's typically how it works best," Alan replied.

Alan had been erasing potential Rocks from the whiteboard as the leaders selected them as individual Rocks. When everyone had concluded and Sue had agreed to complete the Rock Sheet (see page 189), five items were left. Alan read through the remaining items one by one, asking the team whether each potential Rock needed to be added to the Issues List. He grabbed a green marker and transferred "Document and Simplify Core Processes" and "Define HR/IT Seats" to the rather large list of issues.

"That brings us to the eighth and final question on the V/TO," Alan announced. "What are your issues? To answer that question, I first want to go back to something we discussed earlier when we were talking about compartmentalizing. I know it's been a long day, but do you remember when I mentioned that issues fall into two categories?"

"Yes," said Sue as she flipped back to check her notes. "I spend enough time managing the Issues List on our Level 10 Meeting agenda that I wanted to make sure and get this right. You called them 'long-term issues' and 'short-term issues,' right?"

"Exactly," replied Alan. "Long-term issues belong on your V/TO. Those are things you don't need or want to tackle until your next Quarterly Session, at the earliest. We'll put them on the V/TO because we don't want to get bogged down worrying about them until we're back together on June 24. Short-term issues go on your Level 10 Meeting agenda. These are issues you want or need to solve during the quarter. They're smaller, more pressing obstacles or opportunities that you feel must be addressed before late June. Does that make sense?"

Most of the team nodded.

"With that in mind, let's clean up your Issues List," Alan continued. "I'm going to read down this list of roughly thirty items. When I read an issue, I need the team to shout out one of three things. 'Kill

Swan Services Quarterly Rock Sheet

Future Date: June 24, 20XX
Revenue: $3.5 million
Profit: 5%
Measurables: 8 projects @ $100K +

COMPANY ROCKS

	WHO
1) Focus sales & marketing on target market	Sue
2) Sales rep RPRS (Natalie or hire new)	Sue
3) Close three "A" deals	Sue
4) Roll out EOS foundational tools	Eileen
5) Fill ops leader seat	Eileen
6) Implement project management software	Evan
7)	

SUE

1) Focus sales & marketing on target market
2) Sales rep RPRS (Natalie or hire new)
3) Close three "A" deals
4) Complete account plans for twenty clients
5) Publish proven process
6)
7)

EVAN

1) Implement project management software
2) Implement error-tracking system
3) Document project management process
4)
5)
6)
7)

CAROL

1) Draft 20XX capital expenditure budget
2) Eliminate time-card errors
3) Produce monthly income statements within two weeks
4)
5)
6)
7)

EILEEN

1) Roll Out EOS Foundational Tools
2) Fill Ops Leader Seat
3) Renew credit lines
4)
5)
6)
7)

VIC

1) Create a "key relationship" list and a plan to strengthen them
2) Create an industry event plan for next year
3)
4)
5)
6)
7)

it' means the issue will be solved forever when we complete a goal from the 1-Year Plan, a company Rock, or an individual Rock. 'V/TO' means it's a long-term issue you don't want to be distracted by until your next Quarterly. 'Level 10' means it's a short-term issue that needs to be on your weekly agenda. Is that clear?"

Alan began reading down the list. Every time someone shouted, "Kill it!" and nobody protested, Alan drew a line through the issue. As the number of solved issues mounted, the leaders got more and more excited about how much progress they had made during the day. When the list had been completely reviewed, only ten issues remained. Alan had written "L10" next to three of them and "V/TO" next to seven.

"Sue," he continued, "please transfer the Level 10 issues to next week's meeting agenda. Eileen, the V/TO issues obviously get added to your V/TO, along with all the other work we've completed today. I'll provide more detailed instructions in a moment when we discuss next steps. Before I go there, does anybody have other questions about the Issues List?"

Alan answered a few tactical questions and then concluded the discussion by recapping the four compartments—goals, Rocks, To-Dos, and issues.

"So now you're leaving here with all the moving parts of this business in the right compartment," he explained. "The things you need to get done before year's end are in the first compartment—the goals in your 1-Year Plan. Your priorities for the next ninety days are in compartment two—Rocks. You'll continue to use compartment three—To-Dos—as you complete seven-day action items throughout the quarter. And everything else is an issue—either long-term or short-term. Everything is in its place."

As Alan finished, several members of the team were nodding. Now that they had completed the entire V/TO, removed a significant number of issues from the list, and found a proper home for all the priorities in the business, the system Alan had been sharing with them was becoming clearer and more complete. There was still much work to be done, but nearly everyone on Swan's team felt good about what lay ahead.

Less than a week later, Eileen would present Swan's completed V/TO to the leadership team. (See V/TO on pages 192–193.)

Alan checked his watch and continued. "We're coming into the home stretch," he promised. "So here are the important next steps that will help you capitalize on all the hard work you've done to date and keep gaining momentum as we move forward through the process. First, roll out the foundational tools as described in Eileen's Rock. Eileen, please take all the work we've completed today and fill in every section of the V/TO. Carol, please bring copies of the completed Rock Sheet to the next Level 10 Meeting. Everyone, please stay focused on completing your Rocks. Get a plan, start early, and stay on track through the quarter."

"Eileen," Alan continued, "I'd like your help scheduling a visit to observe one of your Level 10 Meetings this quarter. By the time I visit, these meetings should be darn near perfect, but this'll allow me to help you work out those last few kinks. Last but not least, I'm looking forward to seeing you here June 24 for your first Quarterly Session. I'll check in with you twice between now and then, but I'm here to help in the meantime."

Alan invited questions before moving to conclude the session. He asked the leaders to record their answers to three questions with which they were becoming quite familiar—those asking for feedback, expectations, and a rating.

"Where's my head?" replied Evan right away. "For the first time since we started this process, I can say that I'm truly excited. If you'd have asked me that about six hours ago, I'd have answered differently. But right now I feel relieved, optimistic about the company's future, and confident in my role. My expectations were easily exceeded. Ten."

Sue followed up immediately. "A little overwhelmed," she began. "I have a *huge* load this quarter, and I came here telling myself to be more conservative. But I'm thrilled with the clarity this process has brought to me and the alignment it has brought to the team. Expectations met; ten."

"Wow," said Vic, recalling his answer from the last session. "We covered more ground than I thought was possible today. You helped

THE VISION/TRACTION ORGANIZER

Swan Services – 20XX Q2

VISION

CORE VALUES	1. Be humbly confident 2. Grow or die 3. Help first 4. Do the right thing 5. Do what you say
CORE FOCUS	**Passion:** Building a great company with great people **Niche:** Solving real problems with the right technology
10-YEAR TARGET	$40 million in revenue with 15% net profit

MARKETING STRATEGY	**Target Market/"The List":**
	IT Directors or CFOs at technology-dependent companies (financial services, health care, education, government) with more than $100 million in revenues that are:
	  • Headquartered in the upper Midwest
	  • Comfortable looking outside the organization to solve technology problems
	  • Want a long-term relationship with a strategic partner, not a low-cost vendor
	
	Three Uniques:
	1. We're real people who care
	2. We're experts at using technology to solve business problems
	3. We do what we say
	
	Proven Process:
	
	Guarantee:

3-YEAR PICTURE

Future Date: December 31, 20XX

Revenue: $11 million

Profit: 10%

Measurables: 50 projects @ $100K+

What Does It Look Like?

• 60 RPRS
• Thriving culture
• Strong sales team of 8 people
• New sales office in 1 or more major markets
• New company HQ
• Internal IT seat RPRS
• HR seat RPRS
• Developer/BA/PM recruiting process working
• 40% recurring revenues

THE VISION/TRACTION ORGANIZER

Swan Services – 20XX Q2

TRACTION

1-YEAR PLAN

Future Date: December 31, 20XX
Revenue: $7.25 million
Profit: 5%
Measurables: 20 projects @ $100K+

Goals for the Year:

1. Implement EOS
2. Sales team RPRS
3. Implement marketing strategy
4. Hire ops leader RPRS
5. Core Processes documented, simplified and followed by all
6.
7.

ROCKS

Future Date: June 24, 20XX
Revenue: $3.5 million
Profit: 5%
Measurables: 8 Projects @ $100K+

Rocks for the Quarter:

	Who
1. Focus sales and marketing on target market	Sue
2. Sales rep RPRS (Natalie or hire new)	Sue
3. Close three "A" deals	Sue
4. Roll out EOS foundational tools	Eileen
5. Fill ops leader seat	Eileen
6. Implement project management software	Evan
7.	

ISSUES LIST

1. Measuring utilization
2. Staff-augmentation – Core Focus?
3. Raj RPRS
4. Bill RPRS
5. Terry RPRS
6. Jennifer RPRS
7. Guarantee
8.
9.
10.
11.
12.

us through a couple of prickly situations, and I was actually *on time*! If that doesn't deserve a ten, nothing ever will."

"Expectations?" Alan asked, smiling.

"Oh, of course," Vic replied. "Met, and then some."

"Thank you, Vic," Alan said. "Eileen?"

"Well, I rarely agree word-for-word with Vic," she began, "but I also wrote down 'Wow.' This has been a remarkable two months, and I'm amazed at how far we've come. I'm really proud of everyone on this team—especially Carol, Evan, and Art. All three of you have really taken your lumps through this process, and I'm very grateful that you're all still in the room doing your best to help us move forward. Oh, and Vic, it's a small thing, but thank you for being so good about timeliness these last few weeks. It means a lot to all of us. My expectations were vastly exceeded; ten."

"Great meeting," Art said when Eileen finished. "I'll miss being a part of them, but I like where this team is headed, and feel like my firm and I can continue helping when it makes sense. My expectations were met, and I also say ten."

"Carol?" Alan said gently. "Feedback?"

"On the plus side, Vic *was* on time," she joked, managing a half-smile. "These meetings are still way too long for me, but today I feel we really got a lot of work done. I guess my expectations were met because we completed the vision. So, eight?"

Alan thanked her and addressed the team. "Thank you all for being open and honest in each of our sessions," he began, "even when it meant enduring some awkward moments or engaging in painful conflict. Each of you should be proud of the work you've done together as a team. The progress you've made this far is remarkable, and I'm grateful that you've allowed me to be a part of it. Stay focused, roll out those foundational tools, and make this a great quarter. I can't wait to hear all about it in June."

CHAPTER 6

BIG MOVES

SWAN SERVICES' FOUNDING PARTNERS left Alan's office excited about their newly clear vision and plan for the organization and optimistic about the team's ability to make it happen. Vic was euphoric—for him, clarity and confidence were enough. But for Eileen, those two positive emotions were accompanied by a growing awareness that the next few months were going to be the most tumultuous of her professional career. She shared that concern with her partner the day after their last Vision-Building Session.

"You don't seem very excited," Vic observed innocently over coffee in Eileen's office. "Don't you feel like we're finally on our way to the company we always wanted?"

"Yes," Eileen replied carefully, "but there's an awful lot of work yet to be done!"

"I guess," he agreed. "Your two company Rocks are pretty intense, huh?"

"Oh, piece of cake," she joked. "All I have to do is implement a new way of operating this company and find a new operations leader. Want to trade seats? That visionary thing is starting to sound pretty good."

"No, thanks," Vic protested. "But I *would* like to pitch in. Can I help you get ready for the rollout?"

"Of course," Eileen replied. "And thank you—I'll definitely take you up on that. But there's another issue I wanted to talk to you about."

"Fire away," Vic replied.

"I suspect we'll be replacing *two* members of the leadership team before the end of the year," she explained quietly. "Carol's not going to make it."

"Really?" Vic asked. "I thought she was a lot better yesterday, didn't you?"

"She certainly is making an effort," Eileen agreed. "And while I appreciate that, it isn't likely to last. Deep down, I just don't think she fits our culture. I'm almost certain she'll leave on her own or revert back to her old ways and force us to make a move. I think we need a contingency plan, just in case."

The two quickly agreed to quietly interview individuals and companies that provided interim CFO/controller services. That way, Swan Services could immediately hire someone capable of filling Carol's role on a part-time, contract basis were she to leave suddenly.

Almost immediately after Vic left Eileen's office, Sue popped her head through the door.

"Got a minute?" Sue asked.

"Sure," Eileen said. "What's on your mind?"

"It's about the ops leader seat," she explained. "Unless you've already got a candidate in mind, I think there's someone at my old company who's worth a look."

"Sensi-Tech?" she replied. "Who?"

"Tom Bridgewater," answered Sue. "He's run what they called their delivery department since before I joined the company. His team isn't as large as ours, but Sensi-Tech's project managers, BAs, and developers have been reporting to him for three or four years now."

"Not the account managers?" queried Eileen.

"No," Sue responded. "They report to the director of sales. But everyone in the organization—including the sales and account management teams—really respects him. The people who report to him downright love the guy."

"Hmmm," said Eileen. "Do you think he shares our Core Values?"

"I do," responded Sue, smiling. "Tom's name popped into my head last night on the way home. So I pulled out the Accountability Chart and the Core Values speech and people-analyzed him. In my experience, he's *way* above the bar."

"Sounds like a good idea, Sue," replied Eileen, impressed. "I'm just a little leery because I don't like poaching talent from our competitors."

"I hear ya," agreed Sue, "but word has it Tom's exploring his options. Sensi-Tech is stuck at $3.5 million. They're relying on older technology and are focused on a sector of the market that doesn't have a lot of potential. Tom's the kind of leader who doesn't like to sit still, so I think he's likely to leave regardless. Why don't I grab coffee with him and find out if that's really the case? If he's happy where he is, I won't even mention our opportunity. If I get the sense he's going to leave, I'll ask him to shoot me his resume."

"All right," agreed Eileen, still uneasy. "I'll give some more thought to defining the position in the meantime. Thanks for letting me know."

"You're welcome," Sue said, and left the office.

At the following week's Level 10 Meeting, the leadership team used IDS to agree on a more specific rollout plan for the foundational tools. Eileen left the meeting with a To-Do—to schedule an all-company meeting in mid-May. The team had decided to introduce the V/TO and Accountability Chart at that meeting and to share People Analyzer results one-on-one with each employee shortly thereafter. Sue and Carol planned to begin holding departmental Level 10 Meetings with their direct reports before the Quarterly Session at Alan's office on June 24 but decided to hold off on departmental Rocks and Scorecards until after the next session.

For several weeks, Swan's team settled into a consistent, focused routine. The Level 10 Meetings were running smoothly, everyone's Rocks seemed to be on track, and the numbers on the company Scorecard were heading in the right direction. Eileen had already identified several qualified candidates for the ops leader position, including Tom Bridgewater. For a moment, Swan's integrator allowed herself to think the team had turned the corner—even Carol.

That impression was undone at 5:30 P.M. on a surprisingly warm Friday in early May. Every sane member of the Swan team had long since left to enjoy the spring weather. Eileen was just packing up when she heard shouting coming from the conference room. After a few steps in that direction, she identified the combatants as Carol and Evan.

"You're not even going to be in charge of project management in three months, Evan!" Carol was yelling. "If you're not happy with the project management software I recommended, we'll just have to let the new VP of ops decide!"

"That's ridiculous, Carol," Evan replied, trying to stay calm. "The team agreed that acquiring the software this quarter is a priority. I own the Rock, and until we hire someone new, I own the operations seat. My team field-tested the application you recommended, and it *won't work for us!* I don't care how affordable it is!"

"I see. Well, then, maybe you should have devoted more time to this when it was *my Rock*!" Carol replied condescendingly as Eileen neared the conference room.

"Oh, for Pete's sake, Carol," sighed Evan. "For the hundredth time, *I'm sorry!*"

"Hey, guys," Eileen said as she strode through the door. "Sounds like things are getting a little heated in here. Can I help?"

"Uh, we were just discussing my Rock," said Evan uneasily.

"That sounded like more than a discussion, Evan," said Eileen. "What's the problem, exactly?"

The two leaders started talking at once. Eileen quickly calmed things down and helped the two reach agreement on a plan to move forward with the project management software Rock. Carol rushed out of the conference room, and Evan followed suit, apologizing profusely to his boss for involving her in what he called a "silly argument."

It was after six thirty by the time Eileen headed for home. She'd hoped to have dinner on the patio with her family, but it was now too late for that. Try as she might to forget it, the bickering she'd overheard before entering the conference room kept replaying in her head. With every passing mile, she became more and more angry.

She and Vic spoke briefly about the incident over the weekend and agreed to meet first thing Monday to discuss it further.

"I'd have fired her on the spot," Vic said a little too loudly as he walked through Eileen's office door with two large coffees.

"Shhhhhh!" Eileen replied. "I wasn't happy with *either* of them. Conflict is inevitable, but this had gotten personal and a little nasty."

"Yeah, that's not cool," said Vic. "I'm sure Evan could have handled himself better, but I can't help but think Carol was the one who brought the lighter and gasoline. It sure seems like she's been a real—well—*Carol* lately."

"Really?" Eileen asked. "Have there been other incidents like this that I don't know about?"

"Well, *yeah*," Vic said, as though Eileen should have known. "She's been on her best behavior around *you*, but she's reverted back to the same old Carol when one of the 'little people' wants or needs something."

"For instance?" asked Eileen.

"Last Thursday she and Sue got into it about the commission report," Vic replied. "And earlier in the week she sent a testy email to a couple of Evan's people about their 'tardy, inaccurate' time sheets."

"Why isn't this coming out in our Level 10 Meetings?" Eileen asked.

"Good question," Vic replied. "I know Sue's about ready to throw her on the Issues List—or in front of a bus. But in fairness, this stuff seems like it's all come to a head recently. Until the last few weeks, I think Carol was actually doing a good job of keeping herself in check since your strike one meeting."

After a brief discussion and with Vic's support, Eileen decided to take further action. She first spoke privately with Sue and then Evan to gather more details about the run-ins Vic had mentioned. She took careful notes and reviewed Carol's emails in an effort to thoroughly document how the controller's behavior had been inconsistent with Swan's Core Values. By day's end, Eileen had scheduled a strike two meeting.

At four the following afternoon, Eileen began the meeting by reviewing the run-in with Evan and the other specific events she had learned about from Vic. She used the People Analyzer to illustrate Carol's inability to consistently exhibit Swan's Core Values. Carol was at first combative but soon became sullen and withdrawn. At the end, without making eye contact or uttering a word, she signed the document Eileen had prepared, left the office, and closed the door behind her. Eileen returned to her desk, confident that the Carol saga would be resolved within the month.

The following week, Alan visited Swan Services to observe the leadership team's Level 10 Meeting. The team concluded fifteen minutes early so Alan could provide both positive and constructive feedback. He offered tips for staying focused during the reporting section of the meeting and for improving IDS but overall was quite impressed with the team's mastery of the Level 10 Meeting.

Afterwards, Eileen asked Alan to join her and Vic in her office. They shared their contingency plan for Carol and explained the events of the past month. Eileen asked Alan whether her habit of pulling Vic into one-on-one meetings to discuss sensitive issues like Carol was "permissible."

"Not just permissible," he replied. "It's highly recommended. You'll become a great team and a great company only when you two are consistently on the same page. It's so important that there's a tool in my system called a 'Same Page Meeting.' I suggest you two start holding them regularly. They'll be doubly helpful for you because they will help you resolve any issues you have as owners *or* as the visionary and integrator without bringing them into your leadership team meetings. Without you two on the same page and presenting a united front, it'll be nearly impossible to get everyone else rowing in one direction."

The pair agreed to schedule Same Page Meetings on the first Monday of each month at 3:30 P.M., beginning the following week. Each would come with a list of issues, get them out on the table, prioritize them, and IDS them. Alan explained that they could adjust the frequency of their Same Page Meetings if they needed more or less time together. He offered to help further when needed and left the office a few minutes later.

Three weeks later, Alan got a call from Eileen.

"Carol resigned today," she said.

"Really?" he responded. "Did that come as a surprise to you?"

"Not at all," Eileen replied. "It was still a painful, difficult discussion. But even when she was railing against me and the way things work at Swan Services, I felt amazingly calm and certain this was the right thing for both Carol and the company."

"What do you mean by 'railing against' you and the company?" Alan asked.

"Oh, she gave me an earful," she answered. "We never fully appreciated her, we'll never achieve our vision if we can't hold on to dedicated people like her, we spend way too much time on vision and values and too little getting work done. You get the drill."

"Yes, I do," Alan agreed. "I've heard similar stories from other clients on many occasions. It sounds like you took it all in stride."

"Yes," Eileen replied. "She's gone because she didn't fit our culture. That was clear before she spent a half hour telling me how 'wrong' our culture is. I'm certain we're much better off with Carol in our rearview mirror."

"Agreed," Alan responded. "Though I'd guess that creates another people issue."

"Yes," she said. "But as Vic and I told you a few weeks ago, we have a plan. I'll own the finance seat in Carol's absence, and we're hiring an interim controller who will report to me. I suspect permanently replacing Carol will be a Q3 Rock."

Alan congratulated Eileen on her handling of the difficult people issue and hung up, eager to hear more about Swan Services' journey at the team's next session.

Ninety-Day World

On June 24, Swan's leadership team filed into Alan's office for its first Quarterly Session. Alan greeted each leader warmly, beginning with Sue. Vic wasn't far behind, having been cured of his chronic lateness. Eileen walked in a few minutes before nine.

"Good morning, Alan," she said enthusiastically. "I'd like you to meet Tom Bridgewater, our new VP of operations."

"Hello, Tom," said Alan, shaking the new leader's hand. "Welcome. I've heard a lot about you."

"Good morning, Alan," replied Tom. "And I've heard a lot about you and your Entrepreneurial Operating System, as you might imagine."

"And you still showed up today!" exclaimed Alan, to the amusement of the leaders getting settled around the conference table. "Will Evan be joining us?"

"No," replied Eileen. "He and I had a nice talk yesterday and agreed that Tom had thoroughly integrated himself into the leadership team over the last few weeks."

"Terrific," replied Alan. "Kudos to all of you—especially Evan—for making the transition so smooth and efficient. As you know, it doesn't always work that way."

Alan began the Quarterly Session by reminding the leaders that they had embarked on a journey to strengthen the Six Key

Components of their business. He had drawn the following diagram on the whiteboard.

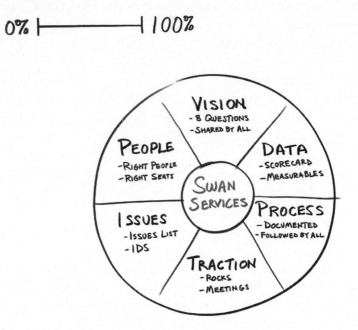

"When you become 80 percent strong or better in each of these Components," he said, "you'll be running a truly great organization. As you may remember, the journey we've embarked on to achieve that goal works like this." He pointed to a diagram of his proven process on the whiteboard.

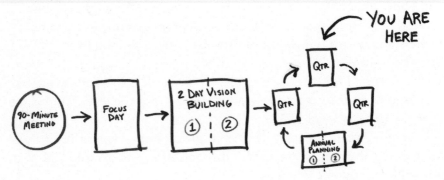

"You are here," Alan said, pointing to the diagram. "At this stage of our journey together, our relationship is all about execution." He then walked the team through the objectives and agenda:

OBJECTIVES

CLEAR VISION
CLEAR PLAN (SAME PAGE)

RESOLVE ALL KEY ISSUES

AGENDA

CHECK-IN
REVIEW Q2
V/TO
SET Q3 ROCKS
IDS
NEXT STEPS
CONCLUDE

"Quarterly Sessions help you create that ninety-day world we've been talking about," Alan explained. "You've been working hard *in* the business for the last ninety days. If you're normal, that means you're starting to fray, you're stuck in the tall grass. Things have become less clear and more complex; you may be getting frustrated with one another. This is our chance to pull it all together and get back on the same page. Today we're going to spend the day working *on* the business. We'll look back on the last ninety days and see how everyone did. We'll recheck your vision and make sure everyone's on the same page with where you're going and how you plan to get there. And we'll make your plan for next quarter crystal clear by setting Rocks. Finally, we'll spend the remainder of the day solving all the key issues with IDS."

Alan then asked the team to check in with bests, an update, and expectations.

Sue went first: "My personal best was a great trip to Napa Valley with Roger. The professional best has to be completing the 'three "A" deals' Rock."

Vic clapped loudly, and the team joined in. Sue smiled and continued.

"Getting the right people in the right seats is working," she continued. "It's been hard and a little painful, but we've made great progress. We've gotten very good at Level 10 Meetings. Our sales and marketing efforts are more focused, but we can continue to get better. Not working? I still don't feel like I have enough time, and I know other people on this team feel the same way. The sales-to-operations handoff isn't working as well as it could. My expectations for today are to get refocused and set priorities for the next quarter."

"Thank you, Sue," Alan responded. "Eileen?"

"My personal best? So far I've been to every one of Henry and Charlie's Little League games," she told them. "That may sound trivial, but it's a major accomplishment for me and something the boys—and my husband, Dan—really appreciate."

"That's great, Eileen," Alan said, smiling.

"At the risk of stroking his ego," she continued, "the professional best is hiring Tom. We were fortunate to find someone to fill the ops leader seat so quickly, and he's hit the ground running. He fits our culture and has gotten a solid handle on the lay of the land over the last four weeks. He's done a brilliant job of gathering information from throughout the organization and working very closely with Evan to gain his confidence and get fully up to speed."

She allowed herself a smile. "They're inseparable," she explained. "When I walk by Tom's office in the morning, they're reviewing project documentation or writing stuff on the whiteboard. Same thing when I leave at night."

A week earlier, Eileen had called Alan to discuss Tom's and Evan's participation in the Quarterly Session. She had originally thought both leaders should attend as a way of formally passing the baton, but Tom's quick ramp-up helped her decide to have him attend the Quarterly on his own. She resolved to have a one-on-one conversation with Evan to let him know.

Though Evan appeared to be comfortable with Tom and his own transition off the leadership team, their conversation *was* extremely emotional. But through it all, Evan's words and actions confirmed that he'd made peace with his new role leading the development team.

"What's working?" she continued. "The rollout meeting really went well. We have some skeptics, and there were some eyes being rolled. But we've been repeating ourselves as often as we can, and I can already see that we'll win them over if we just keep at it. I really like what's happening in sales, and *this* team is more aligned and more focused than ever."

She continued after a short pause. "What's not working is that I'm in two seats now that Carol's left. We have a controller engaged on a contract basis, but getting him up to speed has been difficult. So I'm *buried*. My expectations are that we get a clear plan for the next ninety days that solves that problem and keeps moving the business forward."

Alan thanked Eileen and moved left, asking Vic to check in next. He recounted a great family vacation and mentioned Sue and the sales team as bests.

"What's working is this team," Vic continued. "In one of these sessions, Alan, you said someday we'd absolutely *love* looking into the eyes of everyone around this table—that we'd be confident going into battle with every single member of our leadership team. For the first time, I really feel that way as we sit here today. What's not working is that we need at least one more leader on this team so my partner doesn't *ever* have to miss her kids' baseball games. My expectations are your objectives—to get clear again on our vision, get a solid plan for the quarter, and solve key issues."

"Thank you, Vic," said Alan. "Tom?"

"Thanks, Alan," Tom replied. "My personal and professional bests are the same—being at Swan. I'm so grateful for the opportunity to help this company grow. What's working, as far as I can see after a month, is the clear vision. I also really like the Level 10 Meetings, and that's a remarkable thing to say because I've absolutely *hated* meetings for most of my career! I couldn't even get my previous employer to meet regularly. The only time we ever came together was when a crisis had occurred. What I love about Swan's meetings is that we spend the time solving issues before they turn into crises—sort of heading the train wrecks off at the pass. The other thing I wrote down as working is the way Swan communicated with me during the hiring process. Before I was even offered the job, I had a crystal-clear sense of where the company is going, how it planned to get there, and exactly what my role would be in making it happen. And the

Core Values—well, when Eileen offered me the job, it almost seemed like she was trying to scare me away. She made it painfully clear that if I wasn't a perfect fit for this culture, there's no way I'd be successful here. And I could tell she meant it!"

"That's great stuff, Tom," Alan replied, smiling. "Anything not working?"

"Well, it's early," Tom responded, "but I don't think we're tracking time properly. I also put down 'operations team meetings,' 'invoicing,' and 'estimating.' My expectations are to learn a little more about this process and get a clear plan for the next ninety days and the rest of the year."

Alan thanked Tom and the rest of the team and shared his own bests. He then reminded the team of his expectations for each session.

"As always," he explained, "I expect you to be open and honest. Be open-minded to what other members of the team have to say. You don't always have to agree, but you do need to consider other points of view. And be honest. If there's something you need to say, just say it. Until we get all your issues out of your heads and onto the table, we can't solve them."

With the check-in complete, Alan asked Eileen to distribute copies of the Rock Sheet (see page 207) to each leader and led the team through a Rock review. Beginning with Sue, Alan read through each Rock in its entirety.

"You completed 63 percent of your Rocks this quarter," recapped Alan. "Remember, we're shooting for an 80 percent completion rate, and I'm hoping what you learned this quarter will make you expert Rock setters later today. So what did you learn?"

"Less is more," replied Sue immediately. "I got three company Rocks done, and that was *a lot*. It was silly to sign up for a fourth and fifth."

"What else did you learn?" Alan asked. "Vic?"

"I have to get started earlier in the quarter," replied Vic. "Especially on any Rocks where I have to do research and formulate a plan. Plus, I need to remember that I'm accountable for helping with sales and managing my own accounts."

"Great stuff," replied Alan. "Eileen, what was the key to getting 100 percent of your Rocks done? You certainly had plenty of distractions this quarter!"

Swan Services Quarterly Rock Sheet

Future Date: June 24, 20XX
Revenue: $3.5 million
Profit: 5%
Measurables: 8 projects @ $100K +

COMPANY ROCKS

	WHO	
1) Focus sales & marketing on target market	Sue	Done
2) Sales rep RPRS (Natalie or hire new)	Sue	Done
3) Close three "A" deals	Sue	Done
4) Roll out EOS foundational tools	Eileen	Done
5) Fill ops leader seat	Eileen	Done
6) Implement project management software	Evan	Done
7)		

SUE

1) Focus sales & marketing on target market	Done
2) Sales rep RPRS (Natalie or hire new)	Done
3) Close three "A" deals	Done
4) Complete account plans for twenty clients	ND
5) Publish proven process	ND
6)	
7)	

EVAN (Tom)

1) Implement project management software	Done
2) Implement error-tracking system	ND
3) Document project management process	ND
4)	
5)	
6)	
7)	

EILEEN

1) Roll out EOS foundational tools	Done
2) Fill ops leader seat	Done
3) Renew credit lines	Done
4)	
5)	
6)	
7)	

VIC

1) Create a "key relationship" list and a plan to strengthen them	Done
2) Create an industry event plan for next year	ND
3)	
4)	
5)	
6)	
7)	

CAROL (Eileen)

1) Draft 20XX capital expenditure budget	Done
2) Eliminate time-card errors	ND
3) Produce monthly income statements within two weeks	Done
4)	
5)	
6)	
7)	

"Well, I got started early, stayed on task, and got plenty of help from the team," Eileen replied. "It wasn't easy."

"Next we'll review your financial metrics and key measurable," Alan continued after the Rocks discussion concluded. "With six days left in the quarter, are you on track to hit your numbers for Q2?"

"With Carol gone we're not quite as up-to-date with billing," Eileen admitted. "But I'd say we'll fall a little short of the revenue goal and hit our other two numbers."

"Can you get the revenue number back on track before year-end?" Alan asked.

"You bet," replied Sue. "I wasn't very confident until we booked the third 'A' deal this quarter as part of my Rock. That helped a lot, and the sales pipeline also looks promising. So right now I really feel like we're right on pace to hit the annual numbers."

"Terrific," Alan replied. "So all things considered, how would each of you grade this last ninety days? How'd this team do running the organization? Share a letter grade for the quarter."

"A plus," said Vic right away. "This was an *awesome* ninety days. We dealt with two difficult people issues. We're humming along in sales. We've gotten our numbers back on track. Tom's a great find, and Evan's done a terrific job of helping with the transition. We may have completed only 63 percent of our Rocks, but we're getting much better at predicting and prioritizing. So A plus."

"Thank you, Vic," replied Alan.

The others weren't as enthusiastic, with Sue giving a B and Eileen a B minus, but all agreed that measurable progress had been made.

After a short break, Alan asked Eileen to distribute completed copies of the V/TO.

"The next agenda item," Alan continued, "is reviewing the V/TO one section at a time. We need to make sure we're 100 percent on the same page with where you're going and how you plan to get there."

CORE VALUES	1. Be humbly confident
	2. Grow or die
	3. Help first
	4. Do the right thing
	5. Do what you say

Alan then read each of the Core Values and asked the team to provide yes or no answers to two questions: "Are these Swan Services' Core Values?" and "Are you using them to hire, fire, review, reward, and recognize people?"

The leaders quickly provided yes answers to the first question, and several also answered yes to the second question. Vic paused before he responded.

"I think we're using them to hire people," he said carefully, "as Tom confirmed in his check-in. But I *don't* think we're communicating consistently enough with our existing staff. We're supposed to repeat ourselves often, and I've personally only given the speech once, at our rollout meeting. I've used pieces of it here and there—in the sales Level 10 Meeting and once or twice with an employee. But I can get better, and I'm guessing the rest of this group could, too."

"You're absolutely right," replied Eileen immediately. Sue and Tom also nodded.

"This sounds like an issue," observed Alan, adding it to the list as the leaders nodded in agreement.

"One last question as we review the Core Values," Alan continued. "Are there any new people issues for your Issues List? At this point in the process, we need to name names."

A little surprised, each of the leaders had to think about people. Sue and Eileen instinctively reached for their Accountability Charts.

"Debbie," said Sue after a moment of reflection. "The account manager."

"You don't think she shares the Core Values?" asked Tom, a little defensively.

"Not sure," replied Sue. "Could be Core Values; could be GWC. I just think there's something not quite right. The sales reps worry a bit when she's assigned to their accounts."

"That seems a little harsh," Tom replied. "Are you sure the problem doesn't lie with your reps?"

Sue began to reply reflexively but caught herself. "No, I'm not," she replied calmly. "It may very well be my people, and if you feel any of them is a problem that isn't already up there, let's put them on the Issues List."

"I sure wish you'd have shared this with me before today," Tom said to Sue, frustrated at how she'd called out one of his employees. He had always dealt with people issues behind closed doors—and certainly not with the company owners looking on!

"I'm sorry, Tom," replied Sue sincerely. "I didn't mention Debbie before because it never dawned on me that she might be a wrong person or in the wrong seat until just now. She might be above the bar; I just think it's worth a closer look. Isn't that the way it works, Alan?"

He agreed and helped Tom understand.

"Every quarter there's going to be at least one people issue," Alan explained. "In this environment they just hit you, and the right way to resolve those issues is to get them on the list and IDS them later in the day."

Tom apologized for getting defensive, and the exercise continued. The team identified five people issues that were added to the list and concluded the Core Values discussion. Alan then moved on to review Swan's Core Focus, which the leaders quickly agreed had been accurately defined.

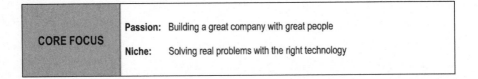

| CORE FOCUS | **Passion:** Building a great company with great people |
| | **Niche:** Solving real problems with the right technology |

"With agreement on your Core Focus," Alan explained, "the next step is making sure all of Swan's people, processes, and systems are aligned to drive the Core Focus with absolute consistency. Are you using your Core Focus as a filter? Is it helping you stay focused? Are you using it to distinguish between opportunities within your sweet spot and shiny stuff?"

A few members of the team nodded, but Tom shifted uncomfortably in his chair and glanced nervously around the room. Alan and Eileen picked up on that right away.

"Open and honest, Tom," Eileen prompted him, beating Alan to the punch.

"Well," Tom responded carefully, "I can see there's a question of whether staff augmentation falls within the Core Focus on the Issues

List already, so I'm not sure if this needs to be brought up. But I have some question as to whether we're still actively selling staff-aug work and other stuff that doesn't fit. Are we selling *only* projects that let us solve real problems with the right technology, or are we bidding on anything we can get our hands on?"

"What deals do you mean, Tom?" asked Sue. It was her turn to get defensive.

"Just a couple of them, Sue," Tom clarified. "The Century Bank proposal Evan worked on with Troy comes to mind. And Natalie wanted to propose some outdated technology for Argosy Industries because she'd been told that's what it would take to get the deal. Remember, you and I talked about that?"

"Yes," she agreed, "but we dealt with that. I think we're being pretty good about staying within our Core Focus."

"Pretty good?" Eileen asked.

"Well, yeah," Sue replied. "I mean, we're all out there fighting hard to uncover every opportunity we can. We've got very aggressive goals, and the team is under a tremendous amount of pressure. I actually like the fact that the team's pushing the envelope and trying everything they can to win more business."

"Me, too," said Vic. "Our problem is *not* a sales team that's too aggressive!"

"I didn't say that," Tom replied, backing off. "Alan asked if we were using the Core Focus as a filter. Eileen asked me to be open and honest, so I answered his question based on my observations over the last few weeks. I certainly didn't mean to ruffle any feathers, but I do think it's an issue."

Alan recorded "Selling outside the Core Focus" on the Issues List, and the Core Focus discussion drew to a close. He then moved to a quick review of the 10-Year Target, with the team quickly confirming its commitment to achieving that long-range, energizing goal.

10-YEAR TARGET	$40 million in revenue with 15% net profit

"Frankly," explained Tom as the discussion concluded, "this is why I'm here. We were standing still at Sensi-Tech, and I'd always dreamed of being part of a team that's building something special. So when I saw Swan's vision, it really excited me. And when I look at the V/TO, that's what I look at first. It still fires me up every time I do it."

Eileen smiled broadly. In one comment, Tom had reminded her how fortunate Swan had been to find him *and* how useful the V/TO would be in clarifying Swan's vision for current and potential employees. After allowing Tom's comments to settle, Alan moved on to Marketing Strategy.

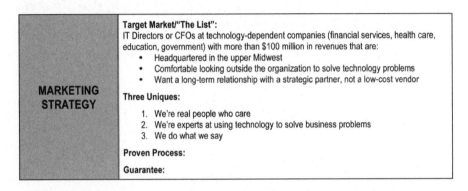

MARKETING STRATEGY

Target Market/"The List":
IT Directors or CFOs at technology-dependent companies (financial services, health care, education, government) with more than $100 million in revenues that are:
- Headquartered in the upper Midwest
- Comfortable looking outside the organization to solve technology problems
- Want a long-term relationship with a strategic partner, not a low-cost vendor

Three Uniques:
1. We're real people who care
2. We're experts at using technology to solve business problems
3. We do what we say

Proven Process:

Guarantee:

Alan began by reading the target market—a description of Swan's ideal prospects—exactly as it had been recorded on the V/TO. The team agreed that the demographic, geographic, and psychographic profiles were "right on."

"Have you compiled 'The List'?" asked Alan. "Have you passed the whole world of prospective clients through a filter and focused all your sales and marketing efforts on those prospects?"

"Yes," Sue replied. "That was my Rock. We're still working to qualify leads from that list. The companies we're calling on fit the demographic and geographic profile, but we have to ask them a few questions before we can tell whether they match our psychographic profile."

"If they don't, do you take them off the list?" asked Tom.

"Yes," Sue said. "We actually had a spirited debate about that in a sales department Level 10 Meeting. Frankly, most of us are so thrilled when someone actually answers the phone or returns our call that we have a hard time taking them off the list. But in the end the team agreed that five pleasant conversations with prospects who will never become clients is a less effective use of time than connecting with one prospect who *will* buy from us someday. That focus has really started paying dividends."

"Have you baked those questions into your sales process?" asked Alan.

"We've started to," replied Sue. "But the sales process won't be completed and fully implemented until this quarter."

With the team completely committed to the target market, Alan directed its attention to the three uniques.

He read them and asked, "Do these three uniques, when taken together, clearly explain why you're different and better than your competition?"

"Yes," Vic replied immediately. "I've started using them faithfully in the sales pitch to answer the 'Why Swan?' question."

"And how's that working?" asked Alan.

"Really well," Vic said, smiling. "To test them last quarter, Sue and I went out and asked our three best clients what they liked most about working with us. Almost unanimously, they agreed with these three things. It was great validation, and it made Sue's reps feel better about using them as well."

"That's a great exercise," Alan replied. "I actually prescribe that approach when my other clients are struggling with their three uniques."

"Even after talking to our best clients," Vic continued, "using the same three points every time hasn't been easy for me. I'm much more comfortable making stuff up as I go along. But I've found that describing our differentiators in the same clear and concise way has made my sales pitch much shorter and much better."

"Shorter?" asked Tom.

"Yeah," Vic explained. "I used to ramble on for ten minutes, touching on key points here and there, talking about our culture, expertise, reliability, responsiveness—basically whatever I thought was going to appeal to the prospect."

"It was actually closer to thirty minutes," joked Sue. Vic laughed out loud, and the team joined in.

"In all seriousness," said Sue, "the three uniques aren't yet the common thread throughout all our sales and marketing efforts, as you recommended last session. The sales team is using them consistently, and we're putting them in our *new* marketing materials, but our old collateral and website still need to be changed. So it's an issue."

Alan added "Using Three Uniques as Common Thread?" to the Issues List. With that, he directed the team's attention to the third part of Marketing Strategy, the proven process.

"Sue, publishing the proven process was one of the Rocks you didn't get done last quarter, right?" Alan asked.

"Right," admitted Sue. "I made some progress and plan to make it a Q3 Rock."

"And the guarantee?" asked Alan about the fourth part of the Marketing Strategy.

"That's on the Issues List—it's not the highest priority right now," Sue answered.

After making sure the team was on the same page with the Marketing Strategy, Alan moved on. "At this point, we now know who we are with our Core Values, what we are with the Core Focus, where we're going with the 10-Year Target, and how we're going to get there with our Marketing Strategy," he summarized. "We now move forward to paint a clear picture of what Swan Services is going to look like in three short years."

3-YEAR PICTURE

Future Date: December 31, 20XX
Revenue: $11 million
Profit: 10%
Measurables: 50 projects @ $100K+

What Does It Look Like?

- 60 RPRS
- Thriving culture
- Strong sales team of 8 people
- New sales office in 1 or more major markets
- New company HQ
- Internal IT seat RPRS
- HR seat RPRS
- Developer/BA/PM recruiting process working
- 40% recurring revenues

Alan started by reviewing the numbers with the team, giving everyone the chance to agree that the goals for revenue, profit, and the key measurable were realistic. The team quickly renewed its commitment to those numbers.

"Now, as I read through all the specific goals one at a time," Alan explained, "listen for anything you have a question about or think is an issue. We'll come back and discuss them after I've read the entire list. So here's what you said the company looks like in three years: It's December 31. You just did $11 million in revenues with a 10 percent profit. You booked fifty projects worth at least $100,000. You have sixty right people in the right seats; a thriving culture; a strong, eight-person sales team; and a new sales office in one or more major markets. You're in a new company headquarters. Your IT and HR seats are filled, your recruiting process is working, and 40 percent of your revenues are recurring. Is everyone still seeing this as your 3-Year Picture? Are each of you still committed to creating that organization over the next two and a half years?"

"Yes!" Vic replied enthusiastically, followed by resounding affirmative responses from the other leaders.

"Good," Alan responded, "because you're the team that has to make it happen."

With everyone committed to achieving the same vision, Alan turned to the traction page of Swan's V/TO, and the rest of the team followed suit.

"We can now bring your vision down to the ground to focus on what really matters," he explained. "Our plan for the remainder of this year." (See 1-Year Plan on page 216.)

One by one, Alan walked the team through the revenue, profit, and key measurable targets the team had created in its last session. In each case, the leaders agreed that the number was still accurate, doable, and on track. Then he moved on to the one-year planning goals, reading each exactly as it was written and asking three questions: "Is this still a goal?" "Is it crystal clear?" and "Is it on track?"

In nearly every case, one or more leaders had a question about the goal before agreeing that it was crystal clear. The team concluded that "Core Processes documented, simplified and FBA" was off track.

1-YEAR PLAN
Future Date: December 31, 20XX
Revenue: $7.25 million
Profit: 5%
Measurables: 20 projects @ $100K+

Goals for the Year:

1.	Implement EOS
2.	Sales team RPRS
3.	Implement marketing strategy
4.	Hire ops leader RPRS
5.	Core Processes documented, simplified and followed by all
6.	
7.	

"Can you get the goal back on track with some concerted effort between now and the end of the year?" asked Alan.

"I think so," replied Eileen, who had raised the issue. "I'd hoped to have more done by now, but with Tom coming on board and Carol's exit, it just hasn't happened."

"Okay, let's capture that as an issue so we're all reminded that we may need to take action this quarter to get it back on track," Alan replied, recording "Core Process Goal Off Track" on the Issues List. "Now that you're 100 percent on the same page with your 1-Year Plan, that should lead and guide all of our Rock setting, decision making, and issues solving for the rest of the day. We've already reviewed your Rocks, so the last thing that requires attention is your Issues List."

Alan motioned toward the whiteboard. "I've recorded these carry-over issues from your last session on the board," he continued. (See V/TO Issues List on page 217.) "But let's take a quick minute to clean them up. I'll read each issue one at a time. If you've solved it in the last ninety days or it's gone away for any reason, just say, 'off,' and I'll erase it. 'On' means it's still an issue, and I'll leave it on the list."

ISSUES LIST	
1.	Billing accuracy
2.	Scorecards and measurables for all
3.	Sue – enough time?
4.	Guarantee?
5.	Define HR seat
6.	Define IT seat
7.	Next gen technology
8.	
9.	
10.	
11.	
12.	

Alan worked through the list quickly, cleaning up several issues along the way.

"With our review of your V/TO done," Alan explained, "it's time to build today's Issues List. Please take five quiet minutes to record all your obstacles, frustrations, ideas, questions, and unrealized opportunities—just get it out of your heads and onto the page. Clear your mind."

While the team thought and wrote down additional issues, Alan added a handful of new issues from the check-in and V/TO review that hadn't already been added to the list on the whiteboard.

Sue volunteered to start, and Alan moved around the table until the Issues List was complete. There were a total of thirty-two issues for the Quarterly Session:

MEASURE UTILIZATION

STAFF AUG IN CORE FOCUS?

NATALIE RPRS

OPS SCORECARD NUMBERS

BILLING ACCURACY

CAROL'S EXIT—EILEEN IN 2 SEATS

RAJ—RPRS

BILL—RPRS

KELLY—RPRS

JENNIFER—RPRS

DEBBIE(AM)—RPRS

VISION SHARED BY ALL

COMMUNICATING CORE VALUES

CORE PROCESS GOAL OFF TRACK

SCORECARDS & MEASURABLES FOR ALL

HOLIDAY PARTY

TRAVEL EXPENSES

SELLING OUTSIDE THE CORE FOCUS

SUE—ENOUGH TIME?

SALES PROCESS

USING 3 UNIQUES AS COMMON THREAD?

PUBLISH PROVEN PROCESS

GUARANTEE?

ART/FIRM—RPRS

PROJECT MANAGEMENT PROCESS

SALES-TO-OPS HANDOFF

ESTIMATING PROCESS

DEFINE HR SEAT

DEFINE IT SEAT

CLIENT SATISFACTION

UPGRADING HARDWARE

NEXT GEN TECHNOLOGY

"Let's take a quick break," Alan said when the list was complete. "When we return, we'll do one of the toughest things you'll ever do in this process: set these issues aside for a while. We've got some bigger fish to fry right now. But remember, ultimately our goal is to solve all the key issues before you leave today."

QUARTERLY ROCKS

"With your vision clear and Issues List complete," Alan said after the break, "it's time to set Q3 Rocks. Look at your 1-Year Plan and your Issues List, and compile a list of the three to seven essential priorities you think the *company* needs to accomplish in the next ninety days. Company Rocks first, individual Rocks second."

After each leader had recorded his or her list, Alan moved left around the conference table, recording thirteen potential company Rocks as he went:

DOCUMENT SALES PROCESS
PUBLISH PROVEN PROCESS
GUARANTEE?
SALES TEAM: RPRS
HIRE CFO
MEASURE UTILIZATION
MEASURE CLIENT SATISFACTION
DOCUMENT PROJECT MANAGEMENT PROCESS
OPS DEPARTMENT: RPRS
SALES-TO-OPS HANDOFF
ESTIMATING PROCESS
SCORECARDS & MEASURABLES FOR ALL
EVENT PLAN FOR NEXT YEAR

After three passes of Keep, Kill, and Combine to prioritize potential Rocks, the team settled on the following list:

DOCUMENT SALES PROCESS
PUBLISH PROVEN PROCESS
HIRE CFO
MEASURE UTILIZATION/CLIENT SATISFACTION
DOCUMENT PROJECT MANAGEMENT PROCESS

Stepping to a section of the whiteboard he had prepared for Swan's Q3 Rock Sheet, Alan then helped the team determine the future date for these goals by scheduling its next Quarterly Session. He tasked Eileen to predict the Q3 goals for revenue, profit, and measurables. Then, one at a time, he helped the team write SMART Rocks, resulting in the following summary:

Q3 ROCKS:

FUTURE DATE: 9/28/XX
REVENUE: $5.25 M
PROFIT: 5%
MEASURABLE: 13 PROJECTS @ $100K+

1. DOCUMENT AND IMPLEMENT SALES PROCESS		SUE
2. DEFINE AND PUBLISH SWAN'S PROVEN PROCESS		SUE
3. HIRE CFO (RPRS)		EILEEN
4. COMPLETE OPS DEPARTMENT SCORECARD (W/UTILIZATION AND CLIENT SATISFACTION)		TOM
5. REFINE AND IMPLEMENT PROJECT MANAGEMENT PROCESS		TOM

The process of prioritizing and writing Rocks involved several interesting discussions. Sue lobbied hard to get Swan's guarantee on the company Rock Sheet, but Eileen felt strongly that a decision about guarantees would best be made after Swan had found its new CFO. Tom argued for "getting a handle on the operations department" as a critical company priority this quarter. He wanted to keep everything on the list, but Alan and the team helped him settle on a few key priorities.

The most interesting discussion occurred during the writing of Eileen's CFO hiring Rock. She'd suggested "Hire CFO (RPRS)," just as she had written the ops leader Rock last quarter.

"Do you really think you can hire the ideal CFO in three months?" Vic challenged. "What if we can't find the right person?"

"Great question, Vic," Alan offered. "Leadership team hires often take my other clients more than one quarter. It's hit or miss: sometimes you find a great fit like Tom in your network; other times you search high and low and still can't find the right person for a while— at times for an entire year. Keep that in mind as you write this Rock."

A brief debate ensued. On the one hand, Eileen and Swan really *needed* a new CFO in the next ninety days. She intended to get this Rock done, but she knew that finding the right person might be difficult. Maybe she should take the safe route and write the Rock in such a way that it might still be "done" if she conducted a thorough search and remained unable to fill the seat.

"The fact is we need a new CFO by September 28," she concluded. "It won't be easy, but I intend to do everything in my power to make it happen. I promise I won't hire the wrong person just to hit the Rock, and I'll accept the accountability if it doesn't get done. But writing a complex Rock just to feel better if I fail is not the answer."

Alan recorded the Rock just as Eileen suggested. The team took a break and settled in for a working lunch. With company Rocks set and Eileen capturing them for the Rock Sheet, Alan then focused the team on individual Rocks.

"Looking at the remaining items," he began, pointing to the list of potential Rocks and issues on the whiteboard, "take five quiet minutes to think about the most important things you must get done this quarter. Those three to seven priorities—hopefully closer to three—are your individual Rocks. Be sure to write them SMART."

When everyone was done, Alan invited the brave one to read his or her entire list to the team. He asked the leaders to listen carefully and provide feedback on two points—whether they were the "right Rocks" and whether they were written SMART. Tom volunteered.

"Thank you, Tom," said Alan. "We have your two company Rocks on the board; just read your additional individual Rocks."

"I wrote down 'fix sales-to-ops handoff,'" he said. "And 'document estimating process.' That's all I have time for now."

"Okay, Tom," Alan said. "Eileen, Vic, Sue, in addition to Tom's two company Rocks, are those two individual Rocks a good use of Tom's time this quarter?"

"Yes," Sue replied immediately, "*if* you can get all that done. If it were me, I'd concentrate on getting the company Rocks done well and save the other two for Q4."

"I was going to say the same thing," replied Vic. "We all learned the hard way, Tom—less is more. Remember, leading the ops department day to day can be a handful without setting aside any time to complete Rocks."

Tom seemed to consider the feedback. He thought about his first month at Swan, filled with ten-hour days and weekend trips to the office. Yet he hadn't even had a Rock last quarter. He looked at Eileen, but she just looked back at him as if she trusted that he'd make the right decision.

"Okay," he said. "I'll take your advice and scratch the 'estimating process.' But I'd like to keep the other one."

"In that case," replied Eileen, "try to write that a little more clearly. It's not really SMART; I'm not sure what you intend to get done in order to fix the handoff."

"I see," Tom replied. "Well, the handoff happens when the sales-person steps away and the ops team—usually an account manager and project manager—takes over day-to-day responsibility for the relationship. That's where things fall through the cracks."

"Hmm," said Sue, thinking out loud. "Say I'm documenting the sales process this quarter and you're documenting the project management process. What if you added 'document account management process' as your individual Rock? That way we can work together on all of them to ensure that no balls get dropped during the transition. Wouldn't that fix what's broken?"

"Yes," Tom replied, beginning to understand the value of writing Rocks well. "I think it would."

Tom scratched out his original individual Rocks and wrote down the new one.

"Any individual Rocks, Sue?" asked Alan.

"Close three 'A' deals," she said. "And for the record, Vic, I'm counting on you for at least one of those."

"Say, Alan," Tom said. "That brings up a question. Is it okay to have something like that as a Rock even if it's part of someone's job? No offense, Sue, but I thought we were counting on you and your team to close three or more 'A' deals *every* quarter. If you don't, we'll never hit our revenue goals or our 'A' client measurable. Right?"

"That's a good question, Tom," replied Alan. "The simplest way to answer it is to ask yourselves if it's one of the three to seven most important things the company or the person needs to get done this quarter. If it is, it's a Rock, regardless of whether it happens to be his or her role."

"I see," Sue replied, a little taken aback by Tom challenging her Rock. She'd forgotten that he had a tendency to be very direct. "It's definitely a priority, so I'd like to leave it as a Rock. Some day winning that many deals may seem routine enough that I don't feel that way, but for now I think it helps keep me focused. I trust that's okay with you, Tom?"

Sue's sarcasm wasn't lost on Tom or on the rest of the team. There was definitely some tension developing between the two talented leaders.

"Okay by me," Tom said innocently. "I'm just trying to understand how this system works."

Eileen said, "Does it make sense to add an 'A' deal measurable to our Scorecard? Wouldn't that help keep you focused on that number each week?"

"Great idea," replied Sue. "I could report the number of 'A' deals in the pipeline each week."

"I'll add '"A" deal Scorecard measure' to your Issues List," replied Alan. "We'll IDS that this afternoon. Any more individual Rocks?"

"I also wrote 'resolve Natalie RPRS question' as an individual Rock. She's gotten herself back above the bar but just barely. By the end of next quarter, I want to either feel she's a great fit or replace her."

Alan nodded, got positive feedback for Sue's Rocks from the team, and moved on to Eileen.

"Meet with three more 'A' clients, and that's it," Eileen said flatly. "With two seats on the leadership team, I have all I can handle."

"Vic?" Alan prompted after the team offered support for Eileen's Rock.

"Develop an industry event plan for next year," Vic read from his list. "It's a carryover Rock from last quarter."

"Anything else?" Alan asked.

"Well, I plan to help Sue with the sales process," he explained. "Is that an individual Rock for me?"

"I'd recommend you not double-count Rocks," Alan replied. "Remember, only one person can drive a Rock, and in this case, that's Sue. If she needs your help, you need to set aside time for that, and she needs to know she can count on you. She won't let you forget. But don't write the same Rock twice—it just leads to complexity and confusion."

Alan invited feedback for Vic's Rock.

"I have a Rock I'd like you to own this quarter," suggested Eileen.

"Are you *integrating* me?" asked Vic, smiling.

"Yes, I am," Eileen replied without missing a beat. "Assuming you're willing to be integrated, I'd like to see you come up with a plan to get our vision shared by all. I think it'll kill two items on the Issues List—'vision shared by all' and 'communicating Core Values.' Make sense?"

"Love it," Vic replied. "I'll write down 'develop and implement plan to get the vision shared by all.'"

"Perfect," replied Eileen.

With the Rock-setting exercise complete, Eileen asked each leader to email his or her individual Rocks to her by Friday, as she planned to complete the Q3 Rock Sheet before the next Level 10 Meeting. Before moving on, Alan had one last order of business—cleaning up the potential Rocks and issues from the whiteboard.

He went through the potential Rocks, erasing everything that had been taken as or combined into a company or individual Rock for the quarter. That left "estimating process" and "Scorecards and measurables for all" as issues. Finally, Alan cleaned up the Issues List, killing anything that had been resolved or would be solved when the Q3 Rocks were completed. The following issues remained:

STAFF AUG IN CORE FOCUS?	SELLING OUTSIDE THE CORE FOCUS
BILLING ACCURACY	MEASURING "A" DEALS
RAJ-RPRS	SUE- ENOUGH TIME?
BILL- RPRS	GUARANTEE?
KELLY-RPRS	ART/FIRM - RPRS
JENNIFER-RPRS	USING 3 UNIQUES AS COMMON THREAD?
DEBBIE(AM)-RPRS	ESTIMATING PROCESS
CORE PROCESS GOAL OFF TRACK	DEFINE HR SEAT
SCORECARDS & MEASURABLES FOR ALL	DEFINE IT SEAT
HOLIDAY PARTY	UPGRADING HARDWARE
TRAVEL EXPENSES	NEXT GEN TECHNOLOGY

"We now have almost four full hours to solve all your key issues," Alan said. "This is the moment I've been waiting for—to see you in your natural habitat of solving issues."

The leaders chuckled and took a quick break, looking forward to their first quarterly issues-solving session. Eileen was eager to watch Alan facilitate IDS. She felt sure the experience would make her better during the Level 10 Meetings. And with Sue and Tom holding departmental Level 10s, she believed it would be good for them as well.

Tom's head was swimming. In one day with Alan and the rest of the Swan team, he'd already spent more time working on the business than in his last year at Sensi-Tech. He began to understand why he had always felt stuck at his old company and why this team seemed to constantly be running in high gear. Furthermore, he was amazed by how comfortable and open the meeting had seemed. There were no sacred cows, no awkward silences—just a group of capable people who liked one another working through challenges together and building something great.

RESOLUTION

The session resumed at one thirty. Armed with a red marker, Alan directed the team's attention to the Issues List and read each item.

"As always," he explained, "the first step to IDS is prioritizing. Let's pick the one, two, and three most important issues on this list."

"Core Process goal off track," said Eileen. Alan recorded a "#1" next to that issue and waited. A few seconds passed.

"Does anyone have a number-two priority?" Alan asked. "Somebody just take a shot over the bow—this shouldn't ever take more than thirty seconds."

"Selling outside the Core Focus?" Vic suggested.

"Measuring 'A' deals," Sue added quickly.

Alan quickly recorded a "#2" next to Vic's issue and a "#3" next to Sue's.

"Issue number one," said Alan, "Core Process goal off track. Eileen, you suggested this as a top priority; what's the issue?"

"Well, we have a couple of Core Process Rocks this quarter already," she explained, "so I'm wondering if it's still an issue or if we ought to do something else this quarter to get that one-year planning goal back on track."

"Got it. Thanks, Eileen," replied Alan. "Does everyone agree that's the issue?"

The other leaders nodded.

"Great," Alan said. "You may recall there's a tool for documenting Core Processes—the Three-Step Process Documenter. I think the best way to resolve the issue is for me to clearly explain the tool so you know what work lies ahead before you can call that goal 'done' at year-end. Okay?"

Alan began writing on a clean section of whiteboard as he continued.

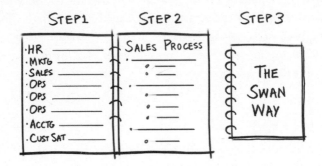

"Step one in the Three-Step Process Documenter is simply getting you all on the same page with what your handful of Core Processes are and with what they're called. Step two is documenting each process at a high level. In one to ten pages—ideally closer to one—you simply identify the *major* steps in the process. This approach documents the 20 percent that gets you 80 percent of the results. We describe the major steps in some detail with a couple of bullet points. This becomes more of a high-level training guide than a detailed SOP manual. It ensures you all agree on how the process should work and the way you want everyone to do it. You'll also discover redundancy and complexity that you can eliminate and simplify. Once your Core Processes are documented, step three is compiling them and placing them in a manual or on a shared drive. This becomes your unique business model—the Swan Services way of doing business. When that's done you can begin training all employees in each process, developing Scorecard numbers and individual measurables around them and ultimately ensuring they're being followed by all."

"I'm really glad I prioritized this," Eileen said, "because we've started in on step two without really having accomplished step one."

"Exactly," agreed Alan, smiling. "You have to understand and agree on the big picture before you start documenting a bunch of processes and procedures. The good news is we can get that done right now."

"Let's do it," replied Eileen. The rest of the team agreed.

"Your Core Processes are the handful of processes that make this business run," Alan reminded the team. "For example, every business has an HR process, a marketing process, a sales process, and one or more operating processes for how you build your products, deliver your services, and take care of your customers. Every company has an accounting process, and many have a customer retention process for how they measure and maintain customer happiness. Those are the kind of big, high-level processes we're looking for here. Take a few moments to make a list of Swan Services' Core Processes."

Once the team had completed this task, he went around the table collecting on the whiteboard the potential Core Processes from every leader, which resulted in the following list:

HR PROCESS
MARKETING PROCESS
SALES PROCESS
ESTIMATING PROCESS
ACCOUNT MANAGEMENT PROCESS
PROJECT MANAGEMENT PROCESS
BUSINESS ANALYSIS PROCESS
DEVELOPMENT PROCESS
PROJECT FULFILLMENT PROCESS
TIME REPORTING PROCESS
BILLING PROCESS
ACCOUNTING PROCESS
PROJECT REVIEW PROCESS
CLIENT SATISFACTION PROCESS

Alan then facilitated some discussion and debate. He moved down the list one item at a time asking, "Is this definitely one of your Core Processes?" During the exercise, the leaders came to understand that many of the suggestions were actually major steps in a higher-level Core Process. Not surprisingly, much of the debate centered on the sales-ops handoff and the number and specificity of the operations processes. Soon the team arrived at a list that every leader felt defined the Swan Services way of operating:

HR PROCESS

MARKETING PROCESS

SALES PROCESS (INCLUDING ESTIMATING)

ACCOUNT MANAGEMENT PROCESS (INCLUDING CLIENT SATISFACTION)

PROJECT FULFILLMENT PROCESS (INCLUDING BA, PM, DEV'T AND PROJECT REVIEW)

ACCOUNTING PROCESS (INCLUDING TIME REPORTING AND BILLING PROCESSES)

"Terrific," Alan said. "Now, this may sound trivial, but it's important that you all begin referring to your Core Processes using these words. That discipline alone will save you and your team hundreds of hours a year in miscommunication. Using the same language as a leadership team is powerful. The work we just did also affects two of your Rocks this quarter. Tom, your project management process Rock just expanded considerably. We have to decide what to do about that. Are you going to document the entire project fulfillment process this quarter, postpone it for a quarter, or rewrite the Rock?"

After a brief discussion, Tom agreed to document the entire project fulfillment process, and Sue agreed to include a step or two in the sales process Rock to cover estimating. Eileen revised the company Rock, and Alan moved on to conclude step one of the Three-Step Process Documenter.

"After Sue and Tom complete their Rocks, you'll have four Core Processes yet to document this year. Would you like to add those to your Issues List, or will your one-year planning goal be the reminder you need to prioritize those next quarter?"

"I think the goal will be an ample reminder, though we have our work cut out for us," said Eileen.

"So do you all believe this issue has been solved?" Alan asked, preparing to erase "Core Process Goal Off Track" from the Issues List.

"Yes," replied the team in unison, smiling.

"Then let's move to issue number two," Alan replied. "Selling outside the Core Focus. Vic, what's the issue?"

"It's what Tom brought up earlier," Vic replied. "We're still selling staff augmentation even though we agree it's outside our Core Focus, and apparently we have some sales reps trying to sell other kinds of projects outside our sweet spot—stuff using outdated technology and that sort of thing."

Tom nodded to signal that Vic got it exactly right.

"So what are we trying to solve, exactly?" Alan asked. "Let's really dig down and identify the issue."

"We haven't clearly defined for the sales team what they can and can't sell," Vic replied. "So we're still selling outside the Core Focus as defined on the V/TO."

"Does everyone agree that's the issue?" Alan got agreement all around.

"Then let's discuss," he said and asked the leaders to find their V/TOs so they could have the Core Focus in clear view while IDSing.

| CORE FOCUS | **Passion:** Building a great company with great people |
| | **Niche:** Solving real problems with the right technology |

"When you talk about clear direction for the sales team," Alan continued, "what exactly do you mean?"

"As Tom said earlier, we seem to be selling or bidding outside the Core Focus in two ways," Sue explained. "The first is that we're actively selling staff-aug work, and the second is that sometimes we're bidding on projects that require us to use the wrong technology. Right, Tom?"

"That's right," Tom replied.

"The second one is easy," Sue explained. "We just shouldn't do it, period. I intend to bake that ground rule into the sales process this quarter."

"Perfect," Tom said. Eileen and Vic agreed.

"Staff aug is a little more difficult," Sue continued. "We have existing relationships that have come to know us as a source of technology talent for their own teams. Plus we have a reputation in the marketplace and have actively pitched that as an offering to prospects for years. And the theory has always been that staff-aug clients can be converted to 'A' clients for project work. So I'd like to propose an interim step."

"I'm all ears," Eileen said.

"I'm proposing we do staff augmentation only as an occasional value-add for 'A' clients who use us for work within our Core Focus. In the current draft of the sales process, there's a qualification step that helps us weed out any prospects primarily interested in staff aug. We've also developed a plan to connect with all current staff-aug clients in an effort to pitch our other services and convert them to 'A' clients."

"I like where you're going," replied Tom, "and forgive me for sounding like the classic ops guy, but I'd like to get more specific. Words like 'primarily' and 'occasional' scare me, especially when somebody from sales uses them."

Tom was smiling when he said it, but Vic and Sue both seemed surprised and a little offended by the statement.

"That's a little harsh," said Eileen, wincing, "don't you think?"

"I didn't mean anything by that," Tom rushed to explain. "Just a software developer trying to be funny and apparently failing miserably."

The team laughed, and the tension dissipated.

Alan then facilitated a discussion to bring more clarity to the sales process, and the team quickly came to the following conclusions:

- The sales team would never lead with staff-aug work and never mention it as one of Swan's services in a sales presentation.
- Staff-aug opportunities added to the sales pipeline would be limited to existing clients.
- Staff-aug proposals accounting for more than 30 percent of an existing client's annual spending would require leadership team approval.

"Have we solved the issue?" asked Alan. Vic, Eileen, and Tom nodded affirmatively, but Sue wasn't completely sure.

"Yes," she finally agreed. "I think we'll have to factor this change into next year's comp plan, but I don't think we need to address that today."

Alan added "Sales Comp Plan" to the Issues List and erased "Selling outside the Core Focus." He then moved on to issue number three.

"Measuring 'A' deals," Alan continued. "What's the issue, Sue?"

"What we discussed earlier when we were setting Rocks," Sue reminded the team. "I'd like to IDS adding one or more 'A' deal measurables to the leadership team and/or sales department Scorecards."

After a quick IDS, Eileen took on a To-Do—add "A" deals in the pipeline to the leadership team Scorecard. Sue agreed to add the same number to the departmental Scorecard and to provide each member of the sales team with a quarterly goal for selling "A" deals. Alan erased the issue from the list and dismissed the team for a quick break.

"Let's prioritize the next top three issues," he said when the team returned.

"Kelly—right person, right seat," Tom said quickly.

The other leaders followed Tom's lead and shouted out priorities right away, with Vic suggesting "holiday party" as issue two and Sue making "travel expenses" issue three.

Alan moved to another section of the whiteboard and quickly began drawing a People Analyzer template.

"You know it's after four o'clock," warned Vic. "Are you sure we should tackle a people issue with less than an hour to IDS?"

"I think we can resolve it," replied Alan. "Please create a People Analyzer, just as I've drawn on the board. Fill in your Core Values and GWC across the top and Kelly's name in the left column."

	Be Humbly Confident	Grow or Die	Help First	Do The Right Thing	Do What You Say	G	W	C
KELLY	+/-	+/-	+	+/-	–	Y	Y	N
THE BAR	+	+	+	+/-	+/-	Y	Y	Y

Alan instructed the leaders to rate Kelly as a plus, plus/minus, or minus for each Core Value and give her a yes or no for "gets it," "wants it," and "has the capacity to do it." Everyone finished in less than two minutes. Alan then went around the room quickly, recording the average score in each column. The exercise clearly identified the people issue: Kelly was below the bar and thus a wrong person in the wrong seat.

The team briefly helped Tom understand exactly why and what that meant. Not only was she not consistently exhibiting Swan's Core Values; she also didn't GWC the seat. Tom volunteered to conduct a coaching conversation with Kelly, using the People Analyzer to illustrate the team's concerns. Eileen explained Swan's three-strike rule and offered to help Tom prepare for that strike one meeting.

Alan asked Sue to add Tom's To-Do to next week's Level 10 Meeting agenda. He then helped the team quickly resolve issues two and three using IDS.

"Okay," Alan continued when all three issues had been solved, "with fourteen minutes left before we move to next steps at 4:45, let's prioritize one more time."

Vic laughed and shook his head. He was beginning to believe they *could* IDS several more issues. The team quickly prioritized the top three and used IDS to resolve the first, "upgrading hardware," by agreeing to acquire one new server and two new laptops for members of Evan's development team.

When that issue had been solved, Alan glanced at his watch.

"We have fifteen minutes left in the day," he said to the team. "If you're ready to conclude at five o'clock as planned, we have to move on to next steps. If you'd like to keep solving issues, I'm game as long as you feel we're still doing good work."

Vic and Tom both looked as though they'd had plenty of issues solving for one day, so the team decided to stop "while we're ahead," as Vic described it. Alan grabbed a red marker and returned to the Issues List.

"There are twelve issues left," Alan stated after quickly counting the remaining items. "Can everyone live with that? Are you okay concluding without resolving them?"

"Yes," Eileen replied. "There's nothing on that list that we have to resolve today."

Sue nodded her approval.

"Very well," Alan responded. "The first next step is cleaning up your Issues List. We have to decide where each of these remaining issues belongs. So as I read down this list, I'd like you to say one of two things: 'V/TO' means it's a long-term issue that you don't want to deal with until your next Quarterly Session in September, at the earliest. 'Level 10' means it's a short-term issue you want or need to resolve this quarter."

BILLING ACCURACY	V/TO	GUARANTEE?	V/TO
BILL- RPRS	L10	ART/FIRM - RPRS	L10
JENNIFER–RPRS	L10	DEFINE HR SEAT	V/TO
DEBBIE(AM)–RPRS	L10	DEFINE IT SEAT	V/TO
SCORECARDS & MEASURABLES FOR ALL	V/TO	NEXT GEN TECHNOLOGY	V/TO
SUE- ENOUGH TIME?	V/TO		

"Cool!" exclaimed Vic. "I'll bet we erased about thirty issues during the course of the day today."

"Twenty-one," replied Eileen. "I was keeping track."

Once again the group had a good laugh, though the thought of solving that many key issues in a single day felt good to everyone.

Alan then ran through next steps for the team, assigning clear ownership and deadlines for all the work. He recapped the To-Dos from the day and asked Eileen to update the V/TO and create the new Rock Sheet. He also introduced a new communication tool to Swan's leadership team.

"One more next step I'd encourage you to begin taking this quarter," Alan suggested, "is something I call a 'State of the Company' message. It's a simple, powerful way to communicate clearly with your entire organization on a quarterly basis. If you want your vision to be shared by all, it's essential. Plus, you have to say it seven times to be heard for the first time. After each Quarterly Session, assemble the troops and use the V/TO and other tools to briefly explain where you've been, where you are, and where you're going. Look at the past, and take a few minutes to celebrate recent successes. Let 'em know how you did on your Rocks. Share the V/TO with them, and explain next quarter's Rocks. If there were any changes to the Accountability Chart, share that, too."

The leaders asked a few questions and supported the idea. Vic agreed to conduct Swan's first State of the Company meeting as part of his "vision shared by all" Rock and to make it part of the organization's Meeting Pulse going forward.

As always, Alan concluded the session with feedback, expectations, and ratings from the team. Everyone's expectations had been met, and the ratings were all tens, with one exception. Tom's rating was nine because he felt he had slowed things down a bit. Eileen closed the session by making a telling point.

"While I hate to cast stones at someone who isn't here to defend herself," she remarked, "the whole atmosphere in this room was different and better without Carol here. It just goes to show how much damage a wrong person can cause if you let the problem fester. I'll never, ever make that mistake again."

MOMENTUM

The following Tuesday morning at 9:00, Swan's leadership team assembled for its first Level 10 Meeting after the Quarterly. Eileen and Sue had updated the Rock Sheet, V/TO, and Accountability Chart (see EOS tools on pages 235–238) and had placed new copies of each around the table.

During the Rock review portion of the meeting, Eileen felt a twinge of guilt when describing the "hire CFO" Rock as on track. She had made little progress in the first week, and she needed every bit of the next twelve weeks to get that Rock done. She resolved to rectify that situation immediately and called Alan afterwards to find out how some of his other clients had filled leadership team seats quickly.

"There's no surefire way to guarantee success," he admitted. "Obviously, the first step is clearly defining the seat, as well as the skills, experiences, and attributes of the kind of person likely to be a great fit for that seat. Most of my clients will send that position description, including the Core Values and the five roles for the seat, to the people in their network. Include everyone who knows you inside and outside the organization. It doesn't work all the time, but it certainly can bear fruit."

"Of course," replied Eileen. "In fact, Tom came from Sue's network. I don't suppose we can find two needles in the same haystack, though."

"Perhaps not," Alan replied. "You may also want to consider using a reputable search firm, especially one that understands the

Swan Services Q3 20XX Rock Sheet

Future Date: September 28, 20XX
Revenue: $5.25 million
Profit: 5%
Measurables: 13 projects @ $100K +

COMPANY ROCKS

	WHO
1) Document and implement sales process	Sue
2) Define and publish Swan's proven process	Sue
3) Hire CFO RPRS	Eileen
4) Complete ops department scorecard (with utilization and client satisfaction)	Tom
5) Refine and implement project fulfillment process	Tom
6)	
7)	

SUE

1) Document and implement sales process	
2) Define and publish Swan's proven process	
3) Resolve Natalie RPRS	
4)	
5)	
6)	
7)	

TOM

1) Complete ops department scorecard (with utilization and client satisfaction)	1)
2) Refine and implement project fulfillment process	2)
3)	3)
4)	4)
5)	5)
6)	6)
7)	7)

EILEEN

1) Hire CFO RPRS	
2) Renew credit lines	
3)	
4)	
5)	
6)	
7)	

VIC

1) Create an industry event plan for next year	
2) Develop and implement plan to get vision shared by all	
3)	
4)	
5)	
6)	
7)	

THE VISION/TRACTION ORGANIZER

Swan Services – 20XX Q3

VISION

CORE VALUES	1. Be humbly confident 2. Grow or die 3. Help first 4. Do the right thing 5. Do what you say
CORE FOCUS	**Passion:** Building a great company with great people **Niche:** Solving real problems with the right technology
10-YEAR TARGET	$40 million in revenue with 15% net profit
MARKETING STRATEGY	**Target Market/"The List":** IT Directors or CFOs at technology-dependent companies (financial services, health care, education, government) with more than $100 million in revenues that are: • Headquartered in the upper Midwest • Comfortable looking outside the organization to solve technology problems • Want a long-term relationship with a strategic partner, not a low-cost vendor **Three Uniques:** 1. We're real people who care 2. We're experts at using technology to solve business problems 3. We do what we say **Proven Process:** **Guarantee:**

3-YEAR PICTURE

Future Date: December 31, 20XX
Revenue: $11 million
Profit: 10%
Measurables: 50 projects @ $100K+

What Does It Look Like?

• 60 RPRS
• Thriving culture
• Strong sales team of 8 people
• New sales office in 1 or more major markets
• New company HQ
• Internal IT seat RPRS
• HR seat RPRS
• Developer/BA/PM recruiting process working
• 40% recurring revenues

THE VISION/TRACTION ORGANIZER

Swan Services – 20XX Q3

TRACTION

1-YEAR PLAN	ROCKS	ISSUES LIST

1-YEAR PLAN

Future Date: December 31, 20XX
Revenue: $7.25 million
Profit: 5%
Measurables: 20 projects @ $100K+

Goals for the Year:

1. Implement EOS
2. Sales team RPRS
3. Implement marketing strategy
4. Hire ops leader RPRS
5. Core Processes documented, simplified and followed by all
6.
7.

ROCKS

Future Date: September 28, 20XX
Revenue: $5.25 million
Profit: 5%
Measurables: 13 projects @ $100K+

Rocks for the Quarter: — Who

1. Document & implement sales process — Sue
2. Define & publish Swan Services' proven process — Sue
3. Hire CFO RPRS — Eileen
4. Complete ops department scorecard (w/ utilization & client satisfaction) — Tom
5. Refine and implement project fulfillment process — Tom
6.
7.

ISSUES LIST

1. Billing accuracy
2. Scorecards and measurables for all
3. Sue – enough time?
4. Guarantee?
5. Define HR seat
6. Define IT seat
7. Next gen technology
8.
9.
10.
11.
12.

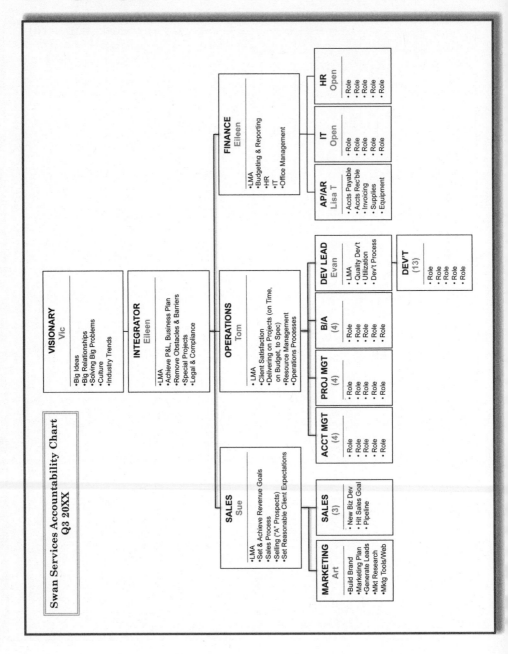

importance of culture fit as well as skills and experience. For a critical position like this, that investment can pay huge dividends. I've also seen some success from online job-posting services."

"I have a couple of reputable search firms in my network," Eileen replied. "I think one of them may specialize in financial professionals. Anything else?"

"Yes," Alan said. "I can't emphasize enough the importance of a solid HR process. The way you handled Tom's hiring was spot on. I think he mentioned you tried to scare him away with the Core Values speech. That alone will seriously reduce the likelihood that a wrong person will accept the job. If one or two slip through the cracks over the years, you'll feel better about exiting those people from the organization faster, because you made your expectations so clear. One of my clients has named that approach 'slow to hire, quick to fire,' and it really works. The only other thing that comes to mind is a technique many of my other clients swear by. When you get close and are down to a couple of top candidates, consider grabbing dinner with each of them or doing something social to get to know the real person. I'm guessing Vic would enjoy that and be really good at it."

"Thanks, Alan," Eileen replied. "That's very helpful."

Alan made it a point to check in with his leadership teams at the midpoint between sessions, so he sent a short message to the Swan Services team about five weeks later. Vic responded by calling him right away.

"I wonder if you can help me come up with some other ways to get our vision shared by all," he said a tad sheepishly. "I haven't made much progress on my Rock."

"Sure, Vic," Alan replied. "Perhaps we could meet to IDS the issue more thoroughly. Would you have time next Monday morning?"

Over coffee, Alan advised Vic that getting the vision shared by all would take time. He helped Vic identify four specific disciplines that would help Swan's leaders repeat themselves often.

"First," he said, "it's vital that you use the Core Values speech when hiring. The second discipline is conducting quarterly State of the Company meetings. The third is to incorporate the People Analyzer into Swan's performance review process. The fourth step I'd recommend is something you can implement right away. Make a point of catching at least one person each week exhibiting a Core Value. Tap that person on the shoulder immediately, and use the Core Values speech to recognize him or her. If you can do it in front of a large crowd, that's even better."

"I love it," replied Vic, genuinely fired up. "I'm kicking myself because I missed an opportunity to do just that last week."

"When you do it the first time," Alan continued, "share it in the Level 10 Meeting as a customer and employee headline. Make a habit of reporting this type of thing each week: Who'd you pat on the back? Are there any bad reports, new people issues? Do that yourself, and then urge the rest of the leadership team to do the same. Eventually this pattern of recognizing people each week will become part of Swan's DNA."

"Great idea, Alan," agreed Vic. "I've thought of doing that many times, but I've never made a habit of it. You know, I can really see how doing these four simple things will help everyone share the vision and build our culture. Best of all, this is exactly the kind of stuff I ought to be doing as visionary."

Just after Labor Day, Eileen called to tell Alan that she'd hired a new CFO—Jeff Chadwick—who was scheduled to start on the Monday before the team's next session.

"Great news, Eileen," Alan replied. "Will he be joining us on the 28th?"

"Well, that's why I was calling," she replied. "Tom did fine, but he was with us for a month before that first session. Do you think having Jeff there in his first week is too much too soon?"

"Not at all," Alan replied. "Whatever you decide is fine, but I'm a proponent of getting a new leader into the room with the whole team as early as possible. He'll learn more about the company in eight hours observing and working with the leadership team than he will in ninety days of working in the company. I've even had a few clients invite leaders to a Quarterly Session *before* their start dates, and that seems to work well. If you're going to scare him away, you might as well do it early."

"Is there any special prep work?" Eileen asked, laughing.

"Spend an hour walking through the foundational tools with him," Alan replied. "The V/TO, Accountability Chart, and Scorecard will be very meaningful. Also review the last few Level 10 Meeting agendas and your Rock Sheet."

"Will do," Eileen replied. "Thanks, Alan. I didn't plan to cut it this close, but I had to interview ten seemingly qualified candidates to find the perfect fit."

"Ten candidates!" Alan exclaimed. "You must not have had time for much more than that this quarter."

"Actually," Eileen replied, "I ended up hiring a retained search firm—Blue Water Group. Miguel had them fill his company's CFO seat. He convinced me the time I spent conducting this search my-self—and poorly by comparison—would easily pay the fee for finding the right person the first time. Even Vic agreed, and he's as skeptical about search firms as he is about consultants!"

Quarterly Pulsing

Three weeks later, the newest member of Swan's leadership team strode through the door. Alan quickly stood up and extended his hand.

"You must be Jeff Chadwick," he said. "Welcome. I'm Alan Roth."

"Thanks, Alan," Jeff replied, smiling and shaking Alan's hand.

"Sorry to be here so early," Jeff added, "but Vic made such a big deal about being on time that I allowed *way* too much time for traffic."

Alan laughed and clued Jeff in to the joke. As Jeff got comfortable, the others filtered in, and the session got started right at nine.

Despite the presence of a brand-new CFO, Swan's leadership team fell quickly into a routine during this second Quarterly Session. The check-in was largely upbeat: Sue reported that the sales team had been hitting its numbers and that she'd let Natalie go during the quarter. Tom had made some real headway in systemizing the operations department and at least identifying and beginning to correct the few people issues that remained. Vic had completed both his Rocks this quarter, and the entire team felt much better about the way the vision was being communicated.

Eileen was "way behind," but she felt hiring Jeff was a key move that would allow her to delegate and elevate. She was eager to focus all her attention on being Swan's integrator, something she'd been hoping to have happen for most of the last nine months. For his part, Jeff was thrilled to be a part of the team and impressed with the clarity and simplicity of the company's vision, plan, and structure.

"I've been here for less than a week," he explained, "and I already know more about where Swan Services wants to go and how it plans to get there than I did at my last company after more than five years! Of course, at my last company, we couldn't plan lunch without a thirty-minute debate."

During the check-in, Alan noticed some friction between Vic and Eileen that hadn't been present in the last few sessions. He couldn't quite pinpoint what was causing the tension, so he resolved to keep his eyes and ears open as the day progressed.

After the check-in, Alan led the team through a Rock review, yielding impressive results. (See the Rock Sheet on page 243.)

Having met its financial targets for the quarter and completed nearly 90 percent of its Rocks, Swan's leadership team rated the quarter an "A minus." Each leader was quite pleased with the progress that had been made but agreed there remained room for improvement. Alan urged the team to spend time celebrating the successes of the past quarter before moving on. He then walked the team through the V/TO, one section at a time. Although Jeff had a few questions, there were no changes to the Core Values and Core Focus. During the review of the 10-year Target, however, Tom raised an issue.

"You know," Tom said to Jeff, "I'm eager to get your opinion about this 10-year Target. At first I was energized by the sheer magnitude of it, but now I'm not so sure. Is this really what we want? It just seems to me that a $40 million technology consulting company is a rare bird for a reason. So I'm wondering if it's really even possible."

Eileen smiled—she'd been wondering the same thing.

"That's a fair question," replied Jeff. "I have no way of answering intelligently until I get a handle on our business model and start running some numbers, but it's probably worth studying."

To make sure everyone was committed to a common vision, Alan led a brief discussion that resulted in the team agreeing to leave the 10-Year Target as is pending Jeff's further study. He grabbed his marker and added "10-Year Target Study" to the Issues List.

Swan Services Q3 20XX Rock Sheet

Future Date: September 28, 20XX

Revenue: $5.25 million On track

Profit: 5% On track

Measurables: 13 projects @ $100K + On track

COMPANY ROCKS

	WHO	
1) Document and implement sales process	Sue	Done
2) Define and publish Swan's proven process	Sue	Done
3) Hire CFO RPRS	Eileen	Done
4) Complete ops department scorecard (with utilization and client satisfaction)	Tom	ND
5) Refine and implement project fulfillment process	Tom	Done
6)		
7)		

SUE

1) Document and implement sales process	Done
2) Define and publish Swan's proven process	Done
3) Resolve Natalie RPRS	Done
4)	
5)	
6)	
7)	

TOM

1) Complete ops department scorecard (with utilization and client satisfaction)	ND
2) Refine and implement project fulfillment process	Done
3)	
4)	
5)	
6)	
7)	

EILEEN

1) Hire CFO RPRS	Done
2) Renew credit lines	Done
3)	
4)	
5)	
6)	
7)	

VIC

1) Create an industry event plan for next year	Done
2) Develop and implement plan to get vision shared by all	Done
3)	
4)	
5)	
6)	
7)	

"Sounds like a Q4 Rock," Vic hinted, elbowing his new CFO in the process. As he did so, Alan noticed a slight grimace register on Eileen's face. He wondered if Vic was getting a little too comfortable—even smug—in his role as Swan's visionary. He realized Vic's check-in had included more than the usual number of barbs and that several had been directed at Eileen.

There were no issues with the Marketing Strategy. Jeff had a few questions about the 3-Year Picture but felt comfortable supporting what the team had come up with for now. The review of the 1-Year Plan went quickly as well.

Having already reviewed last quarter's Rocks, Alan helped the team conclude its V/TO review by cleaning up the Issues List. After a quick break, he asked the leaders to bring up any additional problems, challenges, ideas, and opportunities they wanted to add to the list. That brainstorming session and the morning's check-in helped Alan build the Issues List, in green on the left side of the whiteboard.

BILLING ACCURACY	WORKING OUTSIDE THE CORE FOCUS
SCORECARDS & MEASURABLES FOR ALL	10-YEAR TARGET STUDY
SUE- ENOUGH TIME?	BA SEAT OPEN
GUARANTEE?	BILL- RPRS
DEFINE HR SEAT	RAJ- RPRS
DEFINE IT SEAT	HIRE SALES EXEC (RPRS)
NEXT GEN TECHNOLOGY	MARKETING SEAT ROI
ACQUISITION TARGET?	REVISE FINANCIAL DEPARTMENT STRUCTURE
PTO POLICY	COMMUNITY GIVING
TECHNICAL TRAINING	FINANCE DEPT. LEVEL 10 MEETING
BENCH STRENGTH	FINANCE DEPT. SCORECARDS
DISASTER RECOVERY PLAN	ACCOUNTING SOFTWARE
HR PROCESS	KEY ACCOUNT REVIEWS
MARKETING PROCESS	NEXT YEAR'S BUDGET
ACCOUNT MANAGEMENT PROCESS	MONTHLY FINANCIAL REVIEWS
ACCOUNTING PROCESS	

With the list complete, Alan led the team through a Rock-setting exercise. He began by compiling each leader's list of potential company Rocks on the whiteboard. He led the team through a Keep, Kill, and Combine exercise to help narrow the list of fifteen potential Rocks down to four essential priorities. Alan noticed the tension rising between Vic and Eileen while the team was setting Rocks.

"Gosh, Eileen," Vic exclaimed at one point, "now that we have a full leadership team, you don't need to own all the Rocks!"

The smile on Vic's face showed he intended only good-natured ribbing, but Eileen didn't react well. Alan felt he couldn't let the moment pass without giving the two leaders a chance to be open and honest.

"Vic, Eileen, is there something going on that we need to get on the table?" he asked.

Not being accustomed to Alan's penchant for directness, Jeff nearly dove under the table. A pervading awkwardness descended on the conference room.

"No, no—nothing, Alan," asserted Vic. "I'm sorry, Eileen; I didn't mean to tick you off."

"I'm not ticked off, Vic," she replied icily. "It's just not that funny anymore."

"What's not that funny, Eileen?" asked Alan.

"Vic's constant suggestions that my job as the integrator is easy now that Sue, Tom, and Jeff are in place," she replied. "I'm just getting tired of it."

"Should we leave?" Tom asked, clearing his throat and standing up.

"I don't think that's necessary, Tom," replied Alan. "Vic, Eileen, would you like Tom and the others to give us a few minutes?"

"Heavens no," replied Eileen. "Tom, this is nothing. Vic and I go *way* back. If you're going to be a member of this team, you'll have to get used to some occasional conflict between us. I just felt it was important to let Vic know how I felt about his snide little remarks. As far as I'm concerned, we can move on."

Vic was about to protest; he didn't feel he'd been "constantly suggesting" anything about what Eileen was doing or not doing. He thought for a moment before escalating the argument, and that pause was just enough time to allow Alan to intercede.

"Vic," he said, "have you heard what Eileen has to say? Do you understand that some of your jokes are frustrating her?"

Swan's visionary took a deep breath and tried to understand Eileen's perspective. He looked back on all of the frustrations she'd endured the past year and the challenges she'd helped the company overcome. He realized that she hadn't even spent one week as an integrator leading a healthy, capable, complete leadership team.

"Yes," he said softly. "Yes, I do. Eileen, I'm sorry. Please understand that I don't mean anything by it."

"It's okay, Vic," Eileen replied. "I know it's just your way. But sometimes you don't understand how hurtful your comments can be."

"Point taken," her partner replied. "Thanks for letting me know how you feel."

Alan spent a few moments making sure everyone on the team was satisfied that the issue had been resolved, and lunch was delivered.

The Rock-setting exercise concluded after each leader scoured the remaining list of potential Rocks and issues for additional individual Rocks to complete during the quarter. Eileen captured the work done in the room to create a Q4 Rock Sheet. (See page 247.)

Once company and individual Rocks had been set and Alan cleaned up the Issues List, it had become appreciably smaller:

BILLING ACCURACY	DISASTER RECOVERY PLAN
SCORECARDS & MEASURABLES FOR ALL	MARKETING PROCESS
SUE- ENOUGH TIME?	BONUSES
GUARANTEE?	ACCOUNT MANAGEMENT PROCESS
DEFINE HR SEAT	WORKING OUTSIDE THE CORE FOCUS
DEFINE IT SEAT	COMMUNITY GIVING
ACQUISITION TARGET?	ACCOUNTING SOFTWARE
PTO POLICY	NEXT YEAR'S BUDGET
TECHNICAL TRAINING	KEY ACCOUNT REVIEWS

With the entire afternoon left to tackle issues, Swan's leaders rolled up their sleeves and dug into the Issues List. Alan led the team through the standard prioritization exercise, quickly placing "#1," "#2," and "#3" next to the top issues—Scorecards and measurables for all, bonuses, and monthly financial reviews. As they IDSed the first issue, Alan introduced a technique that would help Swan's leaders save countless hours and resolve more issues in the coming years.

Swan Services Q4 20XX Rock Sheet

Future Date: December 20, 20XX
Revenue: $7.25 million
Profit: 5%
Measurables: 20 projects @ $100K +

COMPANY ROCKS	WHO
1) Document HR process	Eileen
2) Document accounting process (including time and billing)	Jeff
3) Ops department RPRS (open, Bill, Raj)	Tom
4) Sales department RPRS (sales executive, marketing, 20XX staffing plan)	Sue
5)	
6)	
7)	

SUE
1) Sales department RPRS (sales executive, marketing, 20XX staffing plan)
2) Develop 20XX sales and marketing plan
3)
4)
5)
6)
7)

TOM
1) Ops department RPRS (open, Bill, Raj)
2) Implement project fulfillment process and get FBA
3) Develop 20XX staffing plan
4)
5)
6)
7)

JEFF
1) Document accounting process (including time and billing)
2) Create 20XX budget and high-level three- and ten-year financial projections
3) Prepare staff-aug financial analysis and make recommendation re: existing clients
4) Restructure finance department
5) Develop 20XX staffing plan
6)
7)

EILEEN
1) Document HR process
2) Identify at least 3 potential acquisition targets
3)
4)
5)
6)
7)

VIC
1) Conduct quarterly State of the Company meeting and consistently recognize employees
2) Research 3 next generation technologies and recommend further study on the most promising option
3)
4)
5)
6)
7)

While the team tried to help Jeff cobble together a finance department Scorecard, Tom started asking some related questions about a Scorecard for developers. Alan stepped in to get the IDS process back on track.

"Tangent alert!" he said smiling.

Tom and Vic stopped talking, looked up, and smiled back as they realized what had happened. Sue and Eileen laughed out loud. Alan wrote "Development Scorecard" on the whiteboard.

"Sorry we got off on a tangent," Tom said.

"It happens all the time," Alan explained. "I've seen clients veer off onto five separate tangents before realizing they've gotten off the issue at hand. Calling 'tangent alert' on one another is a quick, friendly way of reminding your teammates when they've gotten off track."

With the team refocused, it quickly solved all three issues and moved through eleven more before Alan walked them through next steps just after four thirty. He started by helping clean up the Issues List, compartmentalizing the remaining issues by placing them on the V/TO or the Level 10 Meeting agenda. He made sure Eileen, Sue, and Jeff were clear on their responsibilities for updating the foundational tools and bringing them back to the team's next Level 10 Meeting. And he reminded Vic to get his Rock done by holding the next State of the Company meeting.

"I also want to prep you for your next session," Alan explained, "a very powerful two-day Annual Planning Session that's different from the other work we've done together up to this point. I recommend that we hold this session off-site—away from my office and yours. Sequester yourselves for two meaningful, productive days. Most teams include an overnight stay and some kind of social component. Get out of your routine, go to dinner as a group, and let your hair down."

As he spoke, Alan was summarizing the agenda for each day of Annual Planning on the board:

DAY 1

- REVIEW LAST YEAR/ LAST QUARTER
- TEAM HEALTH
- ORGANIZATIONAL CHECKUP
- SWOT ANALYSIS - ISSUES LIST
- V/TO (THRU 3-YEAR PICTURE)

DAY 2

- 1 YEAR PLAN
  - ROLES & RESPONSIBILITIES
  - NUMBERS
  - DEPARTMENTAL PLANS
- SET Q1 ROCKS
- IDS

"Day one is all about staying at a high level," he explained. "Building team health, challenging yourselves and getting 100 percent on the same page with your vision at thirty thousand feet, and smoking out issues. Day two is completely different—that's when we bring your vision down to the ground, craft a clear plan for next year to achieve it, and resolve all your key issues."

He answered several questions about the agenda, possible venues, and necessary prep work. Eileen agreed to secure an off-site location and handle other logistics. Alan then moved to conclude the Quarterly Session by getting each leader to share with the team his or her feedback, expectations outcome, and rating.

"I'll go first," replied Jeff. "Feedback? Wow. I'm exhausted and definitely a bit overwhelmed. That said, I can't think of a better way to get acquainted with the leadership team and the company than spending a day like this working on the business. The way these tools made it easy for us to jump quickly from high-level strategy to detailed issues was impressive. I can see why you like this system so much. Were my expectations met? You bet. I wanted to learn a lot and contribute a little. The first one was easy; I hope you agree with my thinking on the second one. Rating? I'd say nine. I don't know what ten looks like yet, but this was a darn good start."

Sue and Tom provided similarly positive feedback. Both were thrilled to have nearly cleared the Issues List and walked away with realistic Rocks for the quarter. Sue gave the meeting a ten; Tom gave it a nine.

"I like to begin at the end," said Vic. "My rating is a ten. Great meeting and a great quarter *between* meetings. My expectations were easily met."

"Eileen?" Alan asked when Vic finished.

"Feedback? Frankly, I'm just excited about embarking on a quarter owning one seat, with no major people issues left to resolve," she said. "Jeff, Tom, if I haven't said it often enough yet, hear me now: thanks for joining our team. Today was great. It *was* a little odd, because for once I felt like there was a team of people in the room capable of solving every issue on that list without me being involved. I know that's supposed to excite me, but I'm not quite there yet. My expectations were definitely met. And I'd say nine—only because I kind of floated in and out of the conversation more than normal."

"Great stuff, Eileen. Thank you," replied Alan. "This was a really productive, focused session coming off a truly great quarter. I'm really looking forward to a powerful two-day Annual Planning Session with you on December 20 and 21. Before then, I'd like you all to read Patrick Lencioni's *The Five Dysfunctions of a Team*. It offers a unique and valuable perspective on team health that I think you'll find illuminating."

As he said his good-byes, Alan asked Vic and Eileen to stay behind for a few moments. He queried again about the tension between the two partners. With the other leaders gone, Vic and Eileen acknowledged that they had been arguing about some ownership issues they hadn't yet resolved. The fallout from those discussions had been evident in the room that day, and both partners apologized for the distraction. Alan again urged them to conduct regular Same Page Meetings, which they had gotten away from doing, to help maintain a united front in the business. They compared calendars and agreed to start meeting again on the first Monday of every month beginning the following week.

"Looking forward to seeing you both in December," Alan said as the two partners left his office.

"You too, Alan," replied Vic. "Thanks again."

CHAPTER 7
THE ANNUAL

A S FALL GAVE WAY TO WINTER, Swan's newly focused leadership team continued to gain traction. Jeff and Tom proved to be highly capable leaders who fit Swan's culture. A more focused marketing message was now being used consistently throughout all the company's sales and marketing materials. As a result, Sue and her sales team continued to grow the pipeline and achieve their revenue goals.

Vic really hit his stride as the full-time visionary. His quarterly State of the Company events and the departmental Level 10 Meetings greatly improved communication and helped get everyone in the organization rowing in one direction. Dozens of issues that once languished on the desks of Swan's executives were beginning to be solved—using IDS—by departments or teams.

As Alan learned in two calls with Eileen, however, the team continued to encounter roadblocks. Friction had developed between Tom and Sue. The two passionate leaders often found themselves on different sides of important issues, and their business-related conflicts occasionally led to unproductive sniping and one-on-one politicking.

In terms of technical competence, productivity, and skills as a leader and manager, Jeff had become a tremendous asset to Eileen. Furthermore, his experience helping grow two entrepreneurial organizations brought strategic value to Swan's team and a pervading sense of calm and confidence. But Jeff hadn't yet blended with the team as Eileen had hoped.

"He's a bit of a loner," Eileen told Alan. "He rarely brings issues to the Level 10 Meetings and hardly ever contributes with an opinion or an insight on someone else's issue. He just seems happiest being left to run his own department—which he definitely does well. He seems a little frustrated by the need to pitch in and work together with the other leaders to make them and the company better."

"Does Jeff know you feel this way?" Alan asked.

"Yes. And no," replied Eileen carefully. "I spoke with him briefly about forty-five days into his tenure here and asked him to be a little more engaged in those meetings and when interacting with leaders and other staff members. But things haven't really improved, and I haven't brought the subject up again."

"Open and honest," Alan reminded her. "Try to get this on your Level 10 Issues List or express your concerns one-on-one with Jeff before our next session. If not, I'm confident we'll IDS the issue at your Annual."

Two weeks later, at eight thirty on Wednesday, December 20, Alan prepared to greet the team at the Chambers, a notable hotel in downtown Minneapolis. By 8:55, everyone had arrived, and Alan addressed the team.

"Welcome to the Swan Services two-day Annual Planning Session," he said, stepping to a flip chart at the front of the conference room. "Let's begin by reviewing our objectives for day one."

OBJECTIVES (DAY 1)

- INCREASE TEAM HEALTH
- CLEAR COMPANY VISION
- ISSUES LIST CLEAR

AGENDA (DAY 1)

- CHECK-IN
- REVIEW LAST YEAR/LAST QUARTER
- TEAM HEALTH
- ORGANIZATIONAL CHECKUP
- SWOT ANALYSIS→ ISSUES LIST
- V/TO (THRU 3-YEAR PICTURE)

"Day one is all about staying at a high level," he continued. "Our first objective is to increase team health. That means that whatever degree of team health you walked in with today, it needs to be some degree higher by the time you walk out of here this evening. The second objective is that you leave here crystal clear on Swan Services' vision. When the dust settles at the end of day one, we need you all 100 percent on the same page with where the company is going. The third objective is to build and get clear on your Issues List. Today we're going to smoke out issues; we're not going to solve anything. Day two will feel completely different. That's when we dig into the nitty-gritty, do our planning for next year, set Rocks for Q1, and solve all the key issues. But today we're going to keep things at a high level."

Next Alan walked through the agenda items, explaining how each topic and exercise would help the team improve team health; take a good, hard look at the organization; and align around a common vision for Swan Services. He warned them that an Annual Planning Session Issues List can become quite lengthy but expressed confidence the team would be able to solve most of those issues before concluding on day two.

"When we review your V/TO at an annual," he explained, "*nothing* is sacred. In other words, we're going to go through each section of the V/TO and challenge *everything*. We have to make sure every section is right. Today we're going to go all the way through the vision side of the document, creating a brand-new 3-Year Picture for the organization. We'll throw out the old picture and make a new one because you're smarter, better, and stronger as a team than you were nine months ago when we first created it."

Alan prepared the leaders for a different check-in from the one they had learned in earlier sessions. He asked them to reflect on the year and compile a list of "greats"—three business greats, one personal great, and any unexpected greats that happened during the year. He also asked them to share their specific expectations for the *entire* two-day Annual Planning Session. When everyone stopped writing, Alan asked someone to start by reporting on his or her greats.

"I'll be the brave one," Vic volunteered. "My first great is the visionary role and the ability it's given me to do the things I love most and do best—culture development, relationship building, problem solving, and especially vision building. Sue is the second great. She's allowed me to elevate into that role *and* gotten the sales numbers back on track."

After sharing the third business great—Swan's growing comfort with growth and change—Vic offered his personal great. "My oldest boy made the eighth grade football team," he said, beaming. "In fact, he started every game at quarterback. If anything's better than watching your kid throw a touchdown pass—even in middle school—I sure don't know what it is."

"Any unexpected greats?" Alan asked. "Anything you didn't plan for that just fell in your lap?"

"I'd say Evan stepping out of his role and making way for Tom," Vic replied. "That wasn't only great for Swan; it was great for Evan. I've never seen him so happy. Last week I think he actually threw out that cot he kept in his office!"

The team got a good laugh as Alan moved left to get Sue's check-in. Her three business greats were Vic and Eileen having confidence in her to lead the sales team, the way the sales team responded, and the winning of a very large deal that had recently closed. Her personal great was a clean bill of health for her mother, who had been battling breast cancer. She couldn't think of an unexpected great.

Sitting to Sue's left, Tom went next.

"My personal great is that I'm here at Swan Services," he began. "It's great to be part of a talented, determined leadership team that wants to get better every day. Sue, Eileen, Vic, I can't thank you enough."

The three leaders nodded and smiled.

"I had Evan as a business great, too," he continued. "I was really leery about whether he'd be an asset or a liability, but his attitude *and* his aptitude have been great. And like Vic said, I think he's really happy in his new role."

Tom went on to mention the implementation of the new project management software and a particularly successful project for a major client as his other business greats. Like Sue, he couldn't think of an unexpected great.

"Well, since I've been here for only about four months and I *am* an accountant," began Jeff when Alan asked for his greats, "I've determined I should be responsible for only *one* business great—or one-third the requirement for the rest of you."

He paused, and the other leaders stirred uneasily, not sure what to make of this comment. Alan was about to say something when Jeff continued.

"Only kidding," he said with a wry grin. "Call it CFO humor."

It took a moment for the joke to register, but when it did, the whole team cracked up—more in relief than anything else.

"Odd guy," thought Vic, "but at least he's starting to loosen up."

Jeff went on to recount his business and personal greats—mastering Swan's accounting software, completing the budgets, documenting Swan's accounting process, and his fifteenth wedding anniversary.

"Level 10 Meetings are my unexpected great," he continued. "I've worked with some pretty capable leadership teams, and all of them were *terrible* at meetings. When you told me your weekly meetings were the key to clarity and productivity, I thought you were nuts! But I'm convinced—it's amazing how much we get done each week."

Eileen shot Alan a puzzled glance. As she had explained just two weeks earlier, there was little evidence that Jeff even wanted to *be* in those meetings. Now here he was mentioning them as a highlight of his tenure at Swan. Both Eileen and Alan made a mental note to figure out this puzzle before the two-day session had concluded.

After making sure Jeff was done, Alan moved left and asked Eileen to continue. She spoke first of the EOS process and then of Sue's successful transition from a young talent ready to resign into a vital member of Swan Service's leadership team.

"And that leads me to the third great: the power of right people in the right seats," she continued. "Early in this journey, Alan talked about looking around this table into the eyes of a great leadership team, being proud to be in the room with these people, and confident that together we'd be able to accomplish anything. Vic mentioned it at our last session. It's been a rough journey, but I'm proud to say we're there today."

"My personal great," she continued haltingly, "is my family."

Swan's president paused, momentarily unable to continue. Her eyes moistened, and she struggled to regain her composure. "Frankly, when we started this process, I had become so frustrated and so angry about this business that I carried my troubles home. I was working twelve to fourteen hours a day, and I was an absolute bear. Even when I was with the family, I wasn't really there. I was always thinking about the business, checking in at the office, returning emails—you name it. My husband was frustrated, and my kids—"

Again she paused for a few moments. "Well, they didn't really like me much," she continued. "So my personal great is that I'm getting to know my family again."

The room was silent, charged with emotion.

"Thank you for that, Eileen," Alan said after a long pause. "It's a great reminder that we're all just human beings here, and we need to take the time to reflect and share and grow. It sounds like it's been quite a year. If you're a normal entrepreneurial leadership team, you're charging forward all year, and you never really take a deep breath and celebrate your successes. So right now, and every Annual you do from here on out, is a great chance to stop for five minutes and pat yourselves on the back."

After a moment, Alan moved left around the table again, asking each leader to share his or her expectations for the two-day session. He took careful notes and moved to the next item on the agenda.

"Okay, that's our check-in," he continued. "If there are no other comments, let's review the year and see how you did."

Alan asked Eileen to distribute V/TOs to each leader and drew the team's attention to the 1-Year Plan.

1-YEAR PLAN

Future Date: December 31, 20XX
Revenue: $7.25 million
Profit: 5%
Measurables: 20 projects @ $100K+

Goals for the Year:

1.	Implement EOS
2.	Sales team RPRS
3.	Implement marketing strategy
4.	Hire ops leader RPRS
5.	Core Processes documented, simplified and followed by all
6.	
7.	

"When we created your 1-Year Plan in our third session," Alan began, "you predicted revenues of $7.25 million. With eleven days left in the year, does it look like you're going to achieve that goal?"

"Yes," Jeff and Eileen answered at the same time. Eileen laughed sheepishly before continuing, "Sorry, Jeff, force of habit."

"Well, at least we agree," Jeff replied, smiling. "I looked over our month-to-date numbers last night, and I'd guess we'll finish the year at about $7.6 million."

"Way to go, Sue," Vic said, clapping. "That is truly remarkable."

"Couldn't have reached the goal if Tom and Evan hadn't figured out how to bill all that work in the third and fourth quarters," Sue said earnestly. "And Vic, you closed two monster deals early in Q4; that was key."

"And we predicted a net profit of 5 percent," Alan continued. "Are we going to hit that?"

"Yes," Jeff answered quickly. "Again, these are preliminary numbers, but it'll probably be closer to 6 percent—about $450K—when the dust settles."

"Awesome," said Tom, grinning from ear to ear. Eileen smiled and nodded, more relieved than anything else.

"How about twenty $100K plus projects—will you hit that goal?" Alan asked.

"Well, although the year's not quite done, I have to say no," Tom acknowledged. "I think we'll come in at nineteen—good but not what we predicted."

"So you hit two of your numbers and just missed one," Alan continued. "Now on to the goals."

Alan reviewed Swan's five goals for the year, one at a time.

"Implement EOS," he said. "Again, with eleven days left in the year, will that be done or not done?"

"Done," said several leaders simultaneously. Alan marked goal number one complete on his copy of the V/TO.

"Goal number two: sales team—right people in the right seats?" Alan continued.

"Done," replied Sue. "And so is goal three, 'implement Marketing Strategy.'"

Alan marked both complete and continued. "How about goal number four: hire ops leader—right person, right seat?"

"Done, I hope," Tom replied, getting a good laugh from the other leaders.

"Core Processes documented, simplified, and followed by all," Alan said. "Is goal number five going to be done or not done?"

"I'd have to say not done," replied Eileen. "We've identified all of them and documented most of them but have some work to do to get them followed by all."

Alan then led a quick discussion to ensure that everyone on the team agreed that the goal hadn't been completed as written and to understand the reasons why.

"Although the goal isn't done," Eileen concluded, "we're *miles* ahead of where we were last year. Sue's got the marketing and sales processes documented, her salespeople are trained, and her Scorecard includes several numbers that let her know how consistently those processes are being followed. Tom's made great strides in operations, and Jeff is beginning to get a handle on the Core Processes in his department, as well. So while I know 95 percent done is still not done, I sure feel great about the progress."

"Great stuff, Eileen," replied Alan. "Now I'd like to spend some time really looking back on this last year. What did you learn? What worked? What didn't work? Let's get all your comments, questions, and confessions out on the table. This is what helps you get better."

"For me," Sue explained, "it was all about focus. I kept staring at those sales Scorecard numbers, wondering how the heck I was going to hit them with everything else on my plate. It dawned on me that everyone on the sales team probably felt the same way. At one point early in the year, I just decided that nothing else was as important as hitting these numbers, and I started clearing the decks, making time for what was important and letting go of everything else. And then I helped the sales team do it as well. That was the key. Without that focus and discipline, there's no way we would have hit our numbers."

Vic and Eileen nodded appreciatively, remembering vividly that feeling of having twenty-three top priorities every week and never really finishing anything.

"This is something of a confession," Tom chimed in. "I have to say that early on, I looked at the process-documenting goal more as homework or extra credit than as an essential part of running the operations department. In other words, what was important to me was getting people doing the right stuff all the time, *not* writing it down. That was extra—something that had to be done because your process tells us to, or because Eileen wanted it done, or whatever."

Jeff and Sue were nodding appreciatively, as if they'd felt the same way, too.

"Then I kept seeing Sue's sales numbers each week," Tom continued. "On track, on track, on track—frankly, it was becoming annoying. I mean, whose sales team is always on track? So I asked what her secret was; she hauled out the sales department Scorecard and walked through it with me so I could see how she was running the department on a handful of numbers that linked directly back to her sales process. The lightbulb went on for me when she explained that when Troy or Natalie weren't hitting their numbers, *they* came to *her* for help. Her team was managing *itself.* That's when it occurred to me that what we're doing here is changing the way the business operates—down to the individual staff member—for the better. We're making our lives easier and consistent excellence more commonplace. And that's when I redoubled my efforts to document our Core Processes, train my team, and hold it accountable for following them. It'll definitely be a first-quarter Rock for me."

Jeff took special notice of Tom's "confession." Frankly, he was feeling the same way about lots of the work the team was doing. He'd been a key part of two successful leadership teams, and he'd learned to be effective a certain way. He'd also learned that—in most organizations—outcomes are more important than the methods you use to achieve them. He wasn't ready to change gears and embrace Swan's method quite yet, but Tom's monologue had given him something to think about.

The leaders shared a few other observations before Alan moved to review the fourth quarter.

Alan led the team through a Rock review, learning that Swan's leaders had completed 71 percent of their Rocks. Again, Alan asked the team to comment on what it had learned. During the review, Jeff learned an important lesson about Rocks and accountability. When Alan first read Jeff's fourth and fifth Rocks, he calmly said, "Done." In both cases, his answer elicited surprised looks from the rest of the team—especially Eileen.

"Let's come back to those Rocks when we're done with the Rock review," Alan said before moving on to read Eileen and Vic's Rocks.

"So what was up with Jeff's fourth and fifth Rocks?" Alan asked.

"If they're done, I haven't seen any evidence of that," Eileen explained. The rest of the team nodded in agreement.

"Oh," replied Jeff. "Well, I wasn't aware that those things needed to be shared with the team. I plugged my staffing plan into next year's budget. And I know how I want to structure things as we add people."

A thoughtful discussion followed that gave Jeff a better handle on how Swan's leadership team shared information before considering a Rock done. Eileen explained that she expected to see a revised Accountability Chart for the finance department and that proposed hire dates for any staff additions needed to be clearly agreed upon. That hadn't happened, so Jeff revised those Rocks to "not done." He also promised to work more closely with the team in the future—at least sharing any output from his Rocks and getting feedback from the team during the quarter—before saying "done" at a subsequent session.

With that completed, Alan raised the 1-Year Plan from the V/TO and the Rock Sheet in the air. "That concludes our review of the past," he said. "The only thing we can do with the past is learn from it, let it go, and move on. Now, we hope, we're smarter, better, faster planners. If there are no further comments or questions, let's take a quick break and spend the rest of the day focused on the future."

TEAM HEALTH

"Moving on to team health," Alan began, smiling. "I've been waiting ten months for this moment. So I trust everyone completed the homework assignment and read Patrick Lencioni's *The Five Dysfunctions of a Team*?"

Everyone nodded, and Alan continued. "Lencioni's terrific book teaches you what team health looks like better than I ever could. So let me help you recall what you read by summarizing it."

Alan went on to re-create on the whiteboard and explain Lencioni's five levels of team health—trust, conflict, commitment, accountability, and results—before asking the team to rate itself on each level. That exercise prompted some vivid dialogue, helped expose different viewpoints around the table, and identified specific areas for improvement.

"The key to everything is building trust. If you trust one another—if you're truly open and honest and you're willing to be vulnerable in front of your fellow leaders—all these other things become *effortless*. By building trust and continuing to master the tools in this system, you'll start to see some very tangible benefits. For example, you'll get much better at IDS. It'll become easier to put tough issues on your Issues List. There'll be more open discussion and less politicking. You'll engage in conflict more comfortably and quickly reach decisions to which everyone can commit. You'll all accept accountability for whatever the team decides, and you'll get better at calling one another out when you don't get the results the team needs to gain traction and achieve its vision. Trust is the key, so we're going to work on building trust, raising it from where it was when you walked in here today to a higher level before you walk out of here this evening."

Alan then led the team through an exercise. He called it a "trust builder," one of several activities he'd discovered that help teams learn more about themselves and one another, which builds team trust.

"This exercise is called 'One Thing,'" Alan said. "It's an opportunity to share feedback with your fellow leaders, and there are two parts. In part one, we'll go around the table and tell each leader what we believe is his or her most admirable trait. In part two, we're all going to think of one thing we want that leader to start or stop doing for the greater good of the company and this team—because by not starting or stopping this one thing, the person is actually *hurting* the cause rather than helping."

Several leaders seemed visibly uncomfortable, but Alan calmly answered a few questions and further explained the ground rules. He made it clear that when receiving feedback, the leaders would simply listen and take notes. He encouraged the asking of clarifying questions only—no defending, no discussing, no debating.

"I'll go first," said Vic.

"Thank you, Vic," Alan said. "Do your fellow leaders have your permission to be completely open and honest?"

"Of course," Vic replied.

Alan asked the team members to write down the one thing they most admired about Vic and the one thing they hoped he would start or stop doing.

"Starting to Vic's left with Sue," Alan said when the leaders had finished, "we'll do part one and go around the table. Then we'll do part two. Sue, what is the one thing you most admire about Vic?"

"The thing I most admire about Vic is—" she started before Alan raised his hand to interrupt.

"I'm sorry, Sue," Alan explained. "This exercise works best if you provide your feedback directly to Vic. Please continue."

"All right," Sue said as she turned to face Vic. "The thing I most admire about you is your gift for making other people want to spend time with you. You have this crazy blend of charisma and curiosity that makes prospects, clients, strategic partners—heck, *everyone*— really want to spend time with you."

"Tell me more!" Vic replied, smiling. "Seriously, thank you, Sue."

From there Alan moved around the table. Tom said he most admired Vic's deep caring for the culture and the people at Swan, and Jeff talked about Vic's obvious passion for the business and for Swan's clients.

"Mr. Hightower," said Eileen with an exaggerated sense of formality, "the one thing I admire most about you is your sense of what's possible. When my cup is half empty, you never fail to produce two or three cups that are *overflowing* with possibility. Without that, I truly believe Swan wouldn't exist."

"Gee, partner," said Vic sincerely, "that might be the nicest thing you've ever said to me. Thank you."

"You're welcome," she said, also a little emotional. The room was quiet for a few moments.

"Vic, now that you've had a chance to bask in the glow of all your most admirable qualities," Alan said, "are you ready for a little constructive feedback?"

"Fire away," said Vic, looking around the room.

"This is your chance," Alan told the team, smiling. "You've been saving up for weeks, months, maybe even years. Let's share part two with Vic."

"Okay, here goes," said Sue, taking a deep breath. "Vic, the one thing I want you to stop doing is signing up for stuff and then not getting it done."

Vic started to respond, but Alan stopped him. "Vic, if you don't mind, let's go around the room first. You'll get to ask clarifying questions at the end. Okay?"

Vic nodded, and Alan asked Tom to share his constructive feedback.

"Okay, Vic," continued Tom carefully, "the one thing I need you to stop doing for the greater good of the company is popping in to my meetings. You're always welcome, but when you show up unannounced, it freaks everybody out a little. I know your intentions are good, but in the end, it's more disruptive than helpful."

Vic frowned as he recorded Tom's feedback. This was painful.

"Jeff?" Alan asked.

"Vic," Jeff said, "I'd like to see you start taking a more active interest in Swan's financials."

"And Eileen?" Alan said when Vic was ready.

"Vic," she said carefully, "I'd really like you to stop making smart remarks about how little I have to do now that we have Tom and Jeff here."

"But I—" Vic started to protest and caught himself.

"Vic, with everyone finished providing feedback," Alan said, "the floor is yours. If you'd like to ask a clarifying question of Eileen or anyone else, now is the time. Remember, *just* clarifying questions—don't defend, discuss, or debate."

"Right," said Vic, fighting the urge to argue. "Eileen, um, can you give me an example of when and how I make you feel like I don't think you have enough to do?"

Eileen seemed to consider the question for a moment; the silence made the other leaders fidget.

"I don't think you intend to question my work ethic," said Eileen. "I actually think you're trying to give Sue, Tom, and Jeff the credit they deserve and, in the process, be funny. But several times over the last month or so, you've said—*in public*, mind you—something like, 'Gosh, Eileen, with all these talented leaders around you, what the heck are *you* going to do every day?'"

Vic turned white. As usual, his partner was right—both about his good intentions and his knack for sticking his foot in his mouth while trying to be funny. Once she said it out loud, Vic remembered uttering that statement at last week's Level 10 Meeting.

"I know you don't mean anything by it," repeated Eileen, "but I'm beginning to see just how important and time consuming being an integrator can be. I remember Alan talking about harmoniously integrating the various moving pieces of the business, including this team. That's no walk in the park, Vic. I love it, but I'm not on vacation! What Jeff and Tom do is free me up to be a true integrator. That means keeping the five of us on the same page, running meetings, driving the team to make decisions, and in some cases making them myself. I'm trying to make sure *we* are clear so that we can communicate clearly to our people. I'm working hard to instill discipline and accountability throughout the organization and to *be* disciplined and accountable myself. I'm trying to get better at prioritizing and help other leaders do the same. I'm managing special projects, removing obstacles and barriers—it's a lot!"

"I know, Eileen," Vic said solemnly.

"Plus," she continued, "I'm still *really* struggling to get a little work-life balance here. It's not easy for a card-carrying workaholic like me, but if I don't fix something, my family is really going to suffer. So it doesn't help when you make snide remarks."

"I get it; you're completely right. I'm really sorry," Vic replied, taking a few notes. He asked a clarifying question of Tom as well, gaining insight about how disruptive he can be when he "pops in" to an ops department Level 10 Meeting.

"You *are* an owner of the company," Tom explained. "You may not fully understand the impact that has on the people in operations. They're a little intimidated when you're there; the quality of the meeting suffers. I know your intentions are good, and you're always welcome; I just want you to be aware of the impact."

Once Vic clearly understood the constructive feedback he'd received, Alan prepared the team to share feedback with Sue. One leader at a time, Alan helped the team provide one another with positive and constructive feedback. The exercise produced more than a few surprises and awkward, potentially emotional moments. The most productive of those moments was related to the tension that had been building between Tom and Sue.

Things began coming to a head when Tom suggested Sue "start forecasting closed deals earlier and more accurately." The comment clearly rattled her, although she managed to avoid the temptation to defend herself. Instead, she waited until the end of part two and then calmly asked Tom to provide one or more examples of the kind of deals that had surprised his team. Sue carefully recorded notes as he spoke.

When providing feedback to Tom a few minutes later, Sue was just as pointed.

"Tom," she said when it was her turn, "I'd like you to stop getting so frustrated when I bring up ops department issues in the Level 10 Meetings."

Tom's face turned bright red, but he simply recorded the note and went on. Things got tense when Tom was asking clarifying questions. Ultimately, both leaders came to understand that the occasional surprises, frustrations, and squabbles they had experienced over the past several months were very common challenges faced by sales and operations leaders everywhere. In the end, all the leaders—including Sue and Tom—felt they had gotten a few things off their chests and received valuable information about personal strengths and weaknesses from their peers.

"Thank you all for being open and honest with one another," said Alan. "That exercise alone should have a very positive impact on team health. But if it just ended there—with valuable insight—I really couldn't sleep at night. Because what really matters is putting it into action, and that's what we're going to do next."

He instructed the leaders to review the constructive feedback they'd received from the team and pick "one thing" they would commit to starting or stopping in the coming year. He then asked them to write down that commitment using language he'd just written on the board:

IN THE COMING YEAR, I COMMIT TO START/STOP _____

"There is power in words," Alan said when the writing stopped. "So please state your One Thing commitment exactly as it appears on the board and in your notes."

"In the coming year," began Vic, "I commit to encouraging Eileen to delegate and elevate into her role as the integrator while appreciating the value she brings in that role."

"Thank you, Vic," Eileen replied.

"You're welcome," he responded. "And I intend to work on all that other stuff, too. But I've learned that our friend Alan is quite literal, so when he says 'one thing,' I assume he means it."

"You're right about that," replied Alan, chuckling along with the team. "The more you take on, the less you're going to deliver."

Sue followed Vic's lead by committing to "start demanding accurate, regularly updated sales forecasts from the sales team."

Tom smiled and made eye contact with Sue to indicate how much he appreciated her choice. Tom then committed to "stop being so defensive when ops department issues come up during our Level 10 Meetings."

In response to the clear feedback Eileen had shared with Jeff about his behavior at Level 10 Meetings, Jeff committed to "start staying fully engaged in the Level 10 Meetings for all ninety minutes."

Responding to feedback from most of the team about working too hard and too long, Eileen committed to "start limiting workweeks to no more than fifty hours."

When the leaders had finished reading their commitments, Alan concluded the exercise by carefully explaining next steps.

"Lest you think making these commitments is enough," he explained, "know that we'll be checking your progress every quarter from here on out. At each Quarterly next year, I'll go around the table and ask each of you to read your One Thing commitments. Your fellow leaders will then rate your performance with one word—'better,' 'worse,' or 'same.' Your goal at next year's Annual Planning Session is to hear each leader say that you're 'better' with regard to your keeping your commitment. If you do nothing else but honor these commitments you just made, I have no doubt that trust will increase, team health will improve, and you'll accomplish more next year. Okay, let's take a short break."

When everyone had returned, Alan distributed the organizational checkup. (See pages 268–270.)

Alan asked each leader to complete the checkup based on his or her own perception of the company's progress and then went rapid-fire around the room, gathering each answer. Along the way, he helped the team resolve any range of answers greater than two. This ensured that the team concluded the discussion on the same page about the state of the company. Finally, he helped extract key issues from the exercise—areas where the team agreed there was a need for improvement. The most significant issues were "Core Focus," "everyone has a number," and "Core Processes documented, simplified, and FBA."

Once all the scoring issues had been resolved, Alan asked the team to "do the math" and share its scores. With a low score of 67 and a high score of 73, the team's average score was a 70, which Alan explained meant the team felt it was "70 percent strong in the Six

ORGANIZATIONAL CHECKUP

For each statement below, rank your business on a scale of 1 to 5 where 1 is weak and 5 is strong.

	1	2	3	4	5
1. We have a clear vision in writing that has been properly communicated and is shared by everyone.	☐	☐	☐	☐	☐
2. Our core values are clear, and we are hiring, reviewing, rewarding, and firing around them.	☐	☐	☐	☐	☐
3. Our core business is clear, and our systems and processes reflect that.	☐	☐	☐	☐	☐
4. Our 10-year target is clear and has been communicated to everyone.	☐	☐	☐	☐	☐
5. Our target market is clear, and our sales and marketing efforts are focused on it.	☐	☐	☐	☐	☐
6. Our differentiators are clear, and all of our sales and marketing efforts communicate them.	☐	☐	☐	☐	☐
7. We have a proven process for doing business with our customers. It has been named and visually illustrated, and everyone is adhering to it.	☐	☐	☐	☐	☐
8. All of the people in our organization are the right people.	☐	☐	☐	☐	☐
9. Our accountability chart (organizational chart of roles and responsibilities) is clear, complete, and constantly updated.	☐	☐	☐	☐	☐
10. Everyone is in the right seat.	☐	☐	☐	☐	☐

Continued

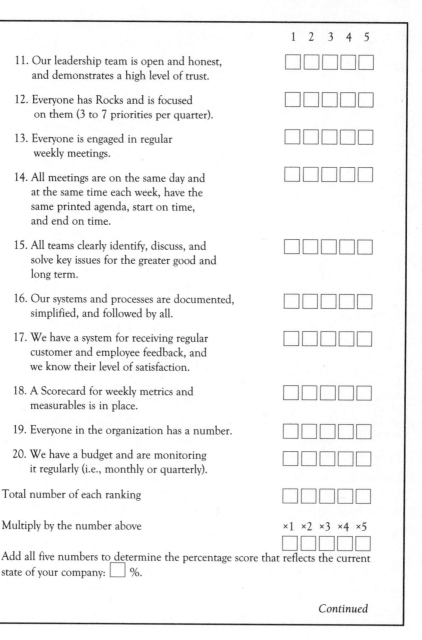

1   2   3   4   5

11. Our leadership team is open and honest,
    and demonstrates a high level of trust. ☐☐☐☐☐

12. Everyone has Rocks and is focused
    on them (3 to 7 priorities per quarter). ☐☐☐☐☐

13. Everyone is engaged in regular
    weekly meetings. ☐☐☐☐☐

14. All meetings are on the same day and
    at the same time each week, have the
    same printed agenda, start on time,
    and end on time. ☐☐☐☐☐

15. All teams clearly identify, discuss, and
    solve key issues for the greater good and
    long term. ☐☐☐☐☐

16. Our systems and processes are documented,
    simplified, and followed by all. ☐☐☐☐☐

17. We have a system for receiving regular
    customer and employee feedback, and
    we know their level of satisfaction. ☐☐☐☐☐

18. A Scorecard for weekly metrics and
    measurables is in place. ☐☐☐☐☐

19. Everyone in the organization has a number. ☐☐☐☐☐

20. We have a budget and are monitoring
    it regularly (i.e., monthly or quarterly). ☐☐☐☐☐

Total number of each ranking ☐☐☐☐☐

Multiply by the number above   ×1 ×2 ×3 ×4 ×5
☐☐☐☐☐

Add all five numbers to determine the percentage score that reflects the current
state of your company: ☐ %.

Continued

SCORING RESULTS
If your score falls between:

20 and 34%   This system and these tools can change your life.

35 and 49%   You are normal. But would you prefer normal or great?

50 and 64%   You are above average, but there is still room
              for improvement.

65 and 79%   You are well above average.

80 and 100%   This is your goal—and where most companies using this system end up.

Key Components." He then helped the leaders understand how continued progress in strengthening those Components would translate directly into results.

"Once we solve the issues we extracted from the organizational checkup," he continued, "you'll easily get to 80 percent or better in each Component, which is the goal. When you get there, you're truly firing on all cylinders."

With that exercise complete, Alan moved quickly to the SWOT analysis. He'd placed four flip chart pages marked "Strengths," "Weaknesses," "Opportunities," and "Threats" on one wall of the hotel conference room. He gave the leaders a few minutes to think carefully about the organization and create a personal set of four lists to go under the titles on the wall. Finally, he moved left around the room, compiling responses from each leader. When all four pages were full, Alan addressed the team.

"Once again," he explained, "everything about this process is designed to be useful and practical. I've completed a lot of SWOT analyses in my day, and one of the things that always bothered me is how often insight that comes from the exercise seems to go nowhere. To make sure that doesn't happen, we'll work through each list to extract *relevant issues* for the coming twelve months. In other words, which items on these pages are issues that need to be tackled in the coming year?"

Alan read each item, asking the team whether the item was a relevant issue. No strengths made the list, which Alan said was not unusual. Eight weaknesses were extracted as issues, and another eight opportunities were added to the list. Six threats were added to the list, and Alan concluded the exercise.

Pointing at two long columns of issues, Alan reminded the team that smoking out dozens of issues on day one of an Annual Planning Session was the goal. In fact, he asked each leader to think again of every idea, obstacle, and frustration that hadn't already been captured, and he added those to the Issues List, resulting in the following:

LEVEL 10 MEETINGS
DEPARTMENTAL SCORECARDS
ACCOUNT MANAGEMENT PROCESS
PROJECT FULFILLMENT PROCESS FBA
ACCOUNTING PROCESS FBA
OTHER OPS PROCESSES?
OTHER FINANCIAL DEPT. PROCESSES?
RESTRUCTURE FINANCIAL DEPT.
FINANCIAL DEPT. STAFFING PLAN
NEXT GEN. TECHNOLOGIES
LEADERSHIP TEAM CONFLICT
STAYING ENGAGED AT L10 MEETINGS
CORE FOCUS- SYSTEM AND PROCESSES
EVERYONE HAS A NUMBER
CORE PROCESSES DOCUMENTED, SIMPLIFIED AND FBA
LEAD GENERATION
LACK OF RECURRING REVENUE
FINDING TALENT
ON-BOARDING NEW HIRES
BENCH STRENGTH IN OPS
MID-LEVEL MANAGEMENT
PREDICTING REVENUES

MANAGING FLUCTUATING WORKLOADS
SENSI-TECH ACQUISITION
NEW OFFICE SPACE
IT RECRUITING
OFF-SHORING (OVERSEAS DEVELOPMENT OFFICE)
"PRODUCTIZING" COMMON SOLUTIONS
CERTIFICATION
LOSING KEY EMPLOYEES
COMPETITORS GETTING STRONGER
OUT-OF-DATE LEGACY TECHNOLOGY
DATA SECURITY
CAPITAL AVAILABILITY (CLIENTS, US)
RISING HEALTH INSURANCE COSTS
SUE-ENOUGH TIME
RAJ - RPRS
PTO POLICY
TECHNICAL TRAINING
DISASTER RECOVERY PLAN
ART/FIRM-RPRS
GUARANTEE
END RUNS

After a break, Alan asked the leaders to grab the updated copies of Swan's V/TO that Eileen had distributed earlier.

"Our goal in reviewing the V/TO today," Alan began, "is to make sure you're all 100 percent on the same page with the vision of the organization, up to and including defining a new 3-Year Picture. With this being the Annual, absolutely nothing is sacred. We're going to review each of the five sections on the vision page of the V/TO; I want you to challenge *everything*. We need to make sure we got it right when we first defined your vision ten months ago, given the growing clarity we all have."

Alan started by reviewing Swan's Core Values, reading them one at a time. The team quickly confirmed the Core Values were right, and all the leaders agreed they'd been thoroughly integrated into the organization's performance review process. Tom and Sue also congratulated Vic for the fine job he'd done helping the team keep the Core Values top of mind.

"Your Core Focus," Alan continued, moving on to the second section of the V/TO, "is 'Building a great company with great people by solving real problems with the right technology.' Is that right? Did we nail it?"

"Yes," replied Tom immediately. "Exactly right. However, we are still doing an awful lot of work outside the Core Focus. I know there's already an issue on our list, but if nothing is sacred at an Annual, I'd like to talk about that."

"Okay, Tom," replied Alan. "If you really believe that this is a fundamental issue, we should resolve it now."

"It's time for us to quit doing staff-aug work," Tom said plainly. "It's the root cause of a half-dozen issues on our list—finding talent, losing key employees, on-boarding new talent, etcetera. It's making it *very* difficult to run an efficient operation, staff properly, and do quality work for clients that want us to work *within* our Core Focus."

"Is everyone clear on what the issue is?" Alan asked the team.

"Yes," Jeff said. "Tom wants us to exit the staff-aug business altogether. I think we've compiled enough data over the last quarter to make an informed decision today. To get my Rock done, I made a recommendation to the team at last week's Level 10 Meeting. We may be able to package the staff-aug portion of our business for sale or form a strategic partnership with a firm that specializes in that type of work. That way we'd be able to derive some economic benefit from our current staff-aug clients. And if we structure the deal properly, Sue's team might be able to direct business to this strategic partner in exchange for some sort of revenue share or referral fee."

"I like that option better than just saying no to clients and prospects," Sue agreed. "We'd have to be confident in the partner's ability, but Jeff's idea could work."

"I like it because we could use the strategic partner to help us with fluctuating workloads," Tom agreed. "Although, as Sue said, we have to find the right partner."

"So let's conclude," Alan continued. "Do we agree that we're going to start searching for a strategic partner?"

"Yes," everyone said in unison.

"It's likely to be a first-quarter Rock," explained Jeff.

"Well done," Alan replied, adding "Staff-Aug Strategic Partner" to the Issues List. "On to 10-Year Target—$40 million with a 15 percent net profit. Is that still the long-term, energizing goal for this organization?"

"I love it," exclaimed Vic. "If anything, I think it might be a little conservative, now that we're starting to hit on all cylinders."

Jeff looked down at his notes and shifted in his seat. He'd been wondering whether to challenge the 10-Year Target for weeks.

"Jeff," Alan asked directly, "what are you thinking?"

"Well," he said slowly, "I'll support whatever the team decides. It's just that..."

"Just say it!" shouted Eileen. "You won't be the first leader at Swan to question Vic's sanity."

Everyone laughed, and Jeff decided to come clean.

"Open and honest," he said carefully, "I hesitated because running a $40 million technology company sounds a lot more fun than it really is. There aren't many of those organizations around—probably for good reason. Do you realize we'd have more than 150 employees at $40 million? We'd probably have a major presence in at least three metro markets. We'd be far less nimble, which is dangerous in any business but deadly for a technology services company."

"Has anyone ever told you you're a real downer?" Vic said, only half in jest.

"It's my job," Jeff replied, also half-joking.

"So what would *your* 10-Year Target be, Jeff?" Eileen asked.

"For me, it's less about revenues than net profit. I think we could easily raise our net profit margin to 20 or 25 percent. We'd have to stay true to our Core Focus, sell within our target market, and find the right partner for our staff-aug business. I've done some financial modeling and believe it's possible. We're actually making those net margins on our best clients today. On revenues of, say, $20 million, that would give us $4 or $5 million in profit. And we could get there with one location and about seventy employees. I like those numbers a lot more than what's on the V/TO right now."

"Are you suggesting we go back to the office next week and tell our employees that we've decided to cut our long-term goal in *half*?" Vic asked. "How the heck can we explain that when things are going so well?"

A spirited debate followed, with every leader chiming in. The team had stumbled on a truly complex issue, and everyone had a valid opinion. Alan kept them focused on the issue at hand and, when people began getting redundant, pushed for a conclusion.

"I'm open to adjusting the profit number upward," Vic said, "but I think we need to leave the revenue number at $40 million and figure out how to get there."

Sue agreed. She'd been energized by the aggressive growth plans and felt Swan's leadership team could break through the ceiling Jeff seemed so concerned about. Despite his enthusiasm for growth, Tom ultimately agreed with Jeff. A more profitable $20 million company with half as many employees seemed a more reasonable, achievable goal than $40 million.

"There's no clear right answer," Alan explained. "So unless someone has something new to say, it's time for the integrator to make the call. Eileen, for the greater good of the business, what's our 10-Year Target?"

"Jeff has expressed some very valid concerns," she replied in a steady, measured tone. "And I think as we grow, it's critical we watch carefully for signs of growing inefficiencies, declining customer and employee satisfaction, and eroding profits." She paused. "While I'd *like* to get to $40 million, I'm just not seeing it. That company's bigger and less nimble than I sense any of us wants to be. I worry a bit about how scaling back our 10-Year Target will affect the troops, but we can simply explain that we've learned a lot over the last year and now believe that running a stable, solid, profitable $25 million business will be better for all of us. It's still nearly *four times* our current size. Vic, can you live with $25 million and 20 percent?"

"That's a $5 million net profit," Vic said. "Yeah, I think I can live with that. And besides, I have nine years to convince you all that you're setting your sights too low."

Eileen smiled, and the team quickly concluded the discussion on a high note.

Alan moved to the Marketing Strategy section of the V/TO. The team quickly agreed the target market and three uniques were right on. Sue explained how well the proven process had been working for the sales team, and she verified that the issue of whether to establish a guarantee had been added to the Issues List. She planned to suggest that as a key issue for the team to IDS during day two.

"Earlier this year," Alan explained after a break, "we created the 3-Year Picture you have on your V/TO. With the additional clarity you've gained over the past ten months, you're better, stronger, and faster. So let's start with a clean slate, move it out another year, and paint a picture of the organization this team plans to build over the *next* three years. First we'll predict the revenue, profit, and measurable for that year."

He gave the team some time to extend their outlook another year and revise their financial predictions. The exercise moved quickly; there were only slight differences of opinion among the team members on each number, and each was quickly resolved.

Once the leaders had agreed on Swan's financial picture, Alan asked them to more thoroughly describe what the organization would look like in three short years. In addition to their prior 3-Year Picture, he asked them to look at the SWOT analysis, Issues List, vision, and Accountability Chart for inspiration.

Moving left around the room, Alan compiled every leader's answers. With the list complete, the team reviewed each item and made a decision about whether it reflected an essential component of Swan's 3-Year Picture, resulting in the following:

3-YEAR PICTURE:

FUTURE DATE: 12/31/20XX
REVENUE: $12M
PROFIT: 12% ($1.44M)
MEASURABLE: 50 PROJECTS @ $100K+

- 50 RPRS
- THRIVING CULTURE
- NEW COMPANY HQ
- NEW SALES OFFICE IN CHICAGO
- STRONG SALES TEAM OF 10 PEOPLE
- HR SEAT (RPRS)
- IT SEAT (RPRS)
- ONE OF MINNESOTA'S "BEST PLACES TO WORK"
- 40% RECURRING REVENUES
- GREAT STAFF-AUG PARTNER IN PLACE
- SEEKING ACQUISITIONS

"With your 3-Year Picture clear," Alan said, "and the whole team 100 percent on the same page with the vision for the organization, we can conclude for the day. Thank you for helping keep things at a high level today. I hope you're looking forward to digging into the nitty-gritty tomorrow. Have a great time together tonight. I'll see you right back here tomorrow morning at nine."

When the session ended a little before five, the team left energized, excited about the journey ahead, and ready to blow off a little steam. Sue, Jeff, and Vic made plans to meet in the hotel's fitness center before dinner. Eileen and Tom retreated to their rooms to get caught up from the day, call home, and freshen up. At seven, the team had cocktails in the lobby before heading to a nearby hot spot for a spectacular dinner. The wine and conversation flowed, the team cut loose, and a good time was had by all.

In three hours over dinner, Eileen learned things about her team that she hadn't discovered in hundreds of hours together at the office. She suddenly regretted not having set aside more time for such activities before and vowed to change that from that point on.

Day Two

Alan wasn't surprised to see a few bleary eyes as Swan's team assembled itself the next morning, a few minutes before nine.

"Welcome to day two of your Annual Planning Session," he began, pointing at the objectives and agenda. "Yesterday was all about keeping things at a high level. Today we roll up our sleeves, dig into the nitty-gritty, and bring Swan's vision down to the ground."

Objectives (Day 2)

- Clear Plan to Achieve Vision
- Clear Plan for Q1
- Resolve Key Issues

Agenda (Day 2)

- Check-In
- Review Issues List/3-Year Picture
- 1-Year Plan
  - Roles and Responsibilities
  - Budget
  - Scorecard
- Establish Q1 Rocks
- IDS
- Next Steps
- Conclude

Alan carefully explained each item on the agenda and invited questions. Hearing none, he instructed the leaders to check in.

"The first thing I'd like to hear from you this morning," he explained, "is your business highlight from yesterday. Then I'd like you to look back at your expectations from yesterday and restate them for me and the team."

After a few minutes, Vic volunteered to go first.

"There were a lot of highlights for me," he admitted, "but the best was the 10-Year Target discussion. That might surprise you because I didn't get my way, but I had a real 'aha' during that discussion. Maybe for the first time, it became clear to me that growth doesn't always have to mean revenues. I mean, if we're dropping $5 million to the bottom line every year, why do I care whether the revenue number is $20 million or $40 million? If we're all living more peaceful, manageable lives and running a stable, profitable operation, that's the *definition* of no worries!"

Vic then reread his expectations from the previous day before Alan turned to Sue for her check-in.

"Hands down, the One Thing exercise," she said. "I enjoyed getting the feedback, and I feel like everyone was really honest with one another and listened carefully to both ends of the spectrum. I think it'll really make a difference for us."

"Tom?" Alan asked after Sue had recounted her expectations from day one.

"The Core Focus decision," he said right away. "And not just because I got what I had hoped for. What I really liked was our ability to decide. We gathered information, analyzed all the options, and made the call. That *never* happened at my old company."

"This is going to sound funny," Jeff said after Tom reread his expectations, "but my highlight was getting called out for being disengaged in our Level 10 Meetings."

"How so?" asked Alan.

"It made me better appreciate how important teamwork and collaboration are in this organization," he admitted. "Everyone talked about that in the hiring process, but yesterday's discussion and the time I got to spend with the team last night prompted some soul searching about what that truly means. I realized that it's never been required anywhere I've worked, so I'm not very good at it. But I *will* learn how I can be a part of this team, and I'm even more excited about what we can accomplish together."

"That's great, Jeff," said Vic.

Jeff completed his check-in by restating yesterday's expectations, and all eyes turned to Eileen.

"There were *lots* of highlights," she said. "I enjoyed looking back on this year and taking the time to both celebrate success and learn from our mistakes. The team health exercise was full of valuable insight and real emotion. But the high point was easily IDSing the staff-aug issue. That's *precisely* the way this business should run—with a bunch of skilled people collecting and analyzing information, evaluating options, and making an informed decision in the best long-term interests of the business." She then restated her expectations for the session.

Moving to the next agenda item, Alan directed the team's attention to the Issues List and 3-Year Picture.

"It's time to review yesterday's work with a fresh set of eyes," he explained. He read through every issue and recited each item in the 3-Year Picture, making sure each leader was clear and on the same page with both.

"With your Issues List and 3-Year Picture clear," he said, "we can now build a solid 1-Year Plan. Let's begin by predicting revenue for the coming year."

"Nine million," said Vic right away.

"I wrote down eight point five," followed Sue.

"Eight and a half," Tom said. "Same as Sue."

"I had eight million," Jeff said, staring at a spreadsheet. "That's only about 10 percent growth over this year, but I'm assuming we'll not be generating staff-aug revenue for the full year. So it's actually closer to 15 percent *real* growth, and it gets us a nice start toward $12 million in three years."

"Sue?" Eileen asked. "Can you and your team make $8 million happen without any new staff-aug business?"

"I think so," Sue replied. "I may want to accelerate my staffing plan, but I think we can get there."

"Tom, can you and your team deliver it?" she asked.

"Yes," he said confidently.

"Then I say $8 million," Eileen replied. "Vic, are you okay with that?"

"Well, normally I'm such a stickler for details," he joked. "Yes, I wasn't thinking about the impact on revenues exiting the staff-aug business would have. I can get on board with that."

Alan recorded $8 million on the flip chart and asked for everyone's profit prediction. The team quickly agreed on 10 percent, or $800,000. A more vigorous debate arose over the number of $100K projects, with the team ultimately arriving at the following financial predictions:

1-Year Plan:

FUTURE DATE:	12/31/20xx
REVENUE:	$8m
PROFIT:	10% ($800K)
MEASURABLE:	30 PROJECTS @ $100K+

"Next we need to come up with the three to seven *most important things* you feel we must do next year to make sure we're on track to achieve your 3-Year Picture," Alan continued.

The leaders began writing immediately. Several members of the team got up to review the 3-Year Picture and Issues List during the exercise and leafed through their foundational tools and notes looking for ideas. When everyone's list was complete, Alan reminded the leaders that they'd take the same one-at-a-time approach to setting one-year planning goals as they had nine months ago.

"All Core Processes documented, simplified, and followed by all," suggested Tom. "That's the only way we're going to grow rapidly *and* increase net profit margin."

"Agreed," said Jeff. Eileen nodded her approval, and both Sue and Vic said they had that on their lists. Alan recorded the goal and asked for another volunteer.

"I wrote down 'Build out the sales and marketing team,'" Sue said. "I've spent the last year getting the right people in the right seats, but as I was working on the budget with Jeff and preparing for this session, it dawned on me that we'll *never* get much more than $7 or 8 million in revenues without adding resources. I'd like to hire one new sales associate in Q1 and another in Q3. I'd also like to internalize marketing in Q1, although that will be an expense-neutral move. I'll spend about two-thirds of the amount we're paying Art's firm on an annual basis to have someone execute on all of our marketing deliverables. I plan to use Art and his team only for research and strategy."

After all agreed, Alan recorded the goal and looked for another suggestion.

"Restructure finance department," said Jeff. "I'm not quite done defining the ideal structure, but I'm thinking that at the very least, we should outsource internal IT to a managed services provider and hire an HR person this year."

"I had 'HR seat' as well," Eileen put in. "I mean, at least a part-time resource. There are an awful lot of HR-related issues on the Issues List that won't go away forever until we get a right person, right seat in the HR seat to take care of them. Jeff's dealing with so many day-to-day people issues that he's becoming the HR person."

This triggered another debate. Tom was on board, but neither Vic nor Sue was sold on the idea. Ultimately, the team agreed to keep it and continued on to add two additional goals.

1-YEAR PLAN:

FUTURE DATE: 12/31/20XX

REVENUE: $8M

PROFIT: 10% ($800K)

MEASURABLE: 30 PROJECTS @ $100K+
1. ALL CORE PROCESSES DOCUMENTED, SIMPLIFIED AND FBA
2. BUILD NEXT GENERATION MKTG/SALES DEPARTMENT
     (2 NEW SALES EXECS, INTERNAL MKTG)
3. RESTRUCTURE FINANCE DEPARTMENT (INCLUDING HR AND IT)
4. SCORECARDS IN EVERY DEPARTMENT & EVERYONE HAS
     A NUMBER
5. INTEGRATE RIGHT STAFF-AUG PARTNER

"Now that we've developed solid goals for next year," Alan said after the team completed its discussion, "there are three agenda items to resolve before your 1-Year Plan is finalized. The first is to answer this question: Are your roles and responsibilities clear? In other words, as you look at your Accountability Chart, do you have everything you need to achieve your 1-Year Plan? Are each of you crystal clear on your role in achieving this plan?"

Alan asked Eileen to distribute the Accountability Chart and worked through it with the team. Again the leaders focused first on structure and then on people. Sue described her plans for the marketing and sales department while Alan illustrated those changes on the whiteboard. The rest of the team asked questions, provided some input, and agreed to support Sue's plan. Tom detailed plans to add a few key resources to the operations department as the year progressed, and Jeff presented his rough plan for building out the finance department.

Once the team members agreed that they had the right structure to support Swan's 1-Year Plan, they focused on identifying any people issues. Alan added several "open seat" issues to the Issues List, as well as a few people one or more members of the team felt might be below the bar.

"The second agenda item is your budget," Alan explained. "Jeff, do you have everything you need to complete your budget for next year?"

"Yes," replied Jeff. "I have a draft budget done already. The decisions we made today and some of the Accountability Chart details we just reviewed will help me get it done before year-end."

"Terrific," Alan said. "On to item number three—your Scorecards. Eileen, can you distribute copies of the leadership team Scorecard so we can review and change it to match our 1-Year Plan?"

Alan walked the team through the Scorecard, one measurable at a time. The leaders updated the goals that would keep Swan on track to achieve its plan for the year. When that exercise was complete, Jeff agreed to make changes to the Scorecard and bring updated copies to the team's next Level 10 Meeting. Alan dismissed the group for a break and readied the room for Rock setting.

"With your 1-Year Plan complete," Alan said as the session resumed, "it's time to set Q1 Rocks. Please review your 1-Year Plan and your Issues List, and record the three to seven priorities you think this company *must get done* in the next ninety days to lay the groundwork for achieving your 1-Year Plan."

With the team beginning to master this process, Rock setting moved more quickly than it had in the past. The list of potential company Rocks was appreciably shorter than it had been in prior sessions, and the process of prioritizing them using Keep, Kill, and Combine went a little faster. The team quickly settled on financial metrics and five company Rocks. Alan then invited the leaders to select individual Rocks. When all was done, Swan's Q1 Rock Sheet looked like the document on page 283.

"Great work," Alan said as the Rock-setting exercise was completed. "We're about to spend the rest of the day solving issues. I know you've all been watching this Issues List grow, and you're chomping at the bit to start solving them."

"You're *so* right, Alan," exclaimed Vic. "I almost snuck back into the room last night and threw away all your green markers!"

"The good news," Alan continued, chuckling, "is that, with your one-year planning goals and Q1 Rocks, you've put plans in place

Swan Services Q1 20XX Rock Sheet

Future Date: March 27, 20XX
Revenue: $2 million
Profit: 7.5%
Measurables: 4 projects @ $100K +

COMPANY ROCKS	WHO
1) Initiate search for staff-aug partner	Eileen
2) Hire new sales associate and marketing coordinator	Sue
3) Structure finance department and define HR seat	Jeff
4) Hire BA, PM, and developer	Tom
5) Make go/no-go decision on next generation technology	Tom
6)	
7)	

SUE
1) Hire new sales associate and marketing coordinator
2) Refine sales department scorecard and individual measurables
3) Get sales process (including pipeline reporting) followed by all
4)
5)
6)
7)

TOM
1) Hire BA, PM, and developer
2) Make go/no-go decision on next generation technology
3) Get project fulfillment process followed by all
4) Refine ops and development department scorecards
5)
6)
7)

JEFF
1) Structure finance department and define HR seat
2) Get accounting process (including time and billing) followed by all
3) Finalize 20XX budget and conduct financial reviews with leadership team within two weeks of month-end
4)
5)
6)
7)

EILEEN
1) Initiate search for staff-aug partner
2) Evaluate Sensi-Tech acquisition opportunity
3) Implement HR process and get followed by all
4)
5)
6)
7)

VIC
1) Evaluate options for increasing recurring revenue and make a recommendation to pursue at least one
2) Conduct at least one trust-builder exercise
3)
4)
5)
6)
7)

that will make some of these issues go away forever. So before we start IDSing, let's go through and clean up this list. I'm going to read through every issue, and if you'll solve it with a goal or a Rock or we've resolved it in the session, just say 'off.' 'On' means it hasn't been solved and we need to leave it on the list."

After several minutes, the unwieldy Issues List had been whittled down to size.

LEVEL 10 MEETINGS	COMPETITORS GETTING STRONGER
LEAD GENERATION	OUT-OF-DATE LEGACY TECHNOLOGY
FINDING TALENT	DATA SECURITY
ON-BOARDING NEW HIRES	CAPITAL AVAILABILITY (CLIENTS, US)
BENCH STRENGTH IN OPS	RISING HEALTH INSURANCE COSTS
MID-LEVEL MANAGEMENT	SUE-ENOUGH TIME
PREDICTING REVENUES	RAJ - RPRS
MANAGING FLUCTUATING WORKLOADS	PTO POLICY
NEW OFFICE SPACE	TECHNICAL TRAINING
IT RECRUITING	DISASTER RECOVERY PLAN
OFF-SHORING (OVERSEAS DEVELOPMENT OFFICE)	GUARANTEE
	END RUNS
"PRODUCTIZING" COMMON SOLUTIONS	LMA
CERTIFICATION	SALES SEAT OPEN (2)
LOSING KEY EMPLOYEES	

"That's *still* cool," said Vic when the list had been scrubbed. "Plus, I can see a bunch more of those going away when we get someone in here who can run with HR."

"Exactly," agreed Jeff.

Again Alan led the team through the discipline of IDS by helping them first prioritize "the one, two, and three most important issues for us to solve here today."

"End runs," Tom said first.

Eileen suggested "Raj—RPRS" and Sue called out, "Predicting revenues." Alan wrote the numerals 1, 2, and 3 next to each issue and then faced the team.

"Let's IDS end runs," Alan began. "Tom, can you identify the exact issue we need to discuss and solve today?"

"Sure," said Tom, a little uncomfortably. "An end run is where one leader goes right to another leader's direct report with a problem—or vice versa—rather than respecting the appropriate chain of command. That happens here too often."

"Can you give us an example?" Eileen asked.

"Sure," Tom said, having prepared for the question. "Vic, you don't do this regularly, but last week I saw you hovering over Matt—the project manager on the Radiation Therapies deal—for about twenty-five minutes. It looked like things were getting a little testy between the two of you, so when the conversation was over, I casually asked him what was up. He explained that Troy had raised a red flag with you about the project."

"Was he upset about our conversation?" Vic asked.

"Before we start discussing," Alan interjected, "are we all clear on the issue?"

The team nodded its agreement, and Alan gestured for Vic and Tom to continue.

"To answer your question," Tom said, "he wasn't upset, per se."

"So then, I'm not sure I understand why it's a problem," Vic replied. "I stopped by Troy's office to ask how things were going. He expressed concern about the project but was too busy working on another proposal to worry about it, so I volunteered to help out. I knew it would be a short conversation, and I sure as heck didn't want to bother *you* with it, so I handled it. How is that a problem?"

Tom was flustered. He'd always been uncomfortable challenging authority. "Tom?" Alan asked calmly. "What problems can an end run cause?"

"Well," he said slowly, "Matt wasn't upset, but you *did* rattle him a bit. You're an owner, Vic. It doesn't matter how laid back and approachable you are. When you pop into someone's cube to resolve a problem, it's intimidating. By the time you left, Matt felt like he'd totally screwed up and was ready to drop everything to focus on the Radiation Therapies project."

"But I didn't accuse him of screwing up!" exclaimed Vic.

"I know you didn't, Vic," Tom replied. "I knew right away that you'd just asked a couple of questions, hoping to figure out what needed to happen to address the client's concerns. But *Matt* didn't understand that. That's why I'd rather you and I talk about issues like that before you go directly to my team members."

"Gosh, Tom," Vic said earnestly, "I have to tell you that that all feels a little corporate to me. That's not our culture! 'Help first' is a Core Value because we've always had a 'whatever it takes, pitch in and help out' mentality. It feels like I'm being attacked for just trying to help."

"Hold on, Vic," Eileen interjected. "I've been listening carefully, and Tom is most certainly *not* attacking you. He's just raised a valid issue and cited a recent example of your behavior to illustrate that issue. He said he *knows* you were just trying to help."

"Right!" said Tom. "I just want you to help *through me* whenever possible. Basically, I'm hoping we can follow the lines of communication as drawn up on the Accountability Chart. When we don't do that, it disrupts my team's sense of priority and sends mixed signals about who's accountable for what."

"You know, Vic," Alan interjected, "this is an issue for many of my clients as they grow. End runs can cut managers off at the knees. Occasionally somebody becomes the 'complaint department' and creates a plague in the organization. But what I hear you saying is that you want to stay accessible to and engaged with all of your employees and preserve your entrepreneurial culture. Right?"

"Yes," replied Vic, curious about where Alan might be going with this.

"I've seen other clients accomplish those goals by following two rules of thumb," he explained. "First, while it's okay and healthy to engage with and talk to employees, you can't solve their problems for them. If you're going to build an organization full of healthy, productive teams, the leader of each team needs to be looked on as the person with the knowledge and authority to help its members solve their own problems."

Vic nodded.

"The second rule," Alan continued, "is that *you* have to look to that manager to solve problems, too. When you're talking with an employee and he or she raises an issue, shares a frustration, or just starts to vent, it's okay to listen, talk things through, and reassure. Before concluding, though, you have to toss the issue back to the manager. A great way to do that is by simply concluding with the question, 'So, are you gonna tell him, or am I gonna tell him?' You have to make it clear that one of you needs to tell the manager. That way you engaged, you listened, and you directed the employee to the right place for help—his or her manager."

In his entire career, Vic had never once closed his office door, and he had only rarely let a closed door on someone else's office stop him. This whole idea of a chain of command rubbed him the wrong way. At the same time, he understood Tom's point about how his good intentions might unwittingly throw employees off their stride.

"So," Vic finally said, "all you're saying is that we should respect one another's roles as leaders and let managers manage?"

"Right," said Tom, relieved.

"I can do that," Vic admitted.

"Is everyone in agreement?" Alan asked.

"Yes," Eileen replied as Jeff nodded, "and I need to get better at avoiding end runs, as well."

"Issue number two," Alan continued after the team agreed it had solved the end run issue. "Is Raj the right person in the right seat? Tom, this is your issue, correct?"

"Yes," he replied.

"Raj has been on the Issues List since before you were here!" exclaimed Eileen.

"I know," Tom agreed. "Evan still thinks he can get him above the bar."

"Okay," Alan replied. "To identify a people issue, we always go right to the People Analyzer."

He instructed the leaders to create a People Analyzer template. The results from the leaders clearly showed Raj was below the bar.

	Be Humbly Confident	Grow or Die	Help First	Do The Right Thing	Do What You Say	G	W	C
RAJ	–	+	+/–	+/–	+	Y	N	Y
THE BAR	+	+	+	+/–	+/–	Y	Y	Y

"Raj is the wrong person in the wrong seat," Alan explained. "Let's discuss."

"Not much to discuss, from my point of view," explained Eileen. "With all due respect to Evan, Raj has been below the bar long enough that we have to exit him. "

"So what's the problem?" Alan asked. "Have you begun consistently using the three-strike rule in your HR process? Have you or Evan had one or two tough conversations with Raj?"

"Two," Tom replied. "Each time he improved for a little while and then started falling back into some old bad habits."

"He's a prima donna," Sue explained. "Super smart, always stays on the cutting edge technology-wise, but he's a pain in the neck. In my opinion, Evan endures the Core Values issues and the 'wants it' problem because he'd have a really hard time replacing Raj's firepower on his team."

"Is that fair, Tom?" Alan asked.

"Yes," he said. "Plus, Raj has some personal issues that keep cropping up every time we start thinking something is the last straw. First one of his parents was sick, then he had some marital problems, and so on. So we decide to wait a little while longer and keep trying to help him improve."

"Ahhhh," said Alan thoughtfully. "Evan's suffering from the 'yeah, buts,' huh?"

"The 'yeah, buts'?" asked Tom.

"That's when you have a clear people issue and everyone on the team thinks you need to invoke the three-strike rule," he explained. "And you just keep saying, 'Yeah, but he's really talented and valuable. Yeah, but he's got some personal problems. Yeah, but it's almost

Christmas, or Easter, or Arbor Day.' And so he just sits on your Issues List holding you back."

Tom chuckled, realizing Alan and the rest of the team were completely right.

"So we have to exit Raj from the organization this quarter," Tom said. "Right?"

"What you have to do is put a plan in place that you and the team believe will make this perpetual people issue go away forever," Alan replied. "Sometimes the extenuating circumstances are good reasons to postpone a termination. Maybe he's vital to a key project or building a demo that will help you win a new 'A' client. If that's the case, all I ask is that you and the team agree on how and when you'll put the wheels in motion for his ultimate exit. Are you going to hire another top-notch developer? Are you going to start cross-training other developers and getting them involved in his active projects to soften the blow of his ultimate departure?"

The team had a healthy, productive discussion about their options. Tom decided to adjust his hiring Rock to include a second developer with the skills necessary to replace Raj. He accepted a To-Do to schedule a meeting with Evan to discuss timing and report back to the team. And he promised that Raj would not be on the Issues List at Swan's next Quarterly Session in March.

Alan then helped the team IDS the third issue, predicting revenues. Confusion and a little conflict had arisen over the quality and consistency of the sales pipeline report on which Tom had been basing his staffing assumptions. In an animated but professional dialogue, the team was able to agree on a few changes to the sales process, the pipeline report itself, and the Scorecard numbers. Sue felt good about resolving the issue, as it gave her a head start on honoring the One Thing commitment she'd made the day before.

With that issue solved, Alan asked the leaders to prioritize the next three most important issues on the list. This time Sue spoke up quickly, making "Guarantee?" issue number one. Eileen suggested Level 10 Meetings as issue number two, and Jeff added data security as issue number three.

"I'd like the team to consider approving a guarantee that can be woven into the sales process," Sue said when Alan asked her to clearly identify the issue. "I think it'll resonate with our target market, be consistent with our Core Focus, and be acceptable from a risk standpoint."

Sue suggested that Swan's guarantee focus *not* on what's delivered but on the speed with which they propose a solution that "solves the client's real problems with the right technology." She spoke passionately about the fact that Swan's prospects were typically quite frustrated by two things: slow response times and the tendency to propose cookie-cutter solutions that wouldn't solve the real problem.

"Not only can we distinguish ourselves with this guarantee," she explained, "but we'll blow everyone else away. We'll start getting invited to meet with more decision makers. We'll start issuing more proposals, and we'll have them in our prospects' hands days—maybe even weeks—before the competition delivers *their* proposal. And we'll be clearly better at pinpointing and resolving the real business problem our prospects are trying to solve than any of our competitors."

Sue fielded a series of questions about the specifics of her idea. She felt Swan should guarantee delivery of a high-level proposal within five business days after a needs analysis meeting. When confronted with a project that didn't match Swan's Core Focus or competencies, she and her sales team were fully prepared to say so and to recommend one or more alternatives to the prospect.

"What happens if we *don't* provide a proposal on time?" asked Jeff.

"Well," Sue said carefully, "if we don't deliver a high-level proposal within five days, and they ultimately select us to do the work, I'd propose we agree to prepare the *detailed* project plan at no cost. Or at least a greatly reduced cost."

The team discussed and debated Sue's proposal vigorously. Ultimately, the leaders believed this type of guarantee would generate more leads and vastly improve Swan's win ratio. Jeff, Tom, and Eileen were concerned about the risks but agreed to endorse the guarantee provided Sue wait to *implement* it until after she and Tom had revised the sales process to minimize cost and risk. Sue added an individual Rock to that effect, and Eileen recorded the following in the Marketing Strategy section of the V/TO: "Swan Services will propose the right technology solution for your real business problem within five business days."

Alan then worked the team through issues two and three. As the afternoon wore on, the team repeatedly prioritized and resolved issues using IDS until a quarter after four, when Vic made a suggestion.

"Alan," he said, waving a piece of notebook paper as though it were a white flag and breathing laboriously for effect, "can I suggest that we prioritize next steps? I don't recover from a late night the way I used to! Does anyone else think we've solved enough issues for one day?"

"Absolutely," Eileen said, laughing. "Actually, I was just about to make the same suggestion—although it would have lacked your sense of drama, Vic."

The others readily agreed, so Alan helped get them clear on next steps. He began by compartmentalizing the Issues List, killing those issues they had solved during the session and putting the remaining issues on either the V/TO or the Level 10 Meeting agenda.

MID-LEVEL MANAGEMENT	V/TO	CAPITAL AVAILABILITY (CLIENTS, US)	V/TO
MANAGING FLUCTUATING WORKLOADS	L10	RISING HEALTH INSURANCE COSTS	L10
NEW OFFICE SPACE	V/TO	SUE-ENOUGH TIME	L10
IT RECRUITING	V/TO	PTO POLICY	L10
OFF-SHORING (OVERSEAS DEV'T OFFICE)	V/TO	TECHNICAL TRAINING	L10
"PRODUCTIZING" COMMON SOLUTIONS	V/TO	DISASTER RECOVERY PLAN	V/TO
CERTIFICATION	V/TO	LMA	V/TO
		SALES SEAT OPEN (2)	V/TO

After walking through next steps and getting the team clear on its homework, Alan moved to conclude the meeting.

"Thank you all for a powerful two days," Alan began. "From my view, you're leaving here healthier as a team, on the same page, and committed to achieving your vision. You have a crystal-clear plan for next year and next quarter, and you solved literally *dozens* of key issues. Thanks for the great work you did together in this room and for all that you've done over the past year to implement this system in your business. Before we leave for the day, please conclude by sharing four things. First, give us some feedback: Where's your head?"

How are you feeling? Then let us know whether your expectations for the two days were met. Third, please be prepared to restate your One Thing commitment for next year. Your rating for the meeting is last. How'd we do over these last two days?"

"I'll start," said Sue when everyone was ready.

"A great two days," she said. "Frankly, I was skeptical—it wasn't easy to imagine spending two days out of the office with all the deals we're trying to close and quotas we're trying to meet. But I'm really glad we did. My expectations were vastly exceeded."

Sue then restated her One Thing commitment and rated the meeting a ten.

Tom's response virtually echoed Sue's. He thanked the group—especially Vic—for allowing him to be open and honest about some things that he'd been holding in for a while. He reiterated how nice it was to be part of a growth-oriented team working together to build something special. After rereading his One Thing commitment, he also rated the meeting a ten.

"I'm with Sue," Jeff said. "After just four months on the job, I wasn't thrilled about two days off-site. And while these two days forced me to work well outside my comfort zone, I'm thrilled with everything that happened here. I know you all a lot better than I did when I walked in here today, and hopefully you feel the same way about me."

The other leaders smiled, all glad to have grown closer to Jeff as well.

"My expectations were absolutely met," he continued. "I'll give the meeting a nine, which I've been told is a ten when it comes from the CFO."

Alan laughed, reminded Jeff to reread his One Thing commitment, and moved on to get Eileen's feedback.

"What a difference a year makes," Eileen began. "After two days with all of you, I can honestly say that I've never been more proud to be part of a team than I am right now. Thank you for pulling together and helping us turn this into the company Vic and I imagined when we had this crazy idea in the first place."

She further explained that the meeting met her expectations, restated her One Thing commitment, and rated the meeting a ten.

"I'll start by rating the meeting a ten," Vic said. "My expectations were met, and next year, I commit to start encouraging Eileen to delegate and elevate into her role as the integrator while appreciating the value she brings in that role. As for feedback, let me say from my heart that I've never felt closer to my partner. This hasn't been an easy journey for either of us. At times—even after we started working with you, Alan—we've wanted to kill one another. This system has helped a lot, but we could not have turned this thing around without everyone in this room. So thank you all. I'm heading into the holidays as happy as I've ever been—and hopeful that next year will be even better."

THE VISION/TRACTION ORGANIZER

Swan Services – 20XX Q1

VISION

		3-YEAR PICTURE
CORE VALUES	1. Be humbly confident 2. Grow or die 3. Help first 4. Do the right thing 5. Do what you say	**Future Date:** December 31, 20XX **Revenue:** $12 million **Profit:** 12% ($1.44 million) **Measurables:** 50 projects @ $100K+ **What Does It Look Like?** • 50 RPRS • Thriving culture • New company HQ • New sales office in Chicago • Strong sales team of 10 people • IT seat RPRS • HR seat RPRS • One of Minnesota's "Best Places to Work" • 40% recurring revenues • Great staff-aug partner in place • Seeking acquisitions
CORE FOCUS	**Passion:** Building a great company with great people **Niche:** Solving real problems with the right technology	
10-YEAR TARGET	$25 million in revenue, 20% net profit	
MARKETING STRATEGY	**Target Market/"The List":** IT directors or CFOs at technology-dependent companies (financial services, health care, education, government) with more than $100 million in revenues that are: • Headquartered in the upper Midwest • Comfortable looking outside the organization to solve technology problems. • Want a long-term relationship with a strategic partner, not a low-cost vendor. **Three Uniques:** 1. We're real people who care 2. We're experts at using technology to solve business problems 3. We do what we say **Proven Process:** see attached **Guarantee:** Swan will propose the right technology solution for your real business problem within five business days	

THE VISION/TRACTION ORGANIZER

Swan Services – 20XX Q1

TRACTION

1-YEAR PLAN	ROCKS	ISSUES LIST

1-YEAR PLAN

Future Date: December 31, 20XX
Revenue: $8 million
Profit: 10% ($800K)
Measurables: 30 projects @ $100K+

Goals for the Year:

1.	All Core Processes documented, simplified and followed by all
2.	Build next generation marketing/sales department (two new sales executives, internal marketing)
3.	Restructure finance department (including HR and IT)
4.	Scorecards in every department and everyone has a number
5.	Find the right staff-augmentation partner
6.	
7.	

ROCKS

Future Date: March 27, 20XX
Revenue: $1.75 million
Profit: 10%
Measurables: 4 projects @ $100K+

Rocks for the Quarter:

		Who
1.	Initiate search for staff-augmentation partner	Eileen
2.	Hire 1 sales associate and marketing coordinator	Sue
3.	Restructure finance department and define HR seat	Jeff
4.	Hire BA, PM, and two developers	Tom
5.	Make go/no-go decision about next generation technology	Tom
6.		
7.		

ISSUES LIST

1.	Mid-level management
2.	New office space
3.	IT recruiting
4.	Off-shoring (overseas development office)
5.	Productizing common solutions
6.	Capital availability (clients, us)
7.	Disaster recovery plan
8.	LMA
9.	Sales seat open
10.	
11.	
12.	

CHAPTER 8
TRACTION

DESPITE A RECORD SNOWFALL that accompanied the dawn of the New Year in Minneapolis, Swan's leadership team continued to gain traction. Alan conducted Quarterly Sessions in March, June, and September, and he enjoyed watching Swan's progress. The company continued to encounter roadblocks, but the tools each leader was now using to run every level of the organization helped Swan overcome even the most significant challenges.

Revenues and profits grew steadily. An improved hiring and onboarding process (compliments of Swan's new HR seat owner) helped Tom and his team manage the backlog and consistently deliver projects on time and under budget to a growing number of delighted clients.

Vic settled comfortably into his role as visionary, pitching in to help Sue and her team open doors, close deals, and strengthen key relationships whenever he was called on. He continued to develop new ways to strengthen Swan's culture and build team health throughout the organization. At least monthly, he brought a new idea or a creative solution to the leadership team's Level 10 Meeting, and more often than not, something of real value resulted from his knack for imagining what might be possible.

The uneasy conflict that existed between Sue, Tom, and Jeff at Swan's Annual Planning Session eased over time. The team occasionally engaged in passionate conflict, but it did so with no hidden agendas, no personal attacks, and everyone focused on the greater good of the business. As a result, Eileen continued to delegate day-to-day responsibilities and focused a growing percentage of her time on key strategic initiatives.

Jeff was able to find an ideal staff-aug partner, and the two organizations spent the year sharing business informally before committing to a formal partnership. Swan immediately began reaping benefits from that alliance, and both organizations flourished as a result.

Even after the staff-aug clients began migrating to the new business partner, Tom and his operations team started getting a better handle on problems with a handful of other clients. These clients seemed to be more difficult to please and less profitable than others. After spending time on such client issues in two successive Quarterlies, Alan introduced a tool he'd seen other organizations use successfully. One of his clients' organizations actually called it the "Dirty Dozen."

"The first step," he explained, "is ranking your clients by overall profitability. At the top of the list are the clients who help you clearly define what they're looking for, consistently provide you access to their people and information you need to keep the project running smoothly, pay promptly, appreciate your work, and become long-time sources of recurring revenue. Conversely, the bottom of the list includes clients who change their scope frequently, don't engage in the project the way you need them to, don't pay promptly, etcetera. These are clients whose projects are therefore less profitable and less enjoyable for your people."

Alan went on to explain how his other clients had made a habit of identifying their least valuable clients each year and how they did one of three things with the clients at the bottom of the list.

"Number *one*," he said, "is working with the clients so they learn to play nice. If they can't or won't change, number *two* is raising their fees to make them more profitable. And if those things don't work, number *three* is a last resort. You may need to exit them and replace them with more profitable, more enjoyable clients."

Swan's leadership team embraced this approach, employing it immediately after the session and using it to steadily increase profits as well as both client and employee satisfaction.

In September, Alan began talking with Eileen and the rest of the team about "graduating" from his process and beginning to run their own sessions. He'd watched the team master most of the tools and begin truly running the business on his system. Everything felt solid and stable. Alan expressed confidence in Eileen's ability to run the Quarterlies and Annuals and pledged to help her make the transition successfully.

At the next Annual, Swan easily surpassed its revenue and profit targets for the year and achieved all five goals from its 1-Year Plan. They scored an 81 on the organizational checkup and left the two days feeling crystal clear on their vision; all focused, disciplined, and accountable for achieving that vision; and healthier as a leadership team.

As planned, Eileen ran Swan's first Quarterly of the following year, a highly rated session, if not entirely smooth. Afterward Eileen called Alan to debrief.

"How's the family?" Alan asked after the two had discussed the meeting and the business.

"For the first time in my life," Eileen said, "I can actually give you a genuine, fully informed answer to that question! Dan's great—he told me last weekend that he feels like we're a team again. You have *no idea* how much that means to me, Alan."

"That's music to my ears, Eileen," Alan replied. "How 'bout the kids?"

"Well, Henry's getting straight A's in eighth grade," she replied, "and Charlie's a star athlete—albeit among eleven-year-olds. I'm proud to say that I've attended nearly every one of their soccer games, school functions, and art exhibits this year. Plus, we actually spent two weeks on vacation over the holidays. That was a first. I'm spending less than fifty hours in the business most weeks, I generally leave work at the office, and I *definitely* sleep better. As a result, I'm really enjoying work again. I feel like being an integrator is what I was born to do."

"That must feel great, Eileen," Alan replied, smiling. "Nothing you tell me could make me happier about the progress you and the team have made."

The two continued chatting for a few minutes and promised to keep in touch. They talked or exchanged emails occasionally. Several months later, after Eileen had run two more Quarterly Sessions, she again thought of Alan and realized just how far she and her team had come.

She left the office early that afternoon to help set up for a Business Roundtable group social event. At about a quarter after five guests began arriving. While helping Bill Pullian check members in for a few minutes, she glanced up to see her friend and fellow Roundtable member John Fredrickson. He didn't look so good.

"Hey, John," she said, extending both arms for a hug. "Everything okay?"

John's face turned red, and Eileen could see the vein on his temple pulsating. He looked even more intense than usual.

"Hey, Eileen," he mumbled, leaning in for a lukewarm embrace. "To be honest, I've been better."

Overcome by a sense of déjà vu, Eileen grabbed John by the hand and headed for the bar. He ran a very successful construction business that was much larger than Swan. Eileen was surprised to see him so frustrated.

"Then let me buy you a drink," she said, "and you can tell me all about it."

With drinks in hand, Eileen led John to a quiet part of the lobby, sat him down, and asked, "What's up?"

"It's the same old stuff," John began. "We're doing okay, but I'm working way too hard, and it seems I spend most of every day ticked off at some*one* or some*thing*."

"Like what?" Eileen asked sincerely. "Or *whom*?"

"Oh, you know," John said, waiving his hand dismissively. "I'm ticked off at my people—none of them really seems to get it or even to really care. We've stopped growing, and we're not making any-where near enough money for a company our size. Frankly, I feel like I've lost control of the business, and no matter what I try, nothing seems to work. Blah, blah, blah."

"Come on, John," Eileen insisted. "I've been there. I really do want to help, even if you just need somebody to listen."

John could tell from the look in her eyes that it was true, and he poured out his guts to Eileen. Over the last eleven years, he'd built a successful business from scratch, relying mostly on his own strong will and determination. He'd had fun for the first eight years, but the last three had been rough. He was averaging seventy hours a week in the business and lying awake most nights worrying about what he hadn't had time to fix earlier that day.

When Eileen asked about his leadership team, John laughed sarcastically. He'd spent the last two years running through a string of unsuccessful internal promotions, external hires, and consultants.

"I wouldn't refer to any of them as a real leader," he lamented. "And we've never even gotten close to functioning as a team! I know it's my fault—frankly, in this condition, I can't be an easy guy to work for. Honestly, Eileen, if I can't figure this out, I'm going to sell the damn company and start over."

"Believe it or not," Eileen said, smiling broadly, "I know *exactly* what that feels like. Three years ago, at an event like this one, a good friend did something for me that I'll never forget."

She reached into her purse and pulled out a business card. John watched her write something on the back of the card before sliding it across the table to him.

"On your way home tonight," she said emphatically, "I want you to call my friend Alan Roth. If you really want to start getting everything you want from your business, I *promise* he can help you."

And before he knew what had happened, Eileen was gone, rushing across the lobby to greet her husband, Dan. John examined Alan Roth's business card, looking for clues to explain Eileen's strange confidence in this man's ability to help him fix a business he felt was irreparably broken. He flipped the card over to read what Eileen had written.

Traction!

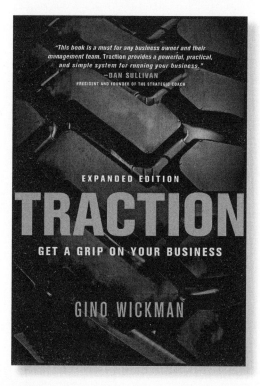

ABOUT THE AUTHORS AND EOS

GINO WICKMAN and MIKE PATON share a passion for helping people get what they want from their businesses. To fulfill that passion, they help companies implement the Entrepreneurial Operating System (EOS), the complete system described in *Get A Grip*, which Gino created. When implemented in an organization, EOS helps leaders run better businesses, get better control, have better life balance, and gain more traction, with the entire organization advancing together as a healthy, functional, and cohesive team.

Gino and Mike spend most of their time as EOS Implementers, working hands-on with the leadership teams of entrepreneurial companies to help them fully implement EOS in their organizations. They're joined by the professional EOS Implementers at EOS Worldwide, a team of successful entrepreneurs from a variety of business backgrounds devoted to helping leaders throughout the world experience all the organizational and personal benefits of implementing EOS.

FOR ADDITIONAL HELP AND INFORMATION

Our goal is to help you get everything you want from your business by offering three ways to fully and purely implement EOS in your organization:

Self-Implementation—Select one of your most capable and dedicated leaders to teach, facilitate, and coach your leadership team through The EOS Process, using free downloadable tools from our website and this book as a guide. You can also use *Get A Grip's* award-winning companion book, *Traction: Get a Grip on Your Business*, as a resource. Written as a how-to guide, it is also published by BenBella Books and is available wherever books are sold.

Supported Self-Implementation—Join the EOS Implementer online Base Camp for a small monthly fee. Base Camp will fully train and support that same leader to become an expert at implementing EOS in your organization; OR.

Professional Implementation—Engage one of our professional EOS Implementers to lead you through The EOS Process.

Visit www.eosworldwide.com to learn more about these three approaches, download free tools, subscribe to our blog for regular helpful tips, find out how to become a professional certified implementer, and schedule keynote speaking engagements or interactive workshops.

If you have any other questions or want more help, call 1-877-EOS-1877 or email info@eosworldwide.com.

Acknowledgments

THIS BOOK would not have been possible without the help and guidance of the following people. We will never be able to thank you enough for your impact on our lives, our work, and this book.

Gino's Family and Friends

Kathy, my strong and beautiful wife, for your love through the good times and the tough times. Thanks for giving me the freedom to be an entrepreneur and for always believing in me. I am truly the luckiest husband in the world. I love you.

Alexis, my wise and beautiful daughter, and Gino, my son with the quick wit and common sense—you both keep me humble, make me laugh, and teach me what life is really about. You are the light of my life. You are amazing individuals and it is a joy to watch you mature into adults. I love you both very much.

Linda Wickman, my mom, for teaching me to be independent, for your amazing quiet strength and wisdom, and for being a great spiritual mentor at this stage in my life.

Floyd Wickman, my dad and my life mentor. This book would not exist without you. You have taught me everything I know about communicating with people, be it one or one thousand. You exemplify every principle in this book.

Neil Pardun, my father-in-law, for teaching me that it is possible to possess wealth and remain humble. You are a rare and special person. I am forever changed through your example.

Karen Grooms, the greatest assistant on earth. Thanks for seventeen years of holding all of the pieces together and protecting me from distractions so that I may remain in my Unique Ability®. I would be lost without you.

Mike Pallin, who I truly believe is my guardian angel. You always place in front of me exactly what I need at that point in my life. This book would not have happened without you.

The "Book Club," aka Curt Rager and Bob Shenefelt, for being incredible friends, an amazing sounding board, and for constantly challenging me. Our annual trip to the mountains gives me tremendous clarity. You are lifers.

Pat Tierney, Rob Tamblyn, and Kevin Brady, my first clients, for letting me practice on you. You gave me the confidence to move forward.

Tyler Smith, for constantly challenging me and not getting caught up in the hype. You are wise beyond your years. Thanks for your friendship, guidance, and honesty.

John Anderson, one of the world's greatest "connectors," for introducing me to six people who have had a huge impact on my success: Verne Harnish, Pat Lencioni, Dan Sullivan, Craig Erlich, Bill Gitre, and John Gallant. You are one of the most selfless people I know.

Rob Dube for your friendship. You have had a huge impact on my life. It has been a pleasure going from your mentor to your protégé. You are an inspiration.

Dan Israel for taking such a huge interest in my business. You have helped me in countless ways. It has been a great pleasure going from your mentor to your protégé. You are the best-kept secret in southeast Michigan.

Mike Paton, my coauthor, you are a dream come true. You're an EOS implementer, writer, partner, friend, and confidant extraordinaire.

Sam Cupp, my business mentor, for teaching me all that I know about business. I would not be where I am without your guidance. I hope I have made you proud.

Dan Sullivan for teaching me how to live in my Unique Ability, Verne Harnish for your inspiration, Pat Lencioni for your advice and teachings, and Jim Collins for your amazing research and findings. You are four thought leaders that have had a huge influence on my teachings. The world is a better place because of your amazing work.

MIKE'S FAMILY AND FRIENDS

Arthur E. Pfeil, my "Pop," a wise, generous teacher loved by thousands of children (including me) who would not be the people they are today without his patient guidance and boundless love. You always wanted me to write this book—I could never have done it without your filling me with a love of learning, teaching, and storytelling. Rest in peace, Pop.

Mary Paton, my mom, whose love and support and confidence in me have never wavered, even when I may not have deserved it. I don't tell you often enough how much I love you and value everything you've done for me.

Jon, Henry, and Charlie—my boys. Your smiles and laughter define joy for me. Jon, I am so proud of the man you've become and eager to see all that you accomplish. Henry, your "world-class hugs" kept me going through many a difficult moment. And Charlie, your seemingly constant happiness is one of the greatest gifts I've ever received. Each of you inspires me—I love you all very much.

My brother, Ozzie, you have been a great friend through many of life's twists and turns. My sister, Lisa, is always in my heart— I miss you every day.

Grandma Jean, thank you for helping me see clearly what true love is—I only hope I can be as lucky as you and Pop were. And Cute Nan (Hester Pfeil), I know you are smiling somewhere and hope you are proud of the man I've become.

Gino Wickman, my mentor, coauthor, and treasured friend— you've helped me discover my life's work and be my best every day. This project has been a joy and your friendship and counsel have meant more to me these last four years than you'll ever know.

To this life's closest friends and teachers—I am so grateful for the gifts you've given me and the love we've shared:

Steve and Mark Hatch, Laura Casale Martin, Kay Shutler, Diane Cresbaugh, David Anderson, Phil Martin, David Radanovich, Jack Thomas, Chip Letzgus, Lisa Phillips, Amy Eddings, Carl Phillips, David Gibbs, Barbara Rigney, Ann Thomas Paton, Brad Smith, Rick Simonton, Betsy Lloyd, Andy Johnson, Bill and Ann Roth, Kerry Roth Paton, Jeff Scholes, Brett and Katie Kaufman, Gino Wickman, Don Tinney, Duane Marshall, CJ DuBe', Billy and Sue McCarthy, Lara Miklasevics, Jon Meyer, Dodd Clasen, Chris Eilers, Jeff Fritz, Susan Broadwell, and Kate Grussing, a lovely surprise and a beautiful gift at just the right time.

Special thanks to Kristen McLinden—a great friend and a better assistant. Put simply, I wouldn't be here without you.

OUR EOS FAMILY

Don Tinney, a great partner, mentor, and friend. Your calm, steady resolve is an inspiration and reminder to us both. Your friendship and wise counsel has made each of us better men. Thank you.

Amber Baird, Lisa Hofmann, and Tyler Smith for your incredible commitment to the EOS Worldwide cause. We couldn't do it without you.

Rene' Boer, Duane Marshall, Ed Callahan, and Steve Smolinski—your feedback on the manuscript was invaluable, and we are both proud to call you friends.

Our team of world-class EOS Implementers—thank you for your commitment to "EOS Pure," for inspiring us to be our best, and for the great work you do every day helping entrepreneurs get what they want from their businesses.

CONTRIBUTORS

The manuscript readers: Rob Dube, Dave Kolb, Stephen Daas, Stephanie Laitala, Karen Feagler, Brett Kaufmann, Chris Nagle, Karen

Andrews, Dan Israel, Curt Rager, Bob Shenefelt, Matt Bergstrom, and Adam Wilberding. Thanks for all of your valuable time and incredible feedback. You are forever a part of this book.

Anne DuBuisson Anderson at Anne Consults; Bethany Brown and Amy Collins at The Cadence Group; Matthew Carnicelli of Carnicelli Literary Services; John Paine of John Paine Editorial Services; Drew Robinson of Spork Design; Ross Slater and Jennifer Tribe of Highspot, Inc.; Glenn Yeffeth and the team at BenBella Books; thank you for helping us tell this story and share it with the world.

And to all of our clients: We are truly blessed that you give us the opportunity to live our dream and work with people we love every day. This book is a by-product of all of our work together, and most of its content comes from you. Thank you for your passion, for being real and raw and vulnerable, and for wanting more from your business. Without you, this book would not exist.

INDEX*

* To learn more about these and other EOS terms, visit www.eosworldwide.com/getagrip/glossary